*The Collected Writings
of
W Hoste*

*The Collected Writings
of
W Hoste*

Volume 2

Prophetic

ISBN 0 946351 75 9

Copyright © 1999 by John Ritchie Ltd.
40 Beansburn, Kilmarnock, Scotland

All rights reserved. No part of this publication may be reproduced, stored in a retrievable system, or transmitted in any form or by any other means – electronic, mechanical, photocopy, recording or otherwise – without prior permission of the copyright owner.

Typeset by John Ritchie Ltd., Kilmarnock
Printed by Bell & Bain Ltd., Glasgow

Foreword

For this second volume of the Collected Writings of Mr. William Hoste five works with a prophetic theme have been selected: *The Kingdom of God; The Great Tribulation; The Mysteries of the New Testament; The Seven Covenants of Holy Scripture; Beyond the Grave*. In these, present day readers may benefit from the encyclopaedic knowledge the author had of the prophetic Scriptures, and from his ability to elucidate their bearing on one another. In addition, the gift of clear exposition which Mr. Hoste used for the benefit of the Lord's people in his own day and generation lives on in these writings for our spiritual blessing and profit today.

The Publishers are grateful to Dr. Bert Cargill of St Monans for compiling and editing this volume, and to Mr. Alan Taylor of Elgin for his assistance in this task by scanning the original booklets into computer based text. The desire and prayer of all involved in the reissue of these valuable writings is that the Lord will be glorified, and His people's affections for Him deepened while we wait for the next event in God's prophetic calendar – the imminent return of His Son from heaven, "even Jesus, which delivered us from the wrath to come". Also, Mr Hoste writes on one of the succeeding pages of this volume, "As all believers hope one day, and rightly so, to share in the coming kingdom, they too should keep their inheritance in view, and walk worthy of their high and holy calling."

Kilmarnock
September 1998

Contents

Foreword v

THE KINGDOM OF GOD–What is it? Whom does it Embrace? ... 2
  1. The Kingdom of God 2
  2. The Kingdom in the Old Testament 10
  3. The Kingdom in the New Testament 17
  4. Who will Share in the Kingdom? 25
  5. The Characteristics of the Future Kingdom 40

THE GREAT TRIBULATION THEORY–Do the Scriptures teach that the Church must go through the Great Tribulation? 52
  1. Confounding the Church with Israel 53
  2. A Fictitious Order of Prophetic Events 56
  3. Confusing the Stages of the Second Coming 62
  4. The Order and Character of the Apocalypse 65
  5. Depriving the Church of her Hope 67

MYSTERIES OF THE NEW TESTAMENT 72
  1. Introduction 72
  2. Seven Great Mysteries 74
  3. Mystery of the Kingdom 77
  4. Mystery of the Heavenly Remnant 81
  5. Mystery of the Great Transformation 86
  6. Mystery of Godliness 94
  7. Mystery of Christ 98
  8. Mystery of God 104
  9. Mystery, Babylon the Great 111
  10. Mystery of Iniquity 118
  11. Mystery of His Will 126

THE SEVEN COVENANTS OF HOLY SCRIPTURE 139
  Introduction 139

1. The Noahic Covenant 139
2. The Abrahamic Covenant 141
3. The Sinaitic Covenant 147
4. The Levitical Covenant 155
5. The Davidic Covenant 157
6. The Covenant with Death 159
7. The New Covenant 164

BEYOND THE GRAVE 168
1. Introduction 168
2. The Intermediate State: (a) Its Reality; (b) Its Denial;
   (c) Its Travesty 171
3. The Millennial Reign and The Everlasting Kingdom 181
4. The Future State of the Redeemed 186
5. The Future of the Wicked 190
6. Universalism 200
7. Conditional Immortality 207

The Kingdom of God

What Is It?   Whom Does It Embrace?

1. THE KINGDOM OF GOD

The Kingdom of God is a theme which may well stir the affections and quicken the interest of all the people of God, for the King will be Jesus, Emmanuel, the Christ of God, their Saviour and their Lord. An earthly prince destined to succeed to his father's kingdom is trained with this in view, and no pains are spared to acquaint him with the history, people and government of his country, and with what is becoming in one of so high a destiny. As all believers hope one day, and rightly so, to share in the coming kingdom, they too should keep their inheritance in view, and walk worthy of their high and holy calling.

The phrase 'Kingdom of God' is employed in various senses in the Word of God. Sometimes it stands for the kingdom as announced by John the Baptist, which, though rejected then, will be eventually manifested in all its glory during the millennial reign. This kingdom will have height as well as breadth, a heavenly and an earthly side. The former is referred to in 1 Corinthians 15:50, as that which "flesh and blood cannot inherit", but the earthly Kingdom will be inherited by men of flesh and blood as we shall see later. Sometimes "Kingdom of God" stands for that which is set up in the hearts of true believers and sometimes more generally for that condition of things brought about in the world by the preaching of the gospel in this age. In this latter aspect the Kingdom will need purging of false profession. Then, lastly, there is "the Eternal Kingdom" of which the millennial Kingdom is the first phase. In this, righteousness will no longer simply rule but will dwell. Then the last enemy shall have been destroyed and God will be all in all. Then at last will the whole universe

THE KINGDOM OF GOD

bow the knee and every tongue confess, even in the fearful regions of the lost, that Jesus Christ is Lord to the glory of God the Father.

We should expect the Kingdom to be a theme much dwelt upon among Christians, but, whether from the difficulty of distinguishing its various phases, or from the mistaken idea that it is not of practical bearing, it is a subject seldom referred to. But its importance in our Lord's estimation is clear from the fact that the Kingdom formed the burden of His instructions to His disciples after His resurrection "being seen of them forty days, and speaking of the things pertaining to the Kingdom of God" (Acts 1:3). True, it was not for them to know then whether the Kingdom would be at once restored to Israel, for that depended on how the nation would treat the Pentecostal message. Their rejection of it showed that the true answer to the disciples' question was in the negative, but the fact remains that the Kingdom in a broader sense did occupy a large place in the early testimony (see Acts 8:12; 14:22; 19:8; 20:25; 28:31).

This last reference at the very close of the Acts is of peculiar interest. It effectually disposes of the theory held by some that all Kingdom teaching is Jewish and was finally superseded for us by the higher revelation of "the Prison Epistles", as they term Ephesians, Philippians and Colossians. This, the last verse of the book, shows us the apostle "preaching the Kingdom of God and teaching the things of Jesus Christ" during this very "prison period". How could his oral and written teaching be in disagreement?

He saw no inconsistency between the "gospel of the grace of God" and Kingdom teaching, as his address to the Ephesian elders shows: "the ministry, which I have received of the Lord Jesus, to testify the gospel of the grace of God. And now, behold, I know that ye all among whom I have gone preaching the Kingdom of God, shall see my face no more" (Acts 20:24-25). The former gives us the privileges of the gospel where all is of grace, the latter the responsibilities of those who are partakers of that grace. We do not enter a sphere of self-pleasing when we believe the gospel, but of Christ-pleasing, and the path that leads to the future Kingdom is not one of soft delights but of "much tribulation".

The prophet Obadiah ends his short but severe prophecy against

Edom with the assurance of Jehovah's ultimate triumph, "The Kingdom shall be the Lord's", but this will only be in the face of the deadly opposition of man and Satan, when Christ returns in person "in power and great glory".

This is quite outside the scope of modern thought. Even the religious world derides the literal fulfilment of what it calls "Jewish Apocalyptics". To such "the Kingdom" means only an improved order of things brought about by religious reform and social legislation. But the King to reign over their renovated world will not be the Christ of God, but the great "Super-Man" of their desire, the product of all that is best in modern thought and progress, with something else thrown in, for another "will give him his own power and seat and authority".

It seems likely indeed that Satan, who is the great counterfeiter of divine truth, will succeed in deceiving the world with a brief semblance of the true reign of peace.

The answer to all this will be a terrible laugh. "He that sitteth in the Heavens shall laugh, the Lord shall have them in derision...Yet have I set My King upon My holy hill of Zion" (Psa 2:4,6). "When they shall say, 'Peace and safety,' then sudden destruction shall come upon them...and they shall not escape" (1 Thess 5:3). The "divine event to which the whole creation moves" is not the final salvation, but the final suppression of every rebel and the complete exaltation of God in Christ. No wonder then that this theme should permeate the Word of God.

Psalmists sang of it. Prophets foretold its rise and glories. Apostles saw it in vision and the Lord Himself proclaimed it. The reason is not hard to find. The setting up of the Kingdom will mark the triumph of Christ, the manifestation of the saints, the restoration of Israel and widespread blessing to the world. Peter describes it in his address to the nation in Acts 3, as "the restitution of all things" – the great antitype of the day of jubilee – when "Ye shall return every man unto his possession and...every man unto his family" (Lev 25:10).

No wonder this was the Spirit-given theme of all the holy prophets since the world began, and that while they told of "the sufferings of Christ", they should also speak with rapture of "the glories that should follow".

What is the Kingdom?

A kingdom has been defined as "the sphere in which the authority of a king is recognised": not an exhaustive definition perhaps, but it will serve our purpose. The Kingdom of God is the sphere in which His authority is recognised.

We must not confound the Kingdom and the Church any more than we would confound Great Britain and the Royal Family. The Kingdom began before the Church was born, and will outlive it down here. Abraham, Isaac, Jacob, and the Old Testament saints who never were in the Church, will sit down in the Kingdom of God (Matt 8:12). The saved of Apocalyptic times who never will be in the Church will reign with Christ (Rev 20:4).

The centre is the same all through, but the circles are different. In the present dispensation all who are in the Church are in the Kingdom, though not exactly in their quality as members of the Church, but rather as "children of the Kingdom". But the Kingdom is not coterminous with the Church but, though including it, stretches out on every side like the atmosphere around an air balloon. The Kingdom now includes the false with the true, all who merely "profess and call themselves Christians", along with the true household of faith. Even in the Millennial Kingdom this will hold good, and along with the true saints there will be those who yield feigned obedience (Psa 18:44; 81:15).

Does it not behove all who "name the Name of Christ to depart from iniquity"? The solemn testing time is nearing: "His fan is in His hand and He shall thoroughly purge His floor, and will gather the wheat into His garner; but the chaff He will burn with fire unquenchable" (Luke 3:17). The mixed sown field is not the Church but the world. When the King comes back the tares will be gathered in bundles and burnt. "All things that offend and they which do iniquity shall be gathered out" of the Kingdom and judged (Matt 13:40). Note carefully that these are not said to be unfaithful children of God, but "children of the evil one".

How Distinguished? – Kingdom of Heaven (lit. of the Heavens) and Kingdom of God

Some say that the "Kingdom of Heaven" includes the false with the true, while the "Kingdom of God" excludes all but the true. This would be very simple if it were true. But, unfortunately, it is not borne out by the Scriptures. The fact that the parable of the mustard seed and leaven are in Matthew 13 referred to the Kingdom of Heaven, and in Luke 13 to the Kingdom of God is enough to show it. Besides, in Matthew 13:11, and Luke 8:10, the expression "mysteries of the Kingdom of Heaven" and "of God" are used interchangeably.

The two terms really mean the same thing from slightly different standpoints. In "Kingdom of God" it is the person who rules who is in view, in the "Kingdom of Heaven" the centre from which He rules, as one might say equally well: the Empire of King George or the Empire of Great Britain. The Kingdom in both aspects ought ideally to be true now – but the enemy has sowed tares and there is confusion.

"Kingdom of Heaven" and the "Heavenly Kingdom"

These must be carefully distinguished as being essentially different. The term "heavenly kingdom" describes that side of the kingdom in which the heavenly saints will have their part. "The Kingdom of Heaven" is the earthly side of the kingdom administered from heaven, and going on as we see in Matthew 13, even now in mystery. In the latter a saved Israel and spared Gentile nations will share. These two aspects of the kingdom are like the upper and lower storeys of the same mansion. Had Israel as a nation accepted the Lord Jesus as their Messiah, His sufferings would have been no less indispensable, but they would not have been inflicted by Israel. Clearly the Romans would not have acquiesced quietly in the setting up of a Jewish kingdom, and by their hands alone He might have died, to the grief of Israel, rather than to their guilt. Had Israel as a nation accepted the testimony of the apostles to a risen Christ "their sins would have been blotted out, times of refreshing" would have been ushered in, and the Lord would have come back and set up His kingdom (Acts 3:19,20).

I believe that the meaning of the disputed words in John 3:12, is to be found in the difference here drawn. "If I have told you earthly things and ye believe not, how shall ye believe if I tell you of heavenly things." The contrast here is not between the "new-birth" and "eternal life". New birth is from above and is essentially a heavenly thing. Nor, indeed, is this contrast found at all, as I judge, in the former and latter parts of our Lord's discourse to Nicodemus. The contrast is rather between what the Lord had previously announced to the Pharisees as the representatives of the nation – "the Kingdom of heaven is at hand" (this was an earthly hope for an earthly people) – and the truth that the Lord was propounding all through to Nicodemus, which was of a different order and on a heavenly plane – the new birth and the possession of eternal life. Entrance into the Kingdom of God in its true and spiritual character entailed "a birth from above". The words of the Lord in fact were in view of the darkness of Nicodemus who represented the Pharisees as a class. 'If you did not believe My simple testimony as regards the national hope of Israel, how could you be expected to believe when I tell you of a spiritual Kingdom?'

Setting Up of the Kingdom

But why should the Kingdom need setting up? Is it not universal? Through the rebellion of angels and men, immense tracts of the moral universe lie today outside the Kingdom of God. Men ask petulantly why God did not prevent it? They forget that the creation of responsible beings capable of moral choice could not but make the misuse of that faculty a possibility, though not a necessity. How could moral freedom be confined and its possible misuse eliminated? As we know too well this faculty of choice has been perverted - hence temporary but terrible confusion in the universe.

The Kingdom of Darkness

When Satan fell, a new kingdom was set up, an "imperium in imperio" – the kingdom of darkness – a dark blot on the hitherto unsullied universe of God. This kingdom is doubtless a highly organised and cunningly devised imitation of the Kingdom of God. For we read of a hierarchy of principalities and powers and rulers in it as in the heavenly sphere. These are governed by Satan as the Prince of the power of the air, with all his perverted wisdom and age-long experience. This kingdom received a vast extension when man fell. We little realise the immense triumph that accrued to Satan, when the whole human race was swept at one blow into his kingdom. Like a phoenix rising from its ashes, he became henceforth the "Prince of this world" and their god. We need not suppose Satan was without legal right to the former title, or our Lord would not have recognised it. Nor was it a false offer he made to Christ, when he offered Him "all the kingdoms of this world and their glory", for how could he have hoped to win the coveted worship with rewards he could not bestow?

After the cross Satan is never called the "Prince of this world". There his power was destroyed and principalities and powers were spoiled. Christ became the owner of this earth by purchase, and its rightful King. But the whole world remains under the Usurper's spell, "lying in the wicked one", while believers are delivered by the Father "from the power of darkness and translated into the Kingdom of the Son of His love" (Col 1:13). "We see not yet all things put under Him" (Heb 2:8), for the time has not yet come to crush His enemies. God can still be just and the justifier of him that believeth in Jesus. To rebel man the message still goes forth: "Be ye reconciled to God". To Christ has been entrusted the double work of mediator and "Repairer of the Breaches". The victory was won on Calvary, manifested at Joseph's empty tomb, and will be consummated when death itself shall be destroyed.

Still mercy holds back the sword of judgment, and "grace reigns through righteousness", but the Lord is returning to set up His Kingdom, and then righteousness will reign. This reign will last a thousand years. It will be overshadowed for a moment by the great final rebellion of man and Satan (Rev 20:8,9) only to shine out again, like the sun after a partial eclipse, in its final and eternal phase – as "the everlasting Kingdom of our Lord and Saviour Jesus Christ". It will be after the last judgment of the Great White Throne – "when the last enemy shall have been destroyed" that the Lord Jesus shall deliver up the Kingdom to His Father, that "God may be all in all" (1 Cor 15:24-26).

"Delivering up the Kingdom"

It is most important to understand this phrase. Can it mean that the Lord will cease to reign? Some have thought so, and have intercalated what I believe to be a purely imaginary period between the millennial Kingdom and the Eternal State. This they have styled "the dispensation of the ages of the ages", at the close of which alone Christ will "deliver up the Kingdom" – but "the ages of the ages" means by New Testament usage eternity and nothing short of it. (See Gal 1:5, Rev 4:9; 11:15; 19:3; 20:10.) Besides, it is "when the last enemy is destroyed" that Christ will deliver up the Kingdom, not "ages of ages" afterwards.

There is another fatal flaw in this interpretation. Though it puts off the final day as long as possible, it admits the eventual end of the reign of Christ, whereas we know this will never be, for Daniel 7:14 tells us "it will never pass away", and Luke 1:33 – "of His Kingdom there shall be no end"; no, not even at the end of a fancied period, "the dispensation of the ages of the ages".

How then do we understand the expression "deliver up the Kingdom"? The identical verb is used in this same chapter (1 Cor 15:3): "I delivered unto you that which I also received". The apostle did not give it up himself when he "delivered it up" to the Corinthians: it might be said "he presented it to them" but kept it himself. So Christ will present back the Kingdom of God purged of every hostile power and influence and fully restored to its allegiance, but without any thought of ceasing to be the Viceroy of Jehovah.

"The Son Himself subject"

But how are we to understand the words in the same chapter, "Then shall the Son also Himself be subject unto Him that put all things under Him, that God may be all in all" (1 Cor 15:28)? Does not this mean, it is asked, that some change will take place in the relationship of Christ to the Father? Or that His humanity will, in some unexplained way, be reabsorbed into the Godhead? No, it means the very opposite. The Lord has for ever "taken upon Himself the form of a servant", and as such He became subject to the Father. He is "the same yesterday, today, and for ever" and can never change. The order of the words in the Greek, as the late Dr. Dale of Birmingham has pointed out, is important. They should read, not "Then shall the Son also", but "Then also shall the Son" be subject. "Also" qualifies the word "then" not "the Son". The words far from denoting a change, preclude it. Then no less than before shall the Son continue to be the servant of Jehovah and as such reign over the new heaven and the new earth.

To compare great things with small, when the Indian Mutiny broke out in 1857, John Lawrence was Governor of the Punjab. He ruled on behalf of the East India Company. On his shoulders fell the chief burden of the great struggle. His mainly was the brain and his the hand that crushed the rebels and handed back the jeopardised provinces to British rule. He did not for that become an independent Sovereign, even less cease to rule, but as Lord Lawrence he ruled on, in a wider sense than ever, as viceroy of the British crown. So the Lord, when He has crushed the great rebellion, destroyed His foes, and handed back the Kingdom to God in enhanced glory and stability, will continue to rule, in a fuller sense even than before, over the new heaven and the new earth, but still only as the Viceroy of Jehovah "that God may be all in all".

The phrase "He must reign till He hath put all enemies under His feet" (1 Cor 15:27) has been taken as an additional reason for asserting that He will cease to reign. But "till" has not necessarily this limited meaning, as reference to such passages as Romans 5:13 will show: "until the law sin was in the world" and afterwards too, as we know too well. (See also Matt 24:38; Acts 7:18; Rev 2:20.) The point is that nothing can really interrupt His reign till His final triumph, no rebellion of man, no inrush of fallen spirits. This is true, however, without prejudice to the continuance of His reign.

2. THE KINGDOM IN THE OLD TESTAMENT

In the following sections we will consider the subject of the Kingdom as revealed:–

in the Old Testament;
in the New Testament;
as to its subjects;
as to its character.

The history of the Kingdom of God divides itself naturally, as all history does, into past, present, and future, but it has this peculiarity over all other history, that it is God-breathed and therefore of divine accuracy, and God-planned and so of divine significance. In Old Testament times the Kingdom was portrayed in figure, and foretold in prophecy and vision as to its future literal manifestation. In the Old Testament certain principles of the Kingdom were revealed, but as their carrying out was entrusted to man, failure came in all along the line, failure apparently hopeless and final.

THE KINGDOM OF GOD

We may divide the consideration of the Kingdom in the Old Testament under the aspects of Theocracy, Autocracy, Viceroyalty, and Interregnum.

1. Theocracy

The first lesson God would teach the universe is that He must be King. This is most reasonable, for He alone has the right, and most desirable, for He alone has the power. It is the last lesson man in his independence will learn. "Our lips are our own, who is Lord over us?" (Psa 12:4) was man's reply to God under law. "We will not have this man to reign over us" (Luke19:14) was man's reply when God revealed Himself in grace. But the heart taught of God humbly confesses, "O Lord our God, other lords besides Thee have had dominion over us: but by Thee only will we make mention of Thy name" (Isa 27:13); "Lord, what wilt Thou have me to do?" (Acts 9:6). The first surrender to Christ is the beginning of eternal blessing.

The first mention of a word in the Scriptures often helps as to its subsequent meaning. The first reference to the Kingdom is in the song of Moses (Exod 15:18), "The Lord shall reign for ever and ever". This is the first recorded song in the Bible, and what was the subject of it? It was Israel's first experience of salvation and they wished to crown their Saviour King. Notice the beautiful order: first, "the salvation of the Lord", then a song before the Lord, lastly, submission to the Lord. Deliverance calls for a *Te Deum* and then an oath of fealty to the Deliverer. "The Lord shall reign for ever and ever": this was a God-given thought, it was His purpose to be their King. "Ye shall be unto Me a kingdom of priests and a holy nation" (Exod 19:6). "He was King in Jeshurun" (Deut 33:5). This was to be a national position, not the prerogative of certain faithful men. The giving of the law was the legislation of the kingdom and though that law was too often broken, the sacrifices permitted Jehovah to retain His seat between the cherubim in the midst of His people. This was theocracy, the personal rule of Jehovah. He was a Shepherd-King, for He led them as a flock through the wilderness. He would "bring them in, and plant them in the mountain of His inheritance" (Exod 15:17). All through the times of Joshua and the Judges, though for their sins He left them for long periods in the hands of their enemies, He never ceased to rule over them, and would have continued to be their King had they been satisfied to go on with Him. But they were not, they must have a king like the nations around, a visible king to lead them against the Ammonites. To be reduced to count upon God alone is, in man's esteem, a terrible pass to be brought to: anything but that, a golden calf, a worldly king, an unconverted leader. This led to the second aspect of the Kingdom.

2. **Autocracy**

This really meant rejection of Jehovah. The rule of the Judges was of a different character. They were raised up by God to bring the people back to Him, but God will not share His throne with another king. Samuel was grieved for was it not he whom Israel was rejecting? "No," answered the Lord, "They have not rejected thee, but they have rejected Me, that I should not reign over them" (1 Sam 8:7). However, He let them have their way that they might learn that it is "an evil thing and a bitter" to forsake the Lord their God (Jer 2:19). He did not, however, grant their request without warning them of what it would mean to have a king: selfishness on his part, the words "he will take", are repeated to them six times; servitude on their part, "ye shall be his servants". We see this illustrated in the whole history of Saul, the man after their own heart. Nearly 400 years later Jehovah reminds Israel of their fatal choice, in case they might even then learn their lesson. "O Israel, thou hast destroyed thyself, but in Me is thine help. I will be thy King. Where is any other that may save thee in all thy cities and thy judges of whom thou saidst, Give me a king and princes? I gave thee a king in mine anger, and took him away in My wrath." (Hos 13:9-11) "He gave them their request but sent leanness into their soul" (Psa 106:15). Saul thus became king in his own right. He acknowledged Jehovah as far as it suited him. God is useful against Philistines but when God saved him from the Philistines and told him to destroy utterly the Amalekites – figure of the flesh and its works – it was another thing. He spared "the best...and all that was good and would not utterly destroy them" (1 Sam 15:9). Many a man will profess to serve God till his pocket suffers, but breaks down under the strain of money. Saul had admirable qualities. He was nature at its best estate, but he was a murderer at heart. He began with rebellion and ended with witchcraft, and stands as a figure of the "Anti-Christ" who will begin with an

THE KINGDOM OF GOD

acknowledgment of God, but will eventually "deny the Father and the Son" (1 John 2:21).

Saul the autocrat rejects the word of the Lord and is himself rejected from being King. Man has had his chance and failed. Now God comes in with His resources. "I have provided Me a King," is His word to Samuel, "a man after mine own heart who shall fulfil all My will." This brings us to the third aspect of the Kingdom.

3. Viceroyalty

The anointing of David introduces the divine ideal: David was to rule in dependence on Jehovah, figure of the true Viceroy to be born in Bethlehem "to be ruler in Israel whose goings forth have been from of old from everlasting" (Mic 5:2).

As has been said, the Kingdom in the Old Testament was in figure only. It could not be otherwise till the true King came. David is the figure of Him that is to come, the anointed Shepherd who showed he was the man of God's choice by slaying Goliath, as Christ did when "through death He destroyed him that had the power of death". It was in His death he proved Himself to the man whose eyes God had opened, to be truly God's King: "Lord remember me when Thou comest into Thy kingdom" (Luke 23:42).

Rejected and pursued, David became the centre for "everyone that was in distress, and everyone that was in debt, and everyone that was bitter of soul". Not very high motives it may be rejoined, but how many come to Christ from high motives? Nevertheless, though Adullam and the desert were not pleasant places, we do not read that a single one of these gathered ones went back to Saul, for they had a heart for David: "Thine are we, David, and on thy side .... for thy God helpeth thee." They had also the word of God represented by Gad the seer, and the priest of God, Abiathar with the ephod. Thus they had, as we have today in Christ, a prophet, priest, and king. Those who came to David in this, the period of his rejection, Benjamites, Gadites, and men of Manasseh were comparatively few. But the chief of them are inscribed by name. The Lord will confess the names of those who confess Him now in the day of His rejection. Those who came to David in Hebron, when he had been crowned king, were numbered by thousands and their names are not given. We may again notice a fact that bears on our general subject that David eventually became king over the whole of Israel, not over a favoured class of those who had been specially faithful to him in his rejection. No doubt these latter had special places of honour but the point is that all were made to share in the kingdom. The period of David's rejection will have a further fulfilment in the days of Anti-Christ, antitype of Saul, the one who will come in his own name and be received by an apostate nation.

The final testimony from the faithful remnant of Israel will then be "the gospel of the kingdom", to be clearly distinguished from "the gospel of the grace of God", though both are based on redemption. The burden of this testimony will be, "The King is coming."

Many of the Psalms belong to this period and describe the sufferings of the faithful witnesses at the hand of Anti-Christ. There are three specially which we may notice, all beginning with the same words, "The Lord reigneth": Psalms 93, 97, 99. In the first, the Psalmist speaks of "the floods lifting up their voice"; in the second, of "all they that serve graven images that boast themselves of idols". The third is addressed to Israel, who are exhorted to tremble. In spite of all "the Lord reigneth", "He is mightier than the waves of the sea"; "He alone is worthy to be worshipped"; "Worship Him, all ye gods."

It is easy to see how such a testimony will be needed, when the idol of the Man of Sin, the great head of the Roman empire, will by satanic power have been quickened into life by Anti-Christ - and set up "where it ought not", probably in the very Holy of Holies of the Temple at Jerusalem (see Matt 24:15). He will sit there personally himself no doubt now and again, but will usually, we may infer, be represented by his "abomination" or idol (2 Thess 2:4; Rev 13:15).

The reign of David, divided into two periods of seven and thirty-three years, shows us Christ reigning in the midst of His enemies, gradually extending His rule to the ends of the earth. This will be a reign of righteousness in which the Lord will "rule the nations with a rod of iron, and dash in pieces like a potter's vessel" those who rebel. Then will be fulfilled the promise of Psalm 2:8, which is often misapplied to the conquests of the gospel: "Ask of Me, and I shall give Thee the heathen for Thine inheritance, and the uttermost parts of the earth for Thy possession".

THE KINGDOM OF GOD

The latter part of David's reign, when "he had been delivered from all his enemies", and specially the glorious times of Solomon's era, seem to apply strictly to the times when God shall have given His Anointed rest from all His enemies, the day of final victory, when the Lord will have put down all authority and power.

Looking back for a moment over the Kingdom in the Old Testament, we see a truth illustrated which runs through the Scriptures that the creature unsustained by divine power sooner or later fails. Lucifer, the anointed cherub, that covered the throne of God and was His representative in universal government, and a light bearer to the universe, failed through pride, another name for independence. What has marked the history of man but self-sufficiency and failure? Of this Adam, Noah, Nadab and Abihu, Korah, and Solomon are examples out of many. Solomon who began so well at Gibeon, afterwards did the very things forbidden to a king (Deut 17:16,17). He multiplied horses from Egypt, silver and gold in abundance and, what is worse, wives. The kingdom was divided. All the kings of Israel were guilty, not by the mere fact that they were kings of the separated tribes, but because they followed the sin of Jeroboam who made Israel to sin. It was the calves that were wrong, not the mere fact of the continuance of the state of division. Every king of Judah failed, even men of faith like Asa, Uzziah, Hezekiah, at least in their closing days. At last, after years of longsuffering such as none but Jehovah could have displayed, the cup was full and judgment fell first on Israel and then on Judah. The kingdom was taken away from them and entrusted to the Gentile powers. This introduces the last great phase of the kingdom in its earthly aspect which has lasted ever since.

4. The Great Interregnum

From Daniel we learn under two prophetic figures that these Gentile powers were to be four, and only four. The Carthaginians came very near to superseding the Roman power and setting up a Punic empire in its place. The Mussulman power later on nearly succeeded in establishing a fifth monarchy, but failed at Tours and Vienna. The word of the Lord by Daniel must hold good. In Nebuchadnezzar's dream the golden head represented Babylon, the silver shoulders the kingdom of the Medes and Persians, the brazen loins Greece, and the iron legs the Roman empire. The metals decrease in value and increase in strength. The kingdoms decrease in moral character but increase in brute force. In the last phase of the Roman empire, an element of weakness, the clay, will be introduced denoting what we see around us today, rule from beneath, the rule of the people – as far removed from God's ideal as the east is from the west. It is as a magnificent image that the Gentile powers stand before the great Babylonian monarch. But to God's prophet, these same powers appear as brute beasts decreasing in moral worth and increasing in ferocity. Here the lion, the king of beasts, represents Babylon in the person of the restored Nebuchadnezzar. The bear represents the Medo-Persian empire "raising itself on one side", the Persian element more powerful than that of Media. The four-winged leopard represents the Grecian empire of Alexander divided among his four generals, namely, Cassander, who seized Macedonia and Greece; Antigonus, to whom fell Asia Minor; Seleucus, whose share was Babylon and the Eastern provinces; and Ptolemy, who became ruler of Egypt. Then, fourthly, the nameless monster, "dreadful and terrible and strong exceedingly", represents the great Roman empire.

Some have thought that these four beasts must represent four nations, whose power will develop remarkably around the shores of the Mediterranean in the last days, possibly Britain, France, Italy, and Greece, and this on the ground that the prophet sees them existing at the same time and that they cannot therefore represent successive monarchies. But the same objection might be raised to the generally accepted interpretation of the image of ch.2. The four empires there, though successive, are seen in the vision as contemporaneous. I think the sense of sequence in the four kingdoms represented by the beasts is clearly conveyed in the interpretation of the vision in ch.7: (e.g. v.23): "The fourth beast shall be the fourth kingdom upon earth...and the ten horns out of his kingdom are the ten kings that shall arise". This last phrase goes on to the final development of the fourth empire and corresponds to the ten toes of the image in ch.2.

The little horn of Daniel 7 will be, I have little doubt, the Man of Sin of 2 Thessalonians 2, the first beast of Revelation 13, the last great governmental head of the revived Roman empire. He is quite distinct from the Anti-Christ, the second beast of Revelation 13, the false prophet, as he is called later – the religious head, if we may so term it, of the last days. These two will, however, work hand in hand and are so closely identified that they are sometimes confused. We must carefully distinguish again from either of these the little horn of Daniel 8, who will, I judge, be the king of the North, at once an opponent of the two former beasts and a deadly enemy of Israel. And these great godless Gentile powers will not be subdued to God by the preaching of the gospel, as some have hoped, but by direct divine interposition. The king of the North will be first dealt with as described in Ezekiel 38 and 39 and Joel 2:20, by judgment from heaven, the beast and the false prophet by the final coming of Christ in power and judgment as described in Revelation 19. "The stone cut out of the mountain without hands", on which Israel has stumbled and been broken, will fall on them and will grind them to powder. These two monsters of iniquity will suffer summary judgment in the lake of fire, and their armies will be slain by the sword of Him who is King of kings and Lord of lords.

Such, then, is an outline of the Kingdom in the Old Testament. It begins in the hands of God, and ends in the hands of the Gentile powers.

3. THE KINGDOM IN THE NEW TESTAMENT

The Gentile interregnum had lasted 600 years when suddenly the wise men from the East arrived with their startling enquiry: "Where is He that is born King of the Jews? for we have seen His star in the East and have come to worship Him" (Matt 2:2). The first question in the Old Testament was God seeking man, here it is man seeking God. The question fell "like a bolt from the blue" on Herod and Jerusalem. "A King! our King! we neither know Him nor want Him," was their reply in effect. King Herod's attitude is easily apprehended, but why should the Jews themselves prefer an Edomite to a king of their own? Because it was perfectly well understood that he who claimed to be their king would prove to be their Messiah (see Matt 2:4), and they were not in a moral state to desire such an one. The wise men will "rise up in the judgment and condemn them". For was it not strange that they should "come from the uttermost parts of the earth" to see only the infant heir to the petty throne of Judea and stranger still that they should desire to worship Him? No doubt God had, in His own way, taught them that the Kingdom of that babe should one day "stretch from shore to shore" and that He would be their King, who was even then worthy of their worship.

The consideration of the Kingdom in the New Testament may be considered in four aspects, as in the case of the former dispensation in the Old Testament, i.e. the Kingdom - Presented; Rejected; In Mystery; Manifested.

1. The Kingdom Presented

When a man claims an inheritance he must show his credentials, much more when he claims a throne. A claimant to the ancient throne of the house of David must satisfy the most exacting tests. Ever since Eden, the world had had the promise of a Deliverer. For centuries His coming, His race, and His tribe, the manner of His birth, and the works He would perform had been the common property of all who could read the Jewish Scriptures. How impossible then for any but the true Messiah to fulfil in His person such manifold conditions! If a man can off-hand produce a key which perfectly fits a complicated lock of nine wards, the chances are the key is the right one and that the man who made the key had something to do with making the lock. In this case the key fits the lock and the heir fits the throne. God did not send His Son to claim the throne of David without authentic and adequate credentials. Let us exhibit nine of them.

(1) He comes of the right stock

Two genealogies are put in, as the legal phrase has it, one by Matthew and the other by Luke. That of Matthew traces down from David through Solomon; that of Luke traces up to David through Solomon's younger brother, Nathan. But in Matthew, Joseph is said to be the son of Jacob, and in Luke the son of Heli. But how can one person have two grandfathers? Only in one way, through his father and mother. The name of Joseph, then, must take the place of Mary in one of the genealogies. There can be no reasonable doubt that this is the true explanation. If the genealogy of Matthew be that of

Joseph, and 1:16 would seem to make it clear, then that of Luke gives us the line of Mary, through whom our Lord became literally of "the seed of David", and, according to the words of Gabriel, "would sit upon the throne of David His father". By Jewish custom, the name of a woman, though it may occur in a genealogy (as for instance Rahab, Ruth, Bathsheba, Tamar, in Matthew 1) must not occur in the direct line: thus, though the names of the daughters of Zelophehad are given in Joshua 17:3, they are only incidentally referred to in the genealogies of Manasseh (1 Chron 7:15). Accordingly the name of Joseph, the son-in-law of Heli, is substituted for Mary, and he is called the father of our Lord. And, indeed, he was so properly by Jewish law, by his marriage with Mary, the child Jesus becoming his legal son and heir. Thus Luke, by tracing the genealogy of our Lord up to Adam, proves His qualification to be the "seed of the woman" foretold in Eden. Matthew, by showing his lineal descent from Abraham, Judah, and David, makes clear that He fulfilled the necessary condition that the Messiah should be at once of the "seed of Abraham" (Gen 13 :15); Shiloh of the tribe of Judah (Gen 49 :10); and a son of the royal house of David (1 Sam 7:14-17). All this proves that the wise men from the East were truly taught of God to recognise in the babe of Bethlehem the royal heir and the Divine Messiah.

(2) He was born of the right kind of mother

She was a virgin, according to the sign proffered to Ahaz by the mouth of Isaiah (7:14). "Before they came together she was found with child of the Holy Ghost", nor "did they come together till she had brought forth her firstborn son". "Now all this was done that it might be fulfilled which was spoken of the Lord by the prophet, saying, Behold a virgin shall be with child and shall bring forth a son, and they shall call His name Emmanuel" (Matt 1:22-23). Cyrus was named 150 years before his birth, and King Josiah 300 years before his. The name of Immanuel was conferred 750 years before the prophecy was fulfilled. It is foolish, as well as false, to pretend that the Virgin Birth is not a fundamental article of faith. If the Lord could not offer this credential, His claim to Messiahship must have failed.

(3) He was born in the right place

Bethlehem was foretold 710 years before by Micah to be the

birthplace of the Messiah (5:2), and certified as such by the chief priests and scribes in answer to the enquiries of Herod: "Out of thee (Bethlehem Ephratah) shall He come forth unto Me that is to be ruler in Israel whose goings forth have been from of old from everlasting." These three credentials, His race, His birth, His birthplace ought to have appealed convincingly to Israel. The next was specially addressed to the Gentiles who had not the Oracles of God.

(4) The right kind of sign

To the wise men of the East, doubtless skilled in astronomical research, what would have appealed more eloquently than a portent in the heavens? What the star exactly was, or how it spoke to them, is not revealed. It left no doubt in their minds whose star it was and what it meant. "We have seen His star in the East and are come to worship Him." It was to them a convincing credential of the birth of the king. Nor was it challenged by the chief priests of Israel. We may compare with this Numbers 24:17, where the appearance of a star is connected with the coming of Him who should rule Israel and destroy His enemies. "A star shall come out of Jacob and a sceptre shall rise out of Israel which shall smite the corners of Moab and destroy all the children of Seth." It would almost seem as if this prophecy of Balaam had been handed down through long generations by the providence of God till the star appeared, and then "the wise understood" the sign. "When they saw the star they rejoiced with exceeding great joy." It was the testimony to the One they sought once more revealed, and it was to Him they offered their gifts, it was Him they worshipped, not His mother.

(5) He received the right kind of testimony from heaven

(a) The testimony of the Father was given at His baptism and on the mount: "This is My Son in whom I am well pleased"; "This is My beloved Son...hear Him" (Matt 3:17; 17:5). The Jews deny that God could have a Son, but their own Scriptures demand that the one who should be king should also be the Son of Jehovah (Psa 2). The one whom Jehovah calls My "King", in v.6, He affirms to be "His Son" in v. 7. See also Isaiah 9:5-6: "The Son given" was to be called "Wonderful, Counsellor, the Mighty God, the Everlasting Father, the Prince of Peace". But when speaking of the Divine Son, we must, of course, avoid the thought of succession in time involved in our terms father and son. He was the Eternal Son: there never was a time when He was not.

(b) The descent of the Spirit upon Him at His baptism fulfilled a necessary condition foretold of the Messiah. It is written in such Scriptures as Isaiah 11:2, "The spirit of the Lord shall rest upon Him"; Isaiah 61:1, "The spirit of the Lord is upon Me because He hath anointed Me". These Scriptures clearly refer to the Messiah, the Anointed One, and were always so understood by the Jews themselves.

(6) He received the right testimony on earth

Consider the testimony of John the Forerunner. It was not "Behold the Man of God", but "Behold the Lamb of God", because every offering for sin, and every burnt offering of the past dispensation, demanded an antitype, and the prophecies demanded a suffering Messiah who should be "led as a lamb to the slaughter", and be "smitten for the transgression of His people".

Consider also the testimony of all to His holiness, because the Lamb must be without blemish. The angel Gabriel, His apostles, His enemies, His judges, His betrayer, the dying robber, the demons themselves (though He refused their testimony) all bore witness that He was the holy, spotless One.

(7) The right fulfilment in His person of the Old Testament predictions

These can be traced throughout Matthew's gospel, e.g. 4:14-16; 8:17; 21:4; 26:54; 27:35.

(8) The right character of His works

Miracles *per se* do not prove a divine Messiah, for the Anti-Christ will perform great wonders (Rev 13:2; 2 Thess 2:9), but the Lord could not have been the Messiah had He, like John the Baptist, done no miracle. He could read out Isaiah 61:1 in the public synagogue, without fear of challenge (Luke 4:18), and could refer to His miracles as a sufficient proof that He was "He that should come" (Matt 11:5; see also John 5:36; 14:11).

(9) The right culmination of His earthly ministry

His death fulfilled Daniel 9:26, "Messiah shall be cut off". His burial fulfilled Isaiah 53:9, "He made His grave with the wicked, and with the rich in His death". His resurrection fulfilled Psalm 16:10, "Thou wilt not leave My soul in hell, neither wilt Thou suffer Thy Holy One to see corruption". And His ascension and session at the right hand of God fulfilled the words of Psalm 110:1, "Sit Thou at My right hand, until I make Thine enemies Thy footstool".

These credentials have been examined and accepted by millions who felt their need of a Saviour, and have found the need more than satisfied in the person and work of Jesus Christ. They have been generally ignored by millions more, but who can deny with the proofs before them that it is unbelief that is unreasonable, not faith?

Summary of Matthew's Gospel

A very brief summary of the Gospel of Matthew will enable us to grasp the first three aspects of the Kingdom in the New Testament. After the formal proclamation on the part of John, and then of the Lord Himself, that the "Kingdom of Heaven was at hand", the laws of the Kingdom are promulgated. Men who acknowledge that they cannot keep the Sinaitic law, desire to place themselves "under the Sermon on the Mount", not perceiving that the latter is broader and deeper and is thus more difficult of fulfilment than the former. I believe this Kingdom code will come into force literally when the Kingdom is once more being announced by the chosen heralds of Israel, sealed with the Spirit for this testimony, and will naturally not cease to apply when the Kingdom is set up, and when "a King shall reign in righteousness", and when He shall early destroy "all the wicked of the earth". But in its application to ourselves, and we can apply it with blessing to our own life and conduct, it must be understood with and be qualified by the rest of the New Testament. Such words as "Give to him that asketh of thee and from him that would borrow of thee turn thou not away", should be taken with other words equally inspired: "If any would not work, neither should he eat"; and again, "Owe no man anything". That it is not intended to apply literally to the present time seems clear from a comparison of John 18:22-23, and Acts 23:2-3, with Matthew 5:39, for neither our Lord nor the Apostle turned the other cheek when smitten. A somewhat shallow objection has been raised to the above exegesis, that it destroys the unity of the word of God. But this unity does not

THE KINGDOM OF GOD

consist in ignoring dispensational truth, but in acknowledging unity of authorship and design. One wonders why such objectors do not carry out Jewish ceremonial, or adopt Matthew 10 as their missionary handbook for the present day.

In chapters 8 and 9 the Lord proves that the Kingdom of God was among them, by showing His authority over disease (8:16), the elements (3:26), demons (8:31), the wills of men (9:9), blindness and death (9:25-29); and then in chapter 11, by communicating the same powers to His disciples. These are the "powers of the world to come" manifested in the early days as long as the setting up of the Kingdom was left still an open question, and which will be seen again before its final establishment.

2. The Kingdom Rejected

This has been foreshadowed from the first by the opposition of the scribes and Pharisees, the responsible representatives of the nation. The accusation of 9:34, repeated in 12:21, "He casteth out devils by Beelzebub the prince of the devils", marks a turning point in our Lord's attitude to the nation, for it discounted His final rejection when He offered Himself in chapter 21 as the promised King. This led on immediately to His crucifixion and death.

The rejection of the Kingdom introduces us to the third and present phase.

3. The Kingdom in Mystery

The miracles and works of the Lord, chapters 8-12, were a proof that the Kingdom of God was with His people. The Pharisees, by imputing these works to Satanic power, rejected the Kingdom. Henceforth the Lord changes His method of address and "without a parable spake He not unto them". The Kingdom was henceforth for the time being "not of this world". For when the King is rejected the Kingdom cannot openly be set up. It did not, however, cease to exist. It assumed a new character, that of a Kingdom in mystery.

A mystery in the New Testament is not something incomprehensible, but an altogether new and unexpected development of a truth already known, resulting in something hitherto unknown*. The mysteries of God are God's answers to

---

* See "Mysteries of the New Testament" p.72-138 of this volume.

man's failures; those of Satan are the full development of those failures. Thus, the coming of Christ in glory was not a mystery. It was clearly revealed in the Old Testament, but that that coming should have a preliminary stage by which His people should be caught away from the evil to come and thus never have to pass through "the great tribulation", or even death, was a mystery revealed in 1 Corinthians 15:51: "Behold I show you a mystery, we shall not all sleep but we shall all be changed". In this sense the Kingdom was not a mystery. The prophets had all foretold it, but always in connection with the King sitting upon the throne. How could it otherwise exist? This was the mystery. The Kingdom exists now in a hidden form. It comes not with observation, but it is there.

The seven parables of Matthew 13 are the mysteries of the Kingdom. The two first explain why the good seems to fare so ill. In the first, the soil is bad; in the second, bad seed is mixed with the good. The next two show why the bad seems to fare so well. The bad becomes great like the great tree and attracts to itself. The bad, like leaven, spreads by its very nature. The culmination of the mustard seed will be the "Man of Sin", and "Anti-Christ"; that of the leavened meal, "mystery Babylon". The next two parables assure us that God's purposes will not fail in spite of man and devil. He will have His treasure, the elect of Israel; His pearl, the whole aggregate of the true children of the Kingdom. We see here a contrast between the human and the divine: the great tree and the great pearl, the hidden leaven and the hidden treasure, professing Christendom and the elect of God. The seventh parable may represent the gospel of the Kingdom in the last days of Israel's testimony in Pentecostal power. Many will be gathered in, but the results will be tested at the end of the age. These seven parables are succeeded in chapters 18-25 by seven other parables, in which principles of right conduct and acceptable service in the Kingdom are illustrated, taking us right on to the time immediately preceding the return of the Son of Man in judgment, when, as has been referred to above, Israel shall be once more God's witnesses on the earth, perhaps the greatest missionaries the world has ever seen, and the most successful.

But in the present the gospel of the grace of God is proclaimed. All who obey it become children of God as to relation, members of the Body of Christ as to distinctive position and privilege, and children of the Kingdom as to responsibility.

This third period of the Kingdom in Mystery, though greatly lengthened by the long-suffering mercy of God, will one day give place to the fourth aspect of the Kingdom.

4. The Kingdom Established

This will not be brought in gradually by gospel effort, much less by civilisation and social reform as many dream, but by the revelation of the Lord Jesus from heaven "in flaming fire, taking vengeance on them that know not God, and that obey not the gospel of our Lord Jesus Christ" (2 Thess 1:8). The stone cut out without hands will fall on the feet of the great image of the Gentile powers and "grind them to powder", and then become a great mountain and fill all the earth. The proclamation shall then go forth: "The kingdoms of the world are become the kingdoms of our Lord and of His Christ, and He shall reign for ever and ever" (Rev 11:15).

4. WHO WILL SHARE IN THE KINGDOM?

A lawyer, whose business it was to be constantly perusing wills, was engaged one day on one when an event occurred which made the monotonous task supremely interesting. He found his own name in the will. We, too, read in the Word of God of a glorious inheritance, "the Kingdom of our God and of His Christ", and we would want to learn if our names are in the will. Can we who have believed in Christ look forward with assurance to one day sharing in the coming Kingdom glories, or is it, as some assert, "a supreme uncertainty"? Surely the enquiry is sufficiently interesting and important. The whole character of our christian walk, of our attitude of soul to God, must depend on whether we are heirs, exhorted to walk worthy of our high calling, or mere claimants on sufferance, doomed to exclusion from the Kingdom unless some unknown standard is attained. The heart of man is legal to the core, and legal conditions may commend themselves to some, but legality never yielded fruit for God. Let us then examine the word of God, and may His grace teach us how to walk and to please Him.

Workings of Grace in the Kingdom

(1) We may notice then, first, that heirship depends on sonship:

"If a son, then an heir of God through Christ" (Gal 4:7). With this agree the words of Peter, "Blessed be the God and Father of our Lord Jesus Christ who...hath begotten us...to an inheritance incorruptible and undefiled reserved in heaven for you" (1 Pet 1:3-4), and those of our Lord to Nicodemus, "Except a man be born of water and of the Spirit he cannot enter the Kingdom of God" (John 3:5). A divine work had to take place for the soul before one sinner could have a right to enter the Kingdom. This is the work of redemption. A divine work must take place in the soul before one sinner could be fit to do so. This is the work of regeneration. The new birth is the "open sesame" of the Kingdom. The Lord's words give no hint of some other undefined condition lurking in the background. If entrance to an exhibition is advertised at two pounds, we should be surprised to find at the turnstile that this was only a preliminary condition of entrance. New birth entails new life, and new life produces new fruit, but all who are born of God will share in the Kingdom of God.

(2) Heirship depends on faith not on faithfulness. Only God can fit us for the Kingdom. The blood of Christ alone can be our title. All saints will be in the Kingdom, that is by grace through faith. All saints will not be in the same place in the Kingdom, that is of reward through faithfulness. James 2:5 tells us that "God hath chosen the poor of this world, rich in faith, and heirs of the Kingdom which God hath prepared for them that love Him". These last words, "them that love Him", is a generic description of all the people of God – rich as well as poor – for if "any man love not the Lord Jesus Christ let him be anathema" (1 Cor 16:22). For those who love Him the Kingdom is prepared; for those who do not, anathema; and there is no third choice.

(3) The believer has already the pledge of the future inheritance. We read, "If any man have not the Spirit of Christ, he is none of His" (Rom 8:9), and the presence of the Spirit in the believer is "the earnest of our inheritance" (Eph 1:14). An earnest is a pledge and guarantee of full blessing to come. He that has the earnest will enjoy the inheritance.

(4) Moreover, the Kingdom is not merely a future promise, it is a present possession. We enter it now, and this fact is used in the

Word as a stimulus to true service. "We receiving a Kingdom which cannot be moved, let us have grace, whereby we may serve God acceptably with reverence and godly fear" (Heb 12:28). Some would reverse this order, and make it read, "Let us serve God acceptably, that we may receive the Kingdom", but the old order is better. To make a part in the Kingdom depend on attainment, is as if some servant had warned the prodigal, when already partaking of the fatted calf, that his father would not receive him unless he served him faithfully. The Kingdom is set up in hearts now: "not meat and drink", not religious forms and observances, "but righteousness, and peace, and joy in the Holy Ghost" (Rom 14:17).

Divine exhortation is not based on a threat of exclusion from the Kingdom, but on our inclusion in Christ. "When Christ, who is our life, shall appear, then shall ye also appear with Him in glory. Mortify, therefore, your members which are upon the earth" (Col 3:4). The apostle indeed prays for many things for the saints of Colosse, (1:9,10) but he does not pray that they may get into the Kingdom; he thanks the Father that they are in it (v.13). We have the same truth addressed to the seven churches: "Unto Him that loved us…and hath made us a Kingdom of priests unto God" (Rev 1:5-6).

(5) There is no thought in Scripture of true believers being turned out of the Kingdom. When Christ comes the Kingdom will be purged. All that offend and work iniquity will be cast out (Matt 13); but are these unfaithful Christians? No, they are "the children of the wicked one", ungodly professors, corresponding to the tares and bad fish of the second and seventh parables. In saying this there is no desire to smooth the pillow of the mere professor but to resist an inverted teaching.

Responsibility in View of the Kingdom

Without doubt there is a danger of minimising the responsibility of the believer and of reducing the Judgment Seat of Christ to the semblance of a mere parade. It is true that only the redeemed will be there, and they in their glorified bodies, and that their sins will not then be remembered, for He who will be Judge will be their Redeemer: but who can lightly think of the solemn possibility of his life work being consumed? Though in certain hymns Christians are encouraged to thank God now for the crown, I know of no scriptural authority for doing so until it be actually obtained. Just as the day of Jubilee influenced all land purchase in Israel, so ought the Judgment Seat of Christ to influence our waking hours, for all will then be seen and weighed in the light of God.

The fact that a boy is his father's heir, and has a place in the house secured, does not make the examinations at the end of the term less real. "We must all be made manifest before the judgment seat of Christ" (2 Cor 5:10). Sins committed before conversion are all and for ever blotted out. Sins incurred since, which have been judged and confessed and forsaken will not, if I judge rightly, be brought up again: "For if we would judge ourselves, we should not be judged" (1 Cor 11:31). These words, though they primarily refer to temporal judgments, seem to contain a general principle of God's government. But how many sins have never really been judged: wrongs inflicted, debts unpaid, promises broken, accusations of false doctrines levelled, unrighteous ways allowed in the home, in the place of business and in the church of God?

The rights and wrongs of things, divisions, quarrels, doctrine, practices, will then be made manifest. Things highly esteemed, even among Christians, may there prove "wood, hay, and stubble", and reputation and character, perhaps, in some cases, stand out in startling contrast. But how much unknown service, hidden prayers, secret gifts, unpublished records, will there shine forth as "gold, silver, and precious stones"? The teaching as to the Kingdom, which is here resisted, is no doubt a reaction against the abounding antinomianism of the present day, but it really substitutes a worse antinomianism in its place. It is like curing a tobacco slave by offering him the opium pipe. It warns professors that they will lose the Kingdom if they are adulterers, fornicators, drunkards, and this is perfectly scriptural, but it hastens to assure them that they may still go to heaven, for heaven is of pure grace, and that is grossly antinomian. Whatever a man's profession may have been, we have no right, as long as his life is openly vicious, to tell him he is a Christian, or indeed to comfort ourselves with the thought that he may be one.

If Christians are Excluded?

When we ask what will become of Christians excluded from

THE KINGDOM OF GOD

the Kingdom, the answers are, as we should expect, perplexingly diverse, for one man's theory is as good as another's. One writer warns us "not to be wise above that which is written", and the next moment attempts to be so. "Some, perhaps," he suggests, "from the lower heavens of Enoch and Elijah, will behold without entering." But this is the mere speculation. What does he know about the heavens of these two prophets? "Others," he affirms, "will return temporarily to corruption and their souls to Hades." He does not explain how "one who has put on incorruption" can return to corruption. It is a contradiction in terms of which there is not one hint in Scripture. "Others are to be cast into outer darkness, where there will be weeping and gnashing of teeth." Gnashing of teeth is used in the Word (see Psa 33:5; 37:12; Acts 7:54) as the expression of hatred and rage. Can this be the attitude of soul of a child of God under what is supposed to be his Father's corrective discipline? This is most subversive doctrine, but there is worse to follow. "The Lord's people guilty of the very gravest offences are temporarily in Gehenna (!) . . . it will continue during the reign of Christ." The comparative emptiness of the lake of fire during the Millennium is adduced as an argument by one of these teachers to point ominously to its use for "wicked Christians", on the same ground, I suppose, that the emptiness of a prison from lack of convicts would clearly indicate that the governor intended filling it with his relations and friends!

One crumb of comfort is thrown to these poor, perishing Christians. "They shall not perish for ever", which, we are assured, is the true meaning of the Greek in John 10:29, instead of "My sheep shall never perish", as we have it in an Authorised and Revised translation. This is the sort of emendation which a man self-taught from an interlinear translation of the Greek Testament might be expected to make, but there is not a scintilla of ground for translating the Greek idiom in this way. The exact form of the Greek with the negative, as we have it here, occurs in five other places, all in John's gospel: 4:14; 8:51,52; 11:26; 13:8. If John 10:28 must be altered, then the same change must be made in all, and a strange sense is the result. Fancy Peter meaning, in John 13:8, when he said, "Thou shalt never wash my feet", that our Lord might wash his feet, but "not for ever". The form of the Greek really excludes perishing at all for the sheep of Christ.

This teaching of a Millennium in the lake of fire for "wicked Christians" as a governmental punishment from God, is the true Romish doctrine of Purgatory, and worse. Those who hold it must be the most anxious or the most self-complacent of men. This doctrine naturally grafts itself on to the deadly doctrine of Universalism, for if some are raised from the second death why indeed not all?

Thank God for His will that none should perish, for His salvation provided for all at the infinite cost of the blood of Christ, and for the promise that all who believe, "being now justified by His blood, shall be saved from wrath through Him", but equally true is it that "He that believeth not the Son shall not see life, but the wrath of God abideth on him". Between these two portions there is a great gulf fixed, and the whole drift of revelation precludes the thought of transference from one to the other after this life.

There is one other explanation put forward to explain the future position of those Christians who are, according to this theory, excluded from the Kingdom: "They will be simply left in their graves." But what will become of those living on the earth when the Lord returns? If they are worthy neither to be taken away nor to inherit the Kingdom, how are they to be disposed of?

A Partial Resurrection and Rapture?

I believe the doctrine of a partial resurrection and rapture is without solid base. The 144,000 of Revelation 14 are said to be these favoured raptured saints! But in chapter 7 we learn they are Israelites chosen in equal number from the 12 tribes. On what principle can Judah, Simeon, Benjamin, mean the church? If this were so then "the church" in which there is no Jew or Gentile, might mean Jewish tribes in which all are Jews. The Bible becomes a gramophone which will say anything you like to put into it. No, the church will have been taken away years before the 144,000 Jewish witnesses even begin their testimony, much more before these are seen with the Lamb on Mount Zion.

But does it not say that "to them that look for Him shall He appear the second time without sin unto salvation" (Heb 9:28)? Yes, but the context does not favour the idea that these are certain faithful Christians. The atmosphere of the chapter is the day of atonement. On that day the altar of incense was supposed to be transferred into the Holiest, being conventionally represented by the golden censer. In Hebrews 9:5 we see this order actually noted, which shows that this special day is in view.

On the day in question Israel was divided into two classes: the High Priest alone in the Holiest, the rest of the nation outside the tabernacle. The antitype is now in progress. The Great High Priest has entered in. Those that look for Him are the people of God in contrast with the world – Amalekites and Edomites – who have no interest in such matters. The word translated "look for" occurs in five other places – Romans 8:23-25, 1 Corinthians 1:7, Galatians 5:5, Philippians 3:10, and always in connection with the coming of Christ. The Apostle takes for granted that all these saints, whether their state was good like that of the Philippians, or low like that of the Corinthians and Galatians, were looking for Christ. If these last named churches were in a bad state they were, according to the "partial rapture" theory, in danger of being left behind, and they ought to have been told so. Why does the apostle not warn them? Why is it to these fallen Galatians he writes, "we through the Spirit wait for the hope of righteousness by faith" (not by faithfulness)? Why is it to these carnal Corinthians he reveals the mystery, "We shall not all sleep, but we shall all be changed . . . the dead shall be raised incorruptible"? Could anything be more inclusive for sleeping and living saints? It was thus the apostle was taught of God to revive these failing saints, not by threats of passing through the great tribulation or of losing their part in the Kingdom, but by unfolding to them the exceeding grace of God.

"Wicked Christians" in Hell?

Even more explicit is 1 Thessalonians 4:16-18: "The dead in Christ shall rise first . . . then we which are alive and remain (lit., are being left) shall be caught up together with them in the clouds, to meet the Lord in the air"; "the dead in Christ", none left in their graves; "we which are alive", none left on the earth. Not a hint of a partial resurrection not a word of any saint being left behind, not a whisper of a third class of unworthy saints, of "wicked Christians", who will be shut up in darkness or hell fire. The apostle closes by exhorting the saints to "comfort one another with these words". How could they if in "supreme uncertainty" of their own fate or that of their beloved dead? It would be like telling a man whose wife had sailed on the "Titanic", to take comfort in the thought that she was alive and well before there was the slightest news that she was. This would be truly to "sing songs to a heavy heart". In the last chapter of this same epistle the apostle adds one word more of assurance to these saints to gladden their hope and encourage them to holiness. "For God hath not appointed us to wrath, but to obtain salvation by our Lord Jesus Christ, who died for us, that, whether we wake (i.e., be wakeful – the same word employed in v.6) or sleep (i.e., be sleepy – the word used in vv.6,7 and quite distinct from the word translated "sleep", in 4:14) we should live together with Him." The Spirit seems to have anticipated this erroneous teaching when he uttered, by the mouth of Zechariah, the words "The Lord my God shall come and all the saints with thee" (14:5), and, by the mouth of Paul, "at the coming of our Lord Jesus Christ with all His saints", and again "when He shall come to be glorified in His saints, and to be admired in all them that believe". How could the Lord come with all His saints, if some had never been taken away? How could all believers admire Him if some are "in outer darkness", "in Hades", or "in the lake of fire"? To ignore the plain teaching of such Scriptures and to build on a disputed interpretation of Revelation 14 and on inferences and analogies, is like a Unitarian going to the book of Exodus to refute the divinity of the Lord, and ruling out the writings of John.

"Attaining unto the Resurrection of the Dead"

But someone may urge that Paul himself was striving "if by any means he might attain to the resurrection of the dead". Yes, but what do the words mean? The noun, which only occurs here, is literally "the out-resurrection". The verb occurs thrice in the New Testament, but never in the sense of resurrection. How could Paul mean that he was striving to attain to physical resurrection, seeing he did not expect to die, see Philippians 1:24-25, but on the contrary to be alive when the Lord returned to share in the blessings of His coming with all his fellow saints (3:20-26). How could this be a matter of reward for faithfulness, if he was sure of it for himself and them?

As has been well said, "A text out of its context is a pretext." Present spiritual experience, not future physical resurrection is, I believe, the thought here.

In Romans 5:2, we see that rejoicing in hope of the glory of God belongs to the justified. This agrees with 8:17, "If children then heirs, heirs of God and joint heirs with Christ, if so be that we suffer with Him that we may be also glorified together with Him".

We suffer with Christ by the fact that we are one with Him. "The suffering with Him," as one has said, "implies a pain due to union." The only other place this exact word occurs is in 1 Corinthians 12:26: "If one member suffer, all the members suffer with it". The suffering is inseparable in one form or another whether the believer is a Great-Heart or a Faint-Heart, for he has Satan against him because he belongs to Christ, the flesh lusting because he is a temple of the Spirit, the world opposing because he is of the Father. But he makes up his mind to be identified with Christ in suffering now, so as to be associated with Him later in glory. That the word translated "if" here does not necessarily imply doubt seems clear from a reference to the only other places where it is used: Rom 3:30; 8:9; 2 Thess 1:6; 1 Cor 8:5; 15:15.

Suffering for Christ is somewhat another thought. This was granted as a special gift to the Philippians: "For unto you it is given in the behalf of Christ, not only to believe on Him but also to suffer for His sake" (Phil 1:29). That a share in the glory is the outcome of faith is clear from two other expressions in Romans 8: v.18, where the apostle speaks unhesitatingly of "the glory which shall be revealed in us", and v.20, where the glory is so assured as to be regarded as already granted, "whom He justified, them He also glorified".

Mistaken Teaching as to the Kingdom

If we are to escape this mistaken teaching as to entrance into the Kingdom, we must avoid the erroneous premises on which it is based.

The first is that all who are called disciples in the Gospels were genuine, and that, therefore, every warning addressed by our Lord to such must apply today to true children of God.

A member of parliament might address a public meeting in his constituency as his electors without any illusion on his part that all were so. The Lord said to some that believed on Him, "If ye continue in My word then are ye My disciples indeed."

Some of those addressed were "sons of the devil" (see John 8:44). In John 6:66 we read, "From that time many of His disciples went back and walked no more with Him", and the Lord had "known from the beginning" that these did not really believe in Him. The word disciple means a learner, and a man might be ever "learning (same word) and never come to the knowledge of the truth". Judas was among the disciples, when the Lord spake of "cutting off the right hand and plucking out the right eye" and might have benefitted by these warnings, but, alas, "he loved the wages of unrighteousness". So it is with the word servant. If Satan is transformed into an angel of light, no wonder his servants take the place of ministers of righteousness. The evil servant of Matthew 24:48 had taken the place of the true servant, but was a hypocrite at heart, and was judged accordingly.

The next mistake is to imagine that all in the early churches were true saints. The epistles were addressed to the saints in the churches, but not all in the churches were therefore saints. As Augustine says, "The church has children among her enemies and enemies among her children." John, speaking of such, says "They went out from us but they were not of us" (1 John 2:19), and Jude speaks of "ungodly men who had crept in unawares...turning the grace of God into lasciviousness" (Jude 4). There were those, too, among the Hebrews, who had forsaken the assembling of themselves together (Heb 10:25) and become in some cases apostates. Such were false professors who, though admitted by error into the local churches, had never possessed true faith in Christ. How fitting then are the warnings imbedded in the epistles. If some taking their place as believers acted like the ungodly, let them take heed lest they should prove to be so. The licentious man of Corinth was not put away as "a failing brother", but as a wicked person, till his deep repentance showed him to be the former. The apostle is careful to make the distinction between a brother and "one that is called a brother". This man was put away, that "the spirit might be saved in the day of the Lord Jesus" (1 Cor 5:5). This has been quoted triumphantly to prove that the apostle recognises him all through as one saved. With all deference I should say it rather proved that he was one who needed to be saved.

What would be more likely to bring a false professor to repentance than the drastic treatment this man received? In 1 Corinthians 6 a condition of disorder is noted. Brother was going to law with brother, and that in the ordinary law courts. Could they not settle these difficulties among themselves? If not, why not suffer unrighteous treatment? But it was they who were acting unrighteously. If they were acting like the unrighteous, let them take care they did not prove to be unrighteous men. Then follows a terrible list: fornicators, idolaters, adulterers, drunkards, revilers, who would not inherit the Kingdom of God. We are asked to believe that this list describes "unfaithful Christians", who will eventually get to heaven after a thousand years of hell fire. But thank God the next verse disproves this. The apostle is describing not Christians at all but types of the unrighteous world, for he goes on to say, "And such were some of you, but ye were washed, ye were sanctified, ye were justified, etc." (1 Cor 6:11). A David may fall into immorality, a Noah into drunkenness, a Lot may settle down in Sodom and a Peter may deny his Lord, even thrice, with oaths and curses; but one swallow does not make a spring, nor does even one grievous fall constitute a believer an unrighteous man. Lot never ceased to be righteous even when living among the Sodomites. David was never characteristically an adulterer, nor Noah a drunkard, nor Peter a blasphemer. But the apostle warns the Corinthians not to give way to unrighteousness, lest they should belie their profession and prove, after all, never to have been in reality anything but unrighteous men. The matter is not really so very difficult; a king issues a proclamation to his kingdom, and as a whole it is suitable to his loyal subjects and only such, but it contains warnings to all and sundry whom it may concern, lest certain tendencies noticed should develop, and some professing to be subjects prove to be only rebels. The epistles are for saints, the warnings in them for professors.

"No whoremonger, nor unclean person, nor covetous man who is an idolater, hath any inheritance in the Kingdom of Christ and of God." This verse has been embodied in a circular widely distributed by post, and is quoted in the interests of this mistaken teaching as "explicitly asserting the exclusion of certain believers (!!) who are warned that their crown is in jeopardy". Is it not shocking to speak of such as "certain believers"?

Then in Galatians 5, after the enumeration of the works of the flesh, the warning note is sounded, "they that do such things shall not inherit the Kingdom of God" (v. 21). These "workers of iniquity" are again supposed to be failing believers, but in the philosophy of these teachers no room is found for the radical distinction that exists between "practising" sin, and being "overtaken in a fault". But the distinction is drawn in the very context of the passage above quoted, in the first verse of the next chapter. Truly the flesh is in the believer, and there is no sin he may not "be overtaken" in (Gal 6:1), but he does not become "a man in the flesh" for that. Abraham, Isaac, Jacob, all fell into lying and other faults, yet they will not spend the Millennium with all liars in the lake of fire, but will sit down, as we have already seen, in the Kingdom of God (Matt 8:12). But murderers, whoremongers, and idolaters are classed with the fearful, the unbelieving, and will have their part in the lake of fire, though they might all have been saved in virtue of the precious blood of Christ, had they been willing to repent of their sins and believe God. To blunt the edge of the warnings to these wicked men by supposing they may be Christians who will eventually enter heaven, is very like "turning the grace of God into lasciviousness". The word of God speaks with no uncertain sound: "without holiness no man shall see the Lord", and where men are characteristically and openly vicious and unholy they will never see the Kingdom nor Heaven either.

A third misconception which lies at the root of this mistaken teaching is that there is a particular class of believers who are described as "overcomers", while the rest are the "overcome". Though many hold this view, I believe it is erroneous. It would be like saying that some living fish swim up stream and some never succeed in doing so, whereas we know there is in every living fish a power that enables it to overcome the current which sweeps away the dead.

Such words as "he that overcometh shall not be hurt of the second death" are pressed by some to show that there are believers who will be hurt of the second death. But the contrast is not between one class of believers and another, but between physical death and eternal death. The promise was for the consolation and strength of the persecuted saints at Smyrna. They might be hurt of the first death, they would never feel the second. "He that overcometh" describes a true believer who is proved to be real. Overcoming does not imply never being overcome, but overcoming at last. A general may suffer reverses and yet conquer in the long run. Then his reverses are forgotten. He is now the conqueror. Of Gad it was said, "a troop shall overcome him but he shall overcome at last". And thus he proved an overcomer. When Joshua fought with Amalek, and Moses held up his hands in prayer, then Israel prevailed, and when he let down his hand Amalek prevailed, but by the power of God Joshua proved to be eventually the victor. And so by grace the church will overcome her Amalek at last.

> "Jehovah is our strength,
> And He shall be our song,
> We shall o'ercome at length
> Although our foes be strong,
> In vain doth Satan now oppose
> For God is stronger than our foes."

The final victor in the great spiritual conflict of this life is the overcomer. Overcoming is the prerogative of the child of God and is by faith. "Whatsoever is born of God overcometh the world: and this is the victory that overcometh the world, even our faith. Who is he that overcometh the world, but he that believeth that Jesus is the Son of God?" (1 John 5:4,5). This overcoming is attributed to those who are of God, because they are of God, and because of the greatness of Him who indwells them. "Ye are of God . . . and have overcome them: because greater is He that is in you, than he that is in the world" (1 John 4:4). "Nay, in all these things we are more than conquerors, through Him that loved us" (Rom 8:37). It may be objected that all the passages quoted from John refer to overcoming the world, whereas the "overcoming" in Revelation 2 and 3 is more general; but what could be more general than the verse just quoted from Romans promising final victory and more than victory over "tribulation, distress, persecution, famine, nakedness, peril or sword", and over the nine-fold opposing forces of the following verses?

On the other hand, if we sum up the promises of recompense to the overcomer, what is there left for these believers who are, by this theory, in no sense overcomers? I do not maintain that "overcoming" is automatic. No true believer would say so; he feels his weakness, he knows the power of the enemy, he watches and prays for overcoming grace. His cry is increasingly, "Hold Thou me up and I shall be safe," but in praying thus he does not prove himself to be an extraordinary Christian, he proves himself to be a Christian.

To refer again to Revelation 21:7,8: "He that overcometh shall inherit all things;...but the fearful, and unbelieving...shall have their part in the lake which burneth with fire and brimstone". Are these "overcome believers"? No, they are expressly said to be unbelievers. Instead of overcoming by the grace of God they have rejected that grace, and are eternally lost. And notice there is no intermediate class.

But does it not say "Blessed and holy is he that hath part in the first resurrection: on such the second death hath no power" (Rev 20:6)? Can it be said that all believers are "blessed and holy"? Will there not, therefore, be some who will not qualify for the first resurrection, and over whom the second death will have power? We have seen that there is no such thing in Scripture as a partial resurrection of the just. "Blessed and holy" is merely a characteristic description of the just, of all the people of God. Not one of such will ever taste of death. And this is exactly what our Lord says, "If a man keep My saying (the equivalent of obey the gospel), he shall never see death" (John 8:51). This is expressed in equivalent terms by the Pharisees: "He shall never taste death" (v. 52). Again, "He that liveth and believeth in Me shall never die" (John 11:26). "This is the bread that came down from heaven, that a man may eat thereof and not die" (John 6:50). Even physical death is abolished for the believer, he sleeps, but does not die; much more will he never taste the second death.

These teachers only ask us to revise our whole conception of

THE KINGDOM OF GOD

scriptural teaching. We thought, and still believe, that the travellers on the broad road are worldlings going down, unless they repent, to a lost eternity; but we are told they may be true Christians on their way to eternal glory, but in danger of forfeiting a place in the Kingdom. So with those described as "adulterers, fornicators, drunkards, etc.", we are asked to believe that they may be citizens of heaven, who must be shut out of "the Kingdom of God", as a punishment for their sins. This kind of difference between heaven and the Kingdom simply does not exist in the word of God. "Entering the Kingdom" is a Scriptural equivalent for being saved. Thus the disciples understood our Lord's words in Luke 18:24,26, and our Lord did not correct their phraseology. "Who then can be saved?" they exclaimed, when the difficulty of a rich man entering the Kingdom of God had been explained. Thus He Himself interpreted the matter by His answer to the question in Luke 13:23, "Lord, are there few that be saved?" "Strive to enter in at the straight gate", for many will seek when it is too late, and find themselves shut out of the Kingdom (see v. 28). The antithesis to being in the Kingdom is being cast out into outer darkness, and there is no hint of any deliverance from that awful condition. It is "the blackness of darkness for ever" (Jude 13). Again, in Matthew 25:31-46, those who do not "inherit the Kingdom" will go into eternal punishment, that "everlasting fire prepared for the devil and his angels". These persons are addressed as "Ye cursed!" Is this the way in which the Lord would address His redeemed, the beloved of the Father, "blessed with all spiritual blessings in Christ"? Truly this teaching is subversive of all sane and sober interpretation of God's Word. These teachers affirm that companies like the wonder workers of Matthew 7:22, the foolish virgins of Matthew 25:12, the professors of Luke 13:24-30, may perfectly well be children of God shut out of the Kingdom but on their way to heaven. But one of the prerogatives of all true sheep is to be known of the Good Shepherd, who said, "I know My sheep and am known of mine". How then can those be sheep to whom the Lord says, "I never knew you"?

Place in the Kingdom

Let us close this chapter with a brief word as to what will determine place in the Kingdom. When the question was asked the Lord, "Who is the greatest in the Kingdom of Heaven?" (Matt 18:1) He did not at once answer the question, but dealt with another first: "Except ye be converted, and become as little children, ye shall not enter the Kingdom of Heaven". They must be sure of entrance first before enquiring as to precedence. Then He takes up their question proper: If you want to be greatest you must humble yourself as a little child: a high place here entails a low place there, the humbler you are here, the more exalted you will be there. We cannot be too clear about this. A man's work shall be tested. That which stands the test will take the prize. Those who have been faithful in that which was another's, will have entrusted to them that which they may call their own. And the reward will be proportional. The man who has turned his pound into ten pounds will rule over ten cities, and so forth. It is not said that the man whose pound remains unfruitful will be cast out of the Kingdom, as in the case of the man with one talent of Matthew 25, but that he will lose his reward and his pound. In Colossians 4:11, the apostle speaks of the Kingdom as the goal where service would be rewarded; in 1 Thessalonians 2:11-12, as the impetus and standard of a worthy walk, charging them "that ye would walk worthy of God, who hath called you unto His kingdom and glory". No doubt is raised as to the call being effectual. 2 Thessalonians 1:5 is in perfect harmony with this. The apostle boasts of their patience in tribulation as that which will manifest the rightness of God's decision to count them worthy of the Kingdom of God. The Thessalonians were proving themselves in the hour of temptation, in which mere stony ground hearers fall away, to be genuine believers destined to share in the Kingdom with all true saints. An abundant entrance into the Kingdom depends on attainment in grace. The Kingdom is never spoken of as the reward or prize in itself, but an incorruptible crown is offered to the one who can win it. Let us so run that we may obtain.

5. THE CHARACTERISTICS OF THE FUTURE KINGDOM

The true Kingdom in its present phase is, as we have seen, hidden from the eyes of men. It is not given to them to know its mysteries. God keeps silence but for the still small voice of grace, drowned for most men by the busy roar of this world's shifting scene. In the absence of the King, the great usurper seeks to hold the balance of power and rule the world for his own ends. As "the god of this world" he blinds men's minds with religious systems, and prepares the way for the acceptance of "the lie". But still there is a remnant of Jews and Gentiles who have ears to hear the call of God. These form the church, the bride of Christ, and are in this age "the children of the Kingdom".

The coming day will be a day of great reversals. "Our God shall come and shall not keep silence." The great powers will be humbled and Israel, now despised, will be exalted. The mighty cities of the world will be levelled to the dust, and Jerusalem will become "the joy of the whole earth". Clearly the Kingdom will have two sides, the earthly and the heavenly, running their course contemporaneously, like the overhead and low level lines of the same railway system, but Christ will be King of them both.

Those who partake of the heavenly calling will enjoy heavenly glory, but flesh and blood will not partake of it. The earthly saints will come into the earthly inheritance promised to Abraham and his seed, and in this, as we have seen, flesh and blood can take part. It is this latter aspect of things that we have chiefly here before us. Necessarily a very brief statement must suffice, otherwise the whole prophetic word must pass in review. We will note seven characteristics of the future kingdom.

1. The Presence of the King

The first characteristic of the world to come will be the presence of the King. That our Lord will be once more in this scene in person may seem strange, but it is certain. Men try and evade the plain meaning of words, or postpone indefinitely their fulfilment, but the words of the heavenly messengers could not be more precise. "This same Jesus...shall so come in like manner as ye have seen Him go into heaven." He went personally, visibly, suddenly. He will return personally, visibly, suddenly. His feet left the Mount of Olives when He ascended to heaven. His feet will stand on that self-same Mount when He returns. This will be not, as some teach, at the end of man's millennium, when the world will have become such a paradise without Him as to constrain Him to return, but before the millennium when all nations shall mourn because of His return. "Every eye shall see Him, and they also which pierced Him" (Rev 1:7). His personal presence is needed and it is assured. "I will overturn, overturn, overturn it: and it shall be no more, until He come whose right it is; and I will give it Him" (Ezek 21:27). His glory will then be manifested, He will come to reign. Not that He will of necessity be continuously on the earth. He will reign over as well as on it. But communication will once more be established between heaven and earth. The true Jacob's ladder will be set up and "the angels of God will be seen ascending and descending upon the Son of Man" (John 1:51). He will be the centre. His glory, His mighty deeds, His divine wisdom will fill the earth. His dominion will stretch from sea to sea. To Him all kings shall bow and offer gifts. All nations shall serve Him and daily shall He be praised.

2. The Sphere of Rewards

All the saints will share in it, but not all will have the same place, rank, reward or responsibility. Some will be nearer the person of the King. Some will have a larger sphere. The difference between the parables of the talents and the pounds may be that, in the first (Matt 25) it is a question of gift and ability. These vary with the individual, but all men, saved and unsaved alike, have gifts for which they will be held responsible. A Balaam, a Judas, a Caiaphas may have gifts as well as a Peter, a John, or a Paul. In the parable of the pounds (Luke 19), it is a question of what only children of God have, the power to serve Him which grace confers. In this sense we are exhorted "not to receive the grace of God in vain". The man who hid his pound lost his pound. The man who hid his talent lost his soul. Some will have ten cities, others five according to faithfulness. The rewards will have been allotted "at the resurrection of the just" before the Judgment Seat of Christ, but will be enjoyed in the Kingdom. The first resurrection will extend over a period. Christ, "the first fruits", the saints who rose immediately after Him form, I judge, a first part of it, then also those who will awake from sleep when He comes and rise to meet Him in the air, and, lastly, the martyred saints of the last great tribulation (Rev 20:4). "This is the first resurrection", as if the apostle would say, "Up to this is the first resurrection." Then all will pass in review: Mary's ointment, Dorcas' garments, Epaphras' prayers, Paul's testimony, and all other life and service for the Lord. The apostles will have a special reward, they will sit on twelve thrones, judging the twelve tribes of Israel (Matt 19:28). Some will have so run so as to obtain the incorruptible crown. To those who faithfully endure will be assigned a crown of life (Jas 1:12); to those who love His appearing a crown of righteousness (2 Tim 4:8). A crown of glory awaits faithful pastors of the flock of Christ (1 Pet 5:4); a crown of rejoicing, those who have won souls for Christ (1 Thess 2:19).

3. A Time of Universal Peace and Prosperity

The promise of Isaiah will at length be fulfilled: "They will beat their swords into ploughshares, and their spears into pruning-hooks; nation shall not lift up sword against nation, neither shall they learn war any more" (Isa 2:4). But this will not be as the result of international conferences or treaties, but by the coming of Him "who maketh wars to cease unto the ends of the earth". But He will "make desolations" first. War from heaven will alone end war on earth. Before swords become ploughshares, ploughshares will have become swords (see Joel 3:10). The guiltiest battle ever fought will be waged when Christ returns. Man will have set himself to measure swords with God. It will be the strangest battle too, for the first act in it will be the summary judgment of the two great rebel leaders, and the last the total annihilation of their great world hosts. Then the groaning creation shall enter into rest. "The wolf also shall dwell with the lamb...and the lion shall eat straw like the ox" (Isa 11:6-7). Humanity will be relieved of its two most crushing burdens, sacerdotal religions and standing armies, and the wasted energies of men will be turned into other channels. The desert and neglected places of the earth, the dark wastes of Africa, the unploughed prairie lands of America, the vast virgin plains of Asia and Australia will be turned to profit. "The desert shall rejoice and blossom as the rose" (Isa 35:1). No doubt this will apply in a special sense to the great desert lands between the Jordan and the Euphrates which are destined to form part of Emmanuel's land, a great triangle nearly as large as India, south of Calcutta and Bombay, but all lands will share in the blessing (Gen 15:18; Deut 11:24). "He shall have dominion from sea to sea, and from the river unto the ends of the earth...His name shall endure for ever...all nations shall call Him blessed" (Psa 72:8,17).

4. A Reign of Righteousness

"A king shall reign in righteousness" (Isa 32:1). This could not possibly have been had an impenitent Israel crowned Him King. The same blood that bought redemption, purchased the inheritance. The Lord will reign by undisputed right. The passages quoted above show that the idea that millennial blessing will be almost limited to Israel whilst the rest of the nations lie in a chronic state of seething rebellion, is an entire exaggeration. But if men do rebel they will find the rod that rules them is a rod of iron. Today men's sins are not imputed in the sense of being summarily dealt with, but then a universal "Habeas Corpus Act" will be in force. "I will early destroy all the wicked of the land, that I may cut off all wicked doers from the city of the Lord" (Psa 101:8). The opening scenes of the Kingdom will be of judgment – of the twelve tribes and of the living nations of the Roman earth and Christendom generally, whose armies will have been slain by the Lord at His return, but during the progress of the millennial reign, immediate judgment, when called for, will at once be meted out. Open evil will no longer be tolerated. The Lord will rule in the midst of His enemies. His rule will be a blessing to the righteous, a scourge to the wicked. Wrongs will be righted, abuses abolished, "every transgression and disobedience" will receive at once "a just recompense of reward".

5. The Absence of Satan

As soon as the Man of Sin and Anti-Christ have been consigned to the lake of fire, and their hosts slain, Satan will be cast into the bottomless pit for a thousand years, "that he should deceive the nations no more, till the thousand years should be fulfilled" (Rev 20:3). That there should be no doubt of the identity of this awful person, he is called here by his four names, "the dragon", the first person of the great triad of evil; "that old serpent", the original seducer of the race; "the devil", the accuser of the brethren; and "Satan", the great adversary of God and man. Doubtless in the name Satan is here included his angels, demons and evil spirits, for they could not be allowed liberty while he is bound. All will be shut up with him, and the world delivered for a thousand years from every Satanic influence (Isa 24:21-23). The bottomless pit, or abyss, must not be confounded with Gehenna. From this last there is no exit possible. From the abyss there is (see Rev 11:7, and Rev 20:7). Accordingly, at the end of the Millennium, Satan will be let loose for a season, to prove that a thousand years in prison will not change him, nor a thousand years of Kingdom glory convert man. Except Israel, and the saved from among the nations of Christendom (Matt 25), all will have a sinful nature, and will certainly have to experience temptations from within, but all Satanic excitement from without will be suppressed. To live in a powder magazine cannot be pleasant at the best of times, how much less when under an enemy's fire! How great the relief were this to be silenced; so too the relief will be immense when the great enemy will be no longer able to harass mankind. When, however, the final test comes, and Satan is set free to deceive the nations, vast numbers, "as the sand of the sea shore for multitude", will flock to his standard, proving, as has already been said, that man apart from the grace of God is incorrigible. A deluge of fire from heaven will destroy them, and the devil will be cast into the lake of fire where the beast and the false prophet are, and they shall be tormented day and night for ever and ever (Rev 20:10).

6. The Universal Knowledge of God

When the sun is shining in its strength it needs neither wit nor grace to see it. When Christ shall appear in glory "the earth shall be filled with the knowledge of the Lord, as the waters cover the sea" (Isa 11:9), or, as Habakkuk 2:14 has it "with the knowledge of the glory of the Lord". This can never be true before the Lord comes, nor will it even then imply universal conversion. Not all will be savingly converted, as we have just seen. As for Israel, all who survive the last great tribulation will be convicted and converted by the coming of Christ. (Zech 12:10). "And so all Israel shall be saved" (Rom 11:26).

Of course, this refers only to those who will be alive when the "Deliverer shall come out of Sion and shall turn away ungodliness from Jacob". These will experience the blessing of the new covenant to be made with them after these days. "I will put My law in their inward parts, and write it in their hearts; and will be their God, and they shall be My people. And they shall teach no more every man his neighbour, and every man his brother, saying, Know the Lord:

for they shall all know Me, from the least of them unto the greatest of them saith the Lord: for I will forgive their iniquity and I will remember their sin no more" (Jer 31:33). I have quoted here in full to show that this is no promise of universal blessing to the nations of the world, much less of universal salvation in the eternal state, as has been perversely put forth, but only of national blessing to Israel, with whom alone the covenant is made, and of whom alone it is said, "Thy people shall be all righteous" (Isa 60:21). And they will continue so, for they will receive a blessing unknown before in any dispensation, not only cleansing from their sins but "a new heart"; God will "take away the stony heart out of their flesh and give them a heart of flesh" (Ezek 11:19), and Jehovah adds, "I will put a new spirit within you, and cause you to walk in My statutes, and ye shall keep My ordinances and do them" (v. 20). Thus they will be sustained by divine power in the path of obedience and holiness, both they and their children; for it is written, "All thy children shall be taught of the Lord; and great shall be the peace of thy children" (Isa 54:13). Besides this, "The inhabitant (i.e., of Jerusalem) shall not say, I am sick: the people that dwell therein shall be forgiven their iniquity" (Isa 33:24), "neither can they die any more: for they are equal unto the angels; and are the children of God, being the children of the resurrection" (Luke 20:36). This not only applies to those who will be raised, but to those who will "be counted worthy to obtain that world", i.e. the Millennial Kingdom. This also applies to those of the nations who are acquitted and blessed at the judgment of nations. They are "the blessed of the Father", and so will "enter the Kingdom", or go "into life eternal" (Matt 25:46). They too, no doubt, will have a physical and spiritual constitution suitable to their new condition, and will be sustained in holiness and blessing throughout the Millennium.

Who then will be those who will join in the post-millennium rebellion? Whence will they come? I believe they will belong to other and outside nations who will not be on trial at the judgment of the nations, just referred to (Matt 25). I think, for various reasons, that those present there will be "all the nations" of Christendom, but not all the nations of the globe. How could such countries as Tibet, Patagonia, the Sudan, etc., be judged according to their treatment of Israelites, in the absence of such among them? No doubt the whole world will have sorely felt the Apocalyptic judgments, but the direct effects of the final catastrophes will fall on the countries of Christendom, and, when these latter are once and for all dealt with, it would seem that large portions of the nations of the earth will be allowed to continue. Otherwise, how understand such an expression as "as concerning the rest of the beasts, they had their dominion taken away: yet their lives were prolonged for a season and time" (Dan 7:12), for this follows immediately on the destruction of the fourth empire? How else explain the fact noted in Isaiah 19:24, that nations will exist as such in these latter times? "In that day shall Israel be the third with Egypt and with Assyria, even a blessing in the midst of the land", or the statement in the last chapter of Isaiah, already referred to, that one of the privileges of Israel in the Millennium will be the carrying of the news of the glory of God to Tarshish, Pul and Lud, "and to the isles afar off that have not heard My fame, neither have seen My glory; and they shall declare My glory among the Gentiles" (Isa 66:19). In the previous verse we read, "I will gather all nations and tongues; and they shall come and see My glory." Who are these nations that will not have seen His glory? Who are those kings of Tarshish, and of the isles, who will bring presents, those kings of Sheba and Zeba that shall offer gifts (Psa 72:10)? Who are those families of the earth who are threatened with judgment if they do not come up to Jerusalem to the feast of Tabernacles? Who are the heathen whom the Lord will rule with a rod of iron? Who else but the spared nations of Asia, Africa, and the isles of the sea, who will not be held responsible as the nations of Christendom will, for positive rejection of the grace of God, and for determined rebellion against His Holy One? No doubt untold millions of these nations will be saved through the testimony of Israel, but the mass will remain unregenerate, and they will be ready to join Satan in his last desperate onslaught on the saints and the Beloved City.

The inhabitants of the millennial earth may thus be divided into three classes. The saved of Israel; the spared of those nations of Christendom who came against Jerusalem (Zech 14:16); and the surviving outside nations, called in Zechariah 11:17, "the families of the earth". The first two classes, as we have seen, will all be saved.

The third class may again be subdivided, from a spiritual point of view, into three divisions:– those who turn to the Lord and are savingly converted; those who are openly rebellious and are summarily dealt with during the course of the millennial reign; and, perhaps the largest class of all, those who "yield feigned obedience" (Psa 66:3 margin), and who will only be manifested in their true character when Satan is loosed.

7. The Hegemony of Israel

Amid the clashing rivalries of the great powers, the idea of hegemony, or world leadership, though usually unexpressed, occupies no small place in the thoughts of men. The question will be settled in an unexpected way. The coming King will "turn the world upside down". Israel, now scattered and downtrodden, will be head, the proud nations of the earth will be tail (Deut 28:13). The old order will give place to the new. Israel will be the masters and "strangers shall stand and feed their flocks and be their vine dressers" (see Isa 61:5). "The nations and the kingdom that will not serve thee shall perish; yea, those nations shall be utterly wasted" (Isa 60:12).

Israel in the Land

Before the Kingdom is set up, yea even before the great and terrible Day of the Lord come, Israel will have been restored in part to their own land, as we see from the prophecy of Joel. They will be at first in a general condition of backsliding from Jehovah, but the menace of the northern army (Gog and Magog, of Ezekiel 38:2), and a call from God, will bring them to repentance. A great revival will take place. God will intervene in power to destroy the Northern army, and grant a period of unexampled material prosperity, restoring to them "the years that the locust hath eaten" (Joel 2:25). But a greater blessing than this awaits them. A great outpouring of the Holy Spirit, compared to which the experiences of Pentecost will be but as the droppings, will be shed forth on the Lord's servants in view of a world wide testimony, and all this before the great and terrible Day of the Lord (Joel 2). This solemn day will be immediately preceded by the gathering together of the nations of the Roman empire against Jerusalem (Joel 3), which will be delivered, in its last extremity, by the personal advent of Jehovah. Him the spared remnant will recognise as the Man of Calvary and their Messiah. Full acknowledgment of their guilt (Zech 11) will lead to full cleansing (Zech 12), and full restoration to Jehovah (Isa 12). Though unfaithful to Him in the past, and as a woman divorced, Israel will be married to Him again. "The remnant shall return, even the remnant of Jacob, unto the Mighty God" (Isa 10:21). "They shall serve the Lord their God, and David their King whom I will raise up unto them" (Jer 30:9), and "out of them shall proceed thanksgiving and the voice of them that make merry" (Jer 30:19). To them the Lord shall say, "Thy people also shall be all righteous: they shall inherit the land for ever" (Isa 60:21).

Israel Restored

There will also be a general gathering and restoration of the scattered flock of Israel. The Lord will seek for His people as a shepherd, "and will deliver them out of all places where they have been scattered in the cloudy and dark day". It "shall come to pass in that day, that the Lord shall set His hand the second time to recover the remnant of His people, which shall be left, from Assyria, and from Egypt...And He shall set up an ensign for the nations, and shall assemble the outcasts of Israel, and gather together the dispersed of Judah from the four corners of the earth" (Isa 11:11-12). "The Lord God which gathereth the outcasts of Israel saith, Yet will I gather others to Him, besides those that are gathered unto Him" (see Isa 49; 56:8). Miraculous events will accompany their restoration, the tongue of the Egyptian sea will be dried up, and the river smitten in, or unto, the seven streams (Isa 11:15; Rev 16:12). This drying up of the Euphrates is generally taken to mean the drying up of the Turkish empire. Does, then, the destruction of the Egyptian sea mean the destruction of Egypt? Surely it ought to, to be consistent. But we know that blessing is reserved for Egypt (Isa 19:21-25). Why not take "the sea" and "the river" to mean what they say and believe that they will be, at least temporarily in the case of the Euphrates, dried up to facilitate the return of Israel from the south and from the east? Then will be fulfilled the words of the prophet, "The ransomed of the Lord shall return, and come to Zion with songs, and everlasting joy upon their heads: they shall obtain joy and gladness, and sighing and sorrow shall flee away" (Isa 35:10).

Jerusalem Rebuilt

Then will Jerusalem be rebuilt on a new and magnificent scale. Jerusalem "shall be builded upon her own heap" (Jer 30:18). "The sons of the strangers shall build up thy walls, and their kings shall minister unto thee" (Isa 60:10). And Jerusalem shall have a new name, "'Jehovah-Shammah' the Lord is there" (Ezek 48:35). "The glory of Lebanon shall come unto thee, the fir tree, the pine tree, and the box together, to beautify the place of My sanctuary" (Isa 60:13). Not only will the city be rebuilt but the temple also, after the pattern shown to Ezekiel, 2,500 years before (Ezek 40, 44). And the land shall be divided to the twelve tribes on a new plan (Ezek 48), Israel and Judah shall no longer be separated kingdoms but one people. "I will take the stick of Joseph, which is in the hand of Ephraim, and the tribes of Israel his fellows, and will put them with him, even with the stick of Judah, and make them one stick, and they shall be one in Mine hand…And I will make them one nation in the land upon the mountains of Israel; and one king shall be king to them all: and they shall be no more two nations, neither shall they be divided into two kingdoms any more at all" (Ezek 37:19-22). "Ephraim shall not envy Judah, and Judah shall not vex Ephraim" (Isa 11:13). They shall be for ever delivered from the abomination of idolatry (Ezek 37:23); and shall become indeed and in truth according to the purpose of Jehovah "a kingdom of priests" unto Him (see Exod 19:6). "Ye shall be named the Priests of the Lord, men shall call you Ministers of our God: ye shall eat the riches of the Gentiles, and in their glory shall ye boast yourselves" (Isa 61:6). For then it will be, as we have already seen, that Jehovah will make with them His new covenant (Jer 31:31), an everlasting covenant (Jer 32:40) as enduring and constant as the Noachian covenant of the day and night (Jer 33:20).

Sacrifices Restored

The sacrifices will be restored in a commemorative sense, not pointing forward like the sacrifices of old, as figures of that which was to come, but looking back, as the symbols of the Lord's Supper do, to that which has been already perfectly done once and for all. "Neither shall the priests the Levites want a man before Me to offer burnt offerings, and to kindle meat offerings, and to do sacrifice continually" (Jer 33:18), and besides, Israel will be as we have seen God's witnesses to a renovated world (Isa 66:19). Thus will Jerusalem become in very deed "the joy of the whole earth", the religious and political centre of all the nations. "All nations shall flow unto it. And many people shall go and say, Come ye, and let us go up to the mountain of the Lord, to the house of the God of Jacob…for out of Zion shall go forth the law and the word of the Lord from Jerusalem" (Isa 2:3). The centre of all will be Him whose "name shall be called Wonderful, Counsellor, The Mighty God, The Everlasting Father, The Prince of Peace" (Isa 9:6) – Jehovah-Jesus. "They shall call Jerusalem the throne of the Lord; and all the nations shall be gathered unto it, to the name of the Lord, to Jerusalem" (Jer 3:17). And if they will not come they will be judged without mercy (Zech 14). Thus will Israel at last be what God intended her to become, His channel of blessing to those of the nations who love her. Such are accordingly called to rejoice in the blessing of His people. "Rejoice ye with Jerusalem, and be glad…that ye may suck, and be satisfied with the breasts of her consolations; that ye may milk out, and be delighted with the abundance of her glory…ye shall be borne upon her sides, and be dandled upon her knees" (Isa 66:10-12). "In that day there shall be a root of Jesse, which shall stand for an ensign of the people; to it shall the Gentiles seek: and His rest shall be glorious" (Isa 11:10). "All the ends of the world shall remember, and turn unto the Lord; and all the kindreds of the nations shall worship before Thee. For the Kingdom is the Lord's: and He is the Governor among the nations…A seed shall serve Him; it shall be accounted to the Lord for a generation. They shall come, and shall declare His righteousness unto a people that shall be born, that He hath done this" (Psa 22:27-28,31).

The Great Tribulation Theory

Do the Scriptures teach that the Church
must pass through "The Great Tribulation?"

It is important to notice the different way in which the Lord speaks of His coming in the great prophetic chapters of the Synoptic Gospels(Matthew 24, Mark 12, Luke 21), and then in His farewell discourse at the end of John. In the first He speaks of Himself as the Son of Man, as indeed was His wont, and of His coming as an event in the far distance, with wars, famines, earthquakes, false Christs, the Great Tribulation, and signs in the heavens to occur first. Then in John He speaks in the first person: "I will come again and receive you unto Myself", with no earthly event to intervene. The same difference is apparent in the Revelation. In chapter 19 the Lord is revealed as "The Faithful and True", coming forth to make war and to judge; and in chapter 22 thrice He speaks of Himself in the first person: "I am coming quickly".

The explanation is simple. Two distinct phases of His coming are in view. The one - the subject of prophecy - when the Lord will be revealed from heaven to the world; the other, the unfolding of a mystery - a previous stage of that coming to take away His own "from the evil to come". The Lord would ever be before His people as the One who died for them, as the One who lives for them, and as the One who is coming for them. Thus the early Christians understood His will. They "turned to God from idols to serve the living and true God: and to wait for His Son from Heaven, whom He raised from the dead, even Jesus, which delivered us from the wrath to come" (1 Thess 1:9,10).

The Tribulation Theory

The object of these pages is to examine a system of interpretation, which I may be allowed for brevity's sake to call "the Tribulation

Theory". It teaches that "the Church" must pass through the Great Tribulation. Those who disseminate these views are doubtless earnest men, but I judge they have been misled by appearances, and have fallen into the common error of drawing general conclusions from particular cases. Thus they put in the forefront of their argument an "order of events" which they think they have proved irrefragably from Matthew 24:29, and Acts 2:20; but the whole idea is built, I believe, on the fallacy of confounding "the day of the Lord", which is a period with "the day of the Lord, that great and notable day" (Acts 2:20, RV), which is a crisis of time. Then, again, they build whole castles on the expression in Isaiah 2:17, "The Lord alone will be exalted in that day", a condition of things which they assert will prevail during the whole period of the day of the Lord, though the words, taken in their context, bear well the meaning that the result of the Lord's judgments will be that He will be alone exalted. To these main arguments we shall refer at length later.

To some people the question may seem unimportant. In reality it is not so. The theory in question tends to obliterate distinctions of the greatest importance. It mixes up the present and the future dispensations. It introduces a weird confusion into the interpretation of the Apocalypse. And in a word, it would nullify at a stroke much of the distinctive teaching which servants of God have been pressing for the last seventy years and more. But, as one has well said, "A tentative hypothesis may account for many facts, but nothing less than a full-orbed scriptural support should satisfy us as to what claims to be the truth of God."

I believe the Tribulation Theory is a mistaken one for the following five reasons which we will examine in their order:

It confounds "the Church" and Israel.

It lays down a fictitious order of prophetic events.

It confuses the stages of the Second Coming.

It upsets the order and character of the Apocalypse.

It deprives the Church of her hope.

1. CONFOUNDING THE CHURCH WITH ISRAEL

The Tribulation Theory tends to break down the distinction between the Church and Israel. From Romans 11 we learn that Israel as a nation, owing to her rejection of the Lord Jesus Christ, has been herself for a time rejected. She is now left "without a king, without a prince, without a sacrifice, without an image, without an ephod, and without teraphim" (Hos 3:4), that is, she is bereft of national and religious privileges, and has been "left empty" by the unclean spirit of idolatry. This spirit will later on return in a form sevenfold worse than before. Now, the setting aside of Israel has left room for the revelation of "the mystery of Christ kept secret since the world began" (Rom 16:25), - a Church composed of believing Jews and Gentiles, between whom the middle wall of partition has been broken down under the headship of a glorified Christ. Israel was an earthly people with an earthly inheritance and a "worldly sanctuary". The Church is a heavenly people with a heavenly calling, priesthood, and inheritance.

The Threefold Division

In 1 Corinthians 10:22 Paul divides the population of Corinth (and the same held good for the whole Roman earth) into the "Jews", rejecting Jesus as Messiah, "the Gentiles", without Christ, without God, and without hope, and "the Church of God", consisting of all from the two first-named classes, who had received Jesus Christ as Lord. As long as "the Church" is on the earth, no Jew or Gentile can receive Christ without being by that very fact at once incorporated into the one body. Witness 1 Corinthians 12:13, RV, where Paul addressing the Corinthians, writes, "In one Spirit were we all baptised into one body, whether Jews or Gentiles." When the Church is gone, then the old distinction will hold good again, and there will be companies of believing Jews and Gentiles, not only distinguished from the world, but from one another. It is clear, then, that if the Scriptures speak to us of a future moment when the temple worship shall be restored in Jerusalem, and saved Israelites be once more recognised as such, the Church will be no longer on the earth.

Now apply this to Matthew 24. We have here a prophetic address delivered to four Jews (see Mark 13:3). They had received Jesus as the promised Christ, but it would be strange had they ceased to be Jews because they had accepted their national Messiah. These four Jews, then, were looking forward to the setting up of Messiah's throne on the earth, or in other words, to that moment when "the kingdom should be restored to Israel". They were, it is true, destined to a higher place; they were later to form part of "the Church which is His body". That, however, was the mystery hid in God (and first officially revealed through the apostle Paul), and of its hopes and destinies they then knew absolutely nothing. The Lord addressed them as representing the faithful Jewish remnant of the last days.

Surely the atmosphere of Matthew 24 is ultra-Jewish. The scene of the events foretold is Jerusalem and Judaea (Matt 24:16; Luke 21:20). The temple destroyed in AD 70 will have been rebuilt, for a certain sign foretold by Daniel concerning "his people" will be seen "in the holy place". Then the faithful ones are to flee, and let them "pray that their flight be not on the Sabbath", for reasons obvious to any pious Jew. Now, what has the Church to do with the Sabbath? And why should the Church be found specially in Jerusalem or Judaea? And what part or lot has she in "the holy places made with hands"? No, there is nothing of the Church in Matthew 24; the very thought is a gross anachronism, but if she were there, then believing Jews, serving God according to the old rites, could not be there at the same time, for they would form part of the Church themselves. But we have just seen that believing Jews are the very people addressed, and therefore we conclude that the Church is excluded from this chapter, and from the Great Tribulation therein described. (When speaking of "the Church" I mean throughout these pages "the body of Christ".)

The "Great Multitude"

Apply the same test to Revelation 7. The "Tribulationists" ask us to believe that the "great multitude" of v. 9 is the Church caught up to heaven. Why, then, is there no mention either of "the Lord's coming" or of "the rapture" in the chapter, and why are the 144,000 faithful Israelites, sealed as servants of God, mentioned before the great multitude? This order is awkward for the Tribulation Theory, so much so that one writer quietly reverses it, and writes as if the "great multitude" were the next thing mentioned after the heavenly signs of chapter 6. It is true that all the events of the Revelation cannot be taken in the sequence as written, but that is no excuse for this tampering with the order of events in chapter 7, in order to fit in with a special theory. But how can the "great multitude" be the

Church, when these 144,000 saved Israelites are existing as such on the earth at the same time? And if the "great multitude" is the raptured Church, why have the 144,000 been left behind? We may be quite sure that neither company represents the Church. The former is, I believe, the fruit of the testimony of the latter - the sealed of Israel.

It may not be perfectly clear who the "great multitude" are, but they are most probably Gentiles converted by the preaching of God's witnesses, and possibly, too, in part, by the proclamation of "the everlasting gospel" of Revelation 14. This gospel is proclaimed to the very four classes from which the "great multitude" is gathered. This is all the more probable, inasmuch as just before the mention of this angelic evangelisation, the 144,000 of chapter 7 reappear on the scene (Rev 14:1). However, whether they be Jews or Gentiles is immaterial to the present discussion. There is one thing they cannot be, that is the Church. When we say that Matthew 24 is Jewish, we do not, of course, mean that it has no voice for us. It is part of Scripture. It is God-breathed. It is profitable. What we do mean is that though in application it is for all who read, in interpretation it is Jewish. We are not the central subject of the Word, but God Himself and His glory.

2. A FICTITIOUS ORDER OF PROPHETIC EVENTS

The second objection to the Tribulation Theory is that it is based on a mistaken exegesis of Matthew 24:29 and Acts 2:20. In the former of these passages the heavenly signs are said to follow the Great Tribulation. In the latter they are said to precede "the great and terrible day of the Lord", and therefore, so the Tribulationists argue, the order of future events will be:- (1) the Great Tribulation; (2) the heavenly signs; (3) the day of the Lord.

This is certainly very clear; but it might have occurred to these teachers that were their theory as true as it is clear it would hardly have been left to our day to make the remarkable discovery. The fallacy of their argument lies in the fact that they have failed to grasp the difference between "the day of the Lord" and "the great and notable day of the Lord". While it does say that the heavenly signs precede the latter, it does not say that they precede "the day of the Lord".

"The Tribulation, the great one" (lit.) of Revelation 7, is to be carefully distinguished, these teachers admit, from the long period of tribulation which is even now leading up to it. Have they not overlooked the difference between "the day of the Lord, the great and notable one" (of Joel 2, Mal 4, and Acts 2), and the long period entitled the "day of the Lord", which precedes as well as succeeds it? This period of time will, I believe, dawn in Revelation 6:1, and continue for a thousand years at least till Revelation 19 (when, according to 2 Peter 3, "The heavens shall pass away with a great noise"). "The great and notable day of the Lord will, on the contrary, be a crisis of time when Christ shall be revealed as "the Sun of Righteousness" to the healing of His people, and "as a burning oven" to the destruction of the ungodly (Mal 4). It is therefore perfectly true to say that "the signs in the heavens" precede "the great and notable day", but they are themselves but an incident in the long period known as "the day of the Lord". I do not mean, of course, that in every passage where "the day of the Lord" is brought before us, the above distinction is necessarily emphasised, but where the two expressions occur in the same passage, as in Joel 2, the distinction is as plain as it is important.

The Order of Events

This being so, I believe that the order of events is not as the "Tribulationists" affirm, but is as follows: (see also the Diagram on page 71)

First there is the Rapture of the Church (divided off by some interval of time not defined in Scripture from the Day of the Lord). Then there is the day of the Lord, which will include: (a) the Great Tribulation; (b) the heavenly signs; (c) the great and notable day of the Lord; and even (d) the millennial reign.

That this order is the right one, I submit the five following proofs:
(1) In several prophecies the day of the Lord has begun before the heavenly signs occur.
(2) We do not read in the prophets of a Great Tribulation preceding the "day of the Lord".
(3) The same characteristics are common to the day of the Lord and to the Great Tribulation.
(4) The same unparalleled character of severity is predicted of both periods.

(5) We do not see either in the Old or New Testament that the Lord is exalted throughout "the day of the Lord".

(1) The Day of the Lord Begun

In several places in Scripture the day of the Lord is described as in full progress before the signs in the heavens are mentioned at all. Thus, in Isaiah 24:23, we read, "Then the moon shall be confounded and the sun ashamed, when the Lord shall reign in Mount Zion". Though the day of the Lord is not specifically named in the twenty-two previous verses, who can doubt that it is referred to in such expressions as "The Lord maketh the earth empty...turning it upside down,...punishing the host of the high ones that are on high, and the kings of the earth upon the earth"? It is, therefore, clear that the "day of the Lord" is said in this chapter to precede the signs in the heavens of v. 23.

Again, in Joel 2:1, "the day of the Lord" is described as at hand. Israel are threatened with it unless they repent. It is a day of darkness and gloominess, and is connected plainly with the judgment of the land of Israel "by the hand of a great people and strong". Then after nine verses, giving a description of their work against Israel, (see v. 6) we have the signs in the heavens in v. 10: "The sun and the moon shall be dark, and the stars shall withdraw their shining". Later on in the same chapter the signs in the heavens are spoken of as preceding "the great and notable day of the Lord". Thus we see that the day of the Lord will have been in progress for some time before the signs in the heavens, which are themselves the heralds of "the great and notable day of the Lord". Does not this clearly justify the distinction between this latter expression, and "the day of the Lord"?

Isaiah 13 is another passage where "the day of the Lord" is spoken of as having begun prior to the signs in the heavens. In v. 6 we read, "The day of the Lord is at hand", and in v. 9 it is described as "cruel both with wrath and fierce anger to lay the land destitute", "He shall destroy the sinners out of it", and then in v. 10 the heavenly signs follow, "The sun shall be darkened in his going forth, and the moon shall not cause her light to shine".

One more passage may suffice. In Isaiah 34:2 we have the indignation of the Lord upon all nations, with its results in v. 3, followed again by the signs in the heaven, described in much the same terms as in Revelation 6.

How, then, is it possible to maintain, in face of such Scriptures, that the "day of the Lord" does not begin until after the signs in the heavens? Nor is there the hard and fast distinction that these teachers would maintain between the "day of the Lord" and "the Great Tribulation", either as to time or character. It would appear rather that the former includes the latter. Even by the showing of the "Tribulationists", "the Great Tribulation" only occupies a part of the whole period, stretching from the opening of the first seal onward. It would be strange had this inclusive period no generic name. I believe it has, and that this name is "the day of the Lord".

As in Egypt during the plagues, so the day of the Lord during part of its course is characterised by the tribulation of God's earthly people at the hands of their enemies by His permission, and at the same time by terrible judgments against the nations of the earth directly from the hand of God, in which His earthly people also share.

(2) Precedence of the Great Tribulation

Again, if "the order of events" is as the advocates of the Tribulation Theory teach, we should not only expect to find the "day of the Lord" preceded by the "heavenly signs" (which we have just seen is not the case) but *a fortiori* by "the Great Tribulation" or by some period which, though not bearing this name, would at any rate correspond to it in character. We have seen that it is impossible at any rate to exclude Israel from the scenes depicted in Matthew 24. Should we not expect to find her decimated and exhausted by the fearful persecutions through which she has just passed?

But where do we find such a state of things in the prophecies? It is the "day of the Lord" with which Israel is threatened if she will not repent (e.g., Isa 2, Joel 2, Amos 1, Zeph 2), as well as the nations of the earth. Again, if the coming of the Lord in Thessalonians 4 is to deliver His Church after "the Great Tribulation", why is there no hint of this latter previously in that chapter?

On the contrary, the exhortation that immediately precedes is, "That ye study to be quiet, and do your own business, and to work with your own hands", advice hardly suitable for a people enduring a raging persecution, as the Tribulation Theory demands. Of course I do not admit for a moment that we have in 1 Thessalonians 4:13-

17 a description of the coming of the Son of Man, as in Matthew 24, but why have we not, even in the following chapter, a hint of tribulation and heavenly signs as likely to precede the "day of the Lord" therein referred to? And why in 2 Thessalonians 2 did the saints imagine that they were in the "day of the Lord", and not in the "Great Tribulation", if this was to take place first?

(3) Likeness of Two Great Events

A third reason for rejecting the Tribulation Theory is that the "order of events" on which it rests necessitates a fictitious distinction between the "day of the Lord" as a time when God alone judges man, and the "Great Tribulation" as a time when man alone afflicts God's people. As a matter of fact the two periods are marked by the same characteristics.

It is not true that the "day of the Lord" is only a time of direct divine judgment on man. In Joel 2, for instance, we see God's judgment on His people, but not directly. He uses "a great people and strong" to chastise them with. Israel are afflicted by man, but this is distinctly called in Joel 2:1 "the day of the Lord". In Luke 21:22, on the other hand, the parallel passage to Matthew 24 where the "Great Tribulation" is spoken of, we read, "These be the days of vengeance, that all things which are written may be fulfilled". Surely the vengeance here spoken of is Jehovah's vengeance by the hand of His enemies. Notice, too, the expression in the same chapter of Luke (v. 23) "wrath upon this people". What people but Israel could possibly be intended? The expression in v. 22, "all things which are written", point to this too, for Israel is the subject of prophecy, not the Church. It is perfectly true that the day of the Lord will also be marked by God's judgments against the nations (see Rev 16), but there is no hint that these latter will have changed one iota in their hatred against those who refuse the mark of the Beast.

We shall see later that the "time of Jacob's trouble" is another way of expressing "the Great Tribulation". But by comparing Isaiah 13:8 with Jeremiah 30:6 we see that the same strange characteristic is common to "the time of Jacob's trouble" and "the day of the Lord". In Isaiah 13 we read that (in "the day of the Lord") "they shall be in pain as a woman that travaileth", and in Jeremiah 30, where it is a question of Jacob's trouble, the words are found, "Ask ye now and see whether a man doth travail with child, wherefore do I see every man with his hands upon his loins". (See also 1 Thess 5:3.) Is not this an additional proof that "the Great Tribulation", or "the time of Jacob's trouble", (call it which you will) is included in "the day of the Lord"?

(4) Unparalleled Severity of Both

A fourth reason for rejecting this fallacious "order of events" and this fictitious distinction between "the day of the Lord" and "the Great Tribulation" is that the same unique and unparalleled character of severity is predicted of both periods.

In Matthew 24:21 we read, "There shall be Great Tribulation, such as was not since the beginning of the world to this time, no, nor ever shall be". In Joel 2:2 it is said of the day of the Lord, "There hath not been ever the like, neither shall be any more after it, even to the years of many generations". In both cases the statements are made in a most general way of all the peoples and times, so that it cannot be said that the two periods are only unique in the experience of some particular class of sufferer. Must not the two periods referred to be the same?

Again in Jeremiah 30:7, we read of "the time of Jacob's trouble", that "there is none like it". The Tribulationists teach that this time comes along after "the Great Tribulation" which, however, is said in Matthew 24:21 above to be also unlike anything before or since. Is it not clear that the two expressions describe, possibly from different standpoints, the same period? As Dr. Tregelles rightly says, "It follows inevitably that the same period is spoken of in both places." (See Tregelles on Daniel, p. 154.)

Again, the "Tribulationists" teach that the Great Tribulation is exclusively a time of man's persecution of God's people, and that the day of the Lord is exclusively a time of God's judgments on man, but, as we have seen above, their theory demands that the Great Tribulation, of which it is said that "no time shall ever be like it", should precede "the day of the Lord", and therefore man's persecution of God's people is more severe than God's judgment on the persecutors, which is incredible. But as it is also said of "the day of the Lord", that there shall never have been any time like it before, we are reduced to saying that the "Great Tribulation" is greater than the "day of the Lord", and that the latter is greater than the Great Tribulation, which is absurd. We may safely affirm, then, that these two expressions, and the "time of Jacob's trouble" are only three ways of describing, from three different points of view, the same concurrent period. But if "the Great Tribulation" is described in Jeremiah 30:7 as the time of Jacob's trouble, it is certain that it is not the Church which will pass through that tribulation, but Israel herself.

(5) The Lord Alone Exalted

It is quite possible to lay too much stress on the expression, "the Lord alone shall be exalted in that day" (Isa 2:17). I believe it does not mean that all through "the day of the Lord" He alone will be exalted, but as the result of God's judgments He alone will be exalted. This interpretation, besides being perfectly natural, has the additional advantage of being in accordance with the facts. Where do we find in Revelation, in those chapters which the "Tribulationists" especially allocate to the day of the Lord, that the name of the Lord alone is exalted? Take chapter 16, for instance, when "the vials" are poured out on the earth. In v. 9 we read, "They blasphemed the name of God,...and they repented not to give Him glory". In v. 11, "They blasphemed the God of Heaven, and repented not of their deeds". Then in vv. 13-16 we have the gathering of the armies of the whole world to Armageddon (with little thought of exalting the Lord alone), and in v. 21 we read, "Men blasphemed God because of the hail."

Do such words as these fit in with this theory, that while the judgments are in progress "the Lord alone is exalted"? We know the final result will be, "His enemies will be made His footstool", and He Himself exalted above all; but this will only happen when Christ appears in person and smites the Man of Sin with the sword of His mouth, and destroys him with the brightness of His coming.

It is really incredible how anyone can seriously maintain that the Lord Himself is alone exalted throughout "the day of the Lord", when at His coming He finds the Beast and the false prophet in red-handed rebellion against Him at the head of their mighty hosts.

3. CONFUSING THE STAGES OF THE SECOND COMING

The Tribulation Theory obliterates the vital distinction between the

THE GREAT TRIBULATION THEORY

coming of the Son of Man to the earth in judgment, and the coming of the Lord in the air to call away His own.

The former of these stages of the Lord's return (really subsequent to the other in the order of events) was foretold in the Old Testament, e.g., Daniel 7:13, "I saw in the night visions one like the Son of Man", and referred to in such passages as Matthew 24, Mark 13, Luke 21. The latter was "a mystery" (that is, kept secret until made known in the New Testament), and revealed specially to Paul, then by him to the Church in his epistles, by a special "word of the Lord" to the Thessalonians, and as a mystery to the Corinthians, "Behold, I show you a mystery" (1 Cor 15:51). After speaking to the former in 1 Thessalonians 4 of what they could not possibly know from the Old Testament, he goes on to speak, in chapter 5, of that which is connected with times and seasons, i.e., the day of the Lord, of which he says, "Ye have no need that I write unto you, for ye yourselves know perfectly...". How could they know this? Because the day of the Lord, and the coming in judgment, "in the great and notable day", were spoken of by the Old Testament prophets, from Isaiah to Malachi. But if the Thessalonians and Corinthians needed special revelations to inform them concerning the "coming of the Lord" for His Church, how could the apostles in Matthew be supposed to have in their minds this coming, which was at that time an unrevealed mystery?

It is really most unscientific, to use a modern phrase, to read back into the apostles' minds that which, had it been there, would have been nothing less than a startling anachronism. No, the Lord was not sent but unto the lost sheep of the house of Israel. Four of these lost sheep He was addressing, who had heard the Shepherd's voice, and they were to Him in the relation of a faithful remnant to their Messiah, and represented that faithful remnant in the last days.

All the surroundings of Matthew 24 are Jewish, as we have seen, and hinge on the destruction of Jerusalem - the tribulation of "this people" (see Luke 21, "great wrath upon this people"), and the coming of the Son of Man to their deliverance as foretold in Zechariah 14. Of course it is not meant by those who emphasise the title here used of "Son of Man" that this is never used where truths directly applicable to the Church are in question. All that is meant is, that where you have "Son of Man coming" the reference is to the coming of the Son of Man as revealed to Daniel.

One writer has referred to the "striking similarity" between the "comings" described in Matthew 24 and 1 Thessalonians 4. Unfortunately he refrained from indicating the points of similarity. We know these exegetes well. The occurrence of the same word in two passages, however divergent, establishes in their facile understanding, close connection between them. They are more occupied with sounds than sense and usually ignore all dispensational differences. Anyone who believes that the Scriptures are God-breathed ought to be more struck with the points of contrast than with their similarity. The words of Scripture are not used haphazardly. Differences which might mean nothing in a mere human book have often a deep significance in the Book of God. True there are certain superficial similarities. In both passages "a coming" is described, and that of the same Person.

But the two events differ as to (1) circumstances, (2) manner, (3) objects.

(1) Different Circumstances

Both passages indeed refer to the same person, but why is that person described as "Son of Man" in Matthew, and as "the Lord Himself" in 1 Thessalonians 4? Again, is there no significance in the fact that "the coming" in Matthew 24 is preceded by "the sign of the Son of Man", by heavenly marvels, and by the Great Tribulation, and is compared to "the Deluge", and has therefore a character of divine judgment, whereas in 1 Thessalonians 4 there is not one word of premonitory signs or tribulation, nor hint of accompanying judgment?

(2) Different Manner

In Matthew 24 the coming is thus described, "Then shall the tribes of the earth mourn, and they shall see the Son of Man coming in the clouds of heaven with power and great glory; and He shall send forth His angels, and they shall gather together His elect...". In 1 Thessalonians 4 angels are not mentioned. ("The voice of the archangel" is literally "with archangel voice" - as though to describe the loudest voice imaginable.) The saints are gathered by the Lord in person and by the trump of God. The action here is instantaneous;

that of sending out angels and gathering by their agency as in Matthew 24, presents the idea of prolonged action.

The coming in Matthew 24 is a public one: "all the tribes of the earth shall mourn" (v. 30). There is no mention of this in connection with the coming of 1 Thessalonians 4. It is all over "in a moment, in the twinkling of an eye" (cf. 1 Cor. 15 where the same coming is described) and the effect on the world at large is not mentioned. It is beside the mark to affirm that because the Lord shouts, therefore the world will hear. In John 12:29 we have an authentic account of God speaking from Heaven in definite words. To some who stood by it was only a clap of thunder. God can make His voice heard to whom He will, and veil it to whom He will.

(3) Different Objects

In Matthew 24 the objects are twofold: (1) the elect; (2) the world. In 1 Thessalonians 4 the objects are also twofold, but different from those just mentioned: (1) the sleeping saints who are raised (there is no mention of resurrection in Matthew 24); (2) the living saints, who are changed. And both together are caught up in the clouds, to be for ever with the Lord. But some one will say, Do we not find rapture spoken of in Matthew 24:40,41? We do, but it is precisely reverse in character to that of 1 Thessalonians 4. Those taken away in this latter chapter are the saints of God removed from a world doomed to judgment. In Matthew 24, if we compare vv.40 and 41 with v.39, we notice that those "taken" correspond with the wicked cut off by the flood, whereas those left behind correspond with Noah and his family, and will be blessed like them. When the Lord comes as in 1 Thessalonians 4 it will be blessed to be taken away. When He comes in His Matthew 24 character it will be blessed to be left behind. In accordance with this, the words for "taken" in Matthew 24 and for "caught up" in 1 Thessalonians 4 are entirely distinct.

4. THE ORDER AND CHARACTER OF THE APOCALYPSE

The order of events in the Revelation, and the Jewish character of the book, are strong arguments against the Tribulation Theory.

In Revelation 1:19 is given the threefold division of the book. Chapter 1 represents the first; chapters 2 - 3 the second, namely, "the things that are", not only messages to seven literal churches, but a prophetic and panoramic view of the Church from the apostolic to the last days; in chapter 4 begins "the things which shall be hereafter", the very phrase being found in v. 1, in slightly stronger form. At this point John is caught up into the open heaven, from which he looks down on the earth, and is henceforth taken up with Israel, Babylon, and the nations. Why does he deal no longer with "the churches"? Because, as I believe, the rapture of John is only representative of the rapture of the whole Church, who may be represented in chapter 4, under the figure of twenty-four white-robed elders. These are seated round the throne, in contrast with the great multitude of chapter 7, who are seen standing before the throne. In chapter 5 the Lord Jesus is spoken of as "the Lion of the tribe of Judah, the Root of David", evidently in relation to Israel (for it is not in such terms that He is presented to us in relation to the Church).

The Lamb

Later on the Lion is seen as "the Lamb", a word used of Him only in the Revelation, and quite distinct from that employed in John 1:29,36; Acts 8:32; and 1 Peter 1:19. It is as "the Lamb" that He purchased the world, and can claim to break the seals of the book, the title deeds of the purchase. It is to Him as "the Lamb" that the living creatures and the twenty-four elders bear witness, as also to "the blood", the purchase price (see Jer 32:8-12). As each of the first four seals is broken, a living creature calls, Come! and at once there is a corresponding manifestation of energy on the earth, which shows that though man proposes and Satan opposes, it is still God who disposes.

The Conqueror

Many believe that the conqueror of chapter 6 is only Satan's counterfeit of that other conqueror on a white horse of Revelation 19, and is none other than the "man of sin" of 2 Thessalonians 2, and the 'coming prince' of Daniel 9, who is destined to make a seven years' covenant, not with the Church, but with Daniel's people, Israel. The fifth seal may very well correspond in measure with the Great Tribulation, consequent on the breaking of that covenant in the midst of the period of seven years. This tribulation, identical, I believe, with the time of Jacob's trouble (Jer 30:6), continues to the end, to that "one day" of Zechariah 14:7.

It is noticeable that in Zechariah 14:1 the Revised Version reads, not "the day of the Lord cometh", but, "a day of the Lord cometh" - a special day - described below as a day "when the light shall not be clear nor dark", "not day nor night", owing may it not be, to the darkening of the heavenly bodies? These signs, we know from Matthew 24, immediately precede the coming of "the Son of Man in power and great glory". I believe this "one day" is the day named in Scripture "the day of the Lord the great and notable one".

It is generally recognised that the Revelation cannot be read consecutively, except within certain limits. The Spirit of God again and again carries us on to the end, although "the end is not yet". Thus chapter 5 leads us on to millennial scenes; chapters 6, 14, and 19, to what appears to be in each case (at least in the two last) the climax of final judgment. But wherever we are, the record is tinged with a Jewish colouring. The very prayer of the souls beneath the altar (ch. 5), which cries for vengeance on their enemies, surely suffices to show that these are not christian but Jewish martyrs, while the reply shows that the day of tribulation was still in progress. The 144,000 Israelites of chapter 7; the rebuilt temple of chapter 11; the character of the testimony of the two witnesses of chapter 11; and that of "the everlasting Gospel" of chapter 14, (which, though of course based on the same foundation as the "gospel of the grace of God" of this dispensation, is surely distinct from this latter, as its terms show,) and many similar points, all go to prove that the Church is not in view in the Apocalypse from chapter 6 and onwards until she comes with her Lord in chapter 19.

5. DEPRIVING THE CHURCH OF HER HOPE

Finally, "the Tribulation Theory" deprives the Church of her hope. The hope of the Christian is neither long life nor painless death. It is neither the conversion of the world nor the judgment of the world. It is neither "the day of the Lord" nor "the Great Tribulation", but the coming of the Lord! The Tribulation Theory eclipses this hope by interposing "the Great Tribulation" between it and the Church. Now one of the last promises of Christ was, "I will come again", and His last assurance before the Book closes,

"Behold, I come quickly". It was Himself, not events on the earth, much less "the Great Tribulation", He would have us wait for.

Somehow I cannot help suspecting that at the back of this theory there lurks, unsuspected by its votaries, legality. The Church has not been what she ought to have been, either collectively or individually, therefore she must go through the Great Tribulation - a kind of Protestant Purgatory – to atone for her manifold failures. Truly, if it were a question of desert, she has deserved worse fires than a Great Tribulation can threaten!

But the same grace that saved us gives us an object to look for - that blessed hope (Tit 2:14). The One who died for our sins is coming to take us to be with Himself for ever. Now, certainly, "the Great Tribulation" is not a blessed hope, and would effectually blot out any such hope beyond it.

An Awkward Parallel

What I can only describe as a very inadequate attempt has been made to get over this difficulty. An effort has been made to suggest a parallel between the Church waiting for her Lord and a company of citizens waiting for the arrival of their king. True, these latter know that their king must be preceded by a squadron of cavalry and a military band, but would this spoil their hope of seeing him? Would they not rather strain eyes and ears to catch the first sight and strains of the head of the procession? So the Tribulationist apologist argues. Very good, but what would correspond in the case of the Church to these joyful strains of music? - the most awful persecution the world has ever known, worse than the massacres of a Tamerlane, fiercer than the *autos da fe* of a Torquemada, more bloody than the butcheries of an Abdul-Ahmid; "a Great Tribulation, such as was not since the beginning of the world to this time, no, nor ever shall be" (Matt 24:21). If, to go back to the supposed parallel, the citizens knew that before their king could possibly appear they must endure three and a half years of prison, torture, and massacre, I maintain it would be idle to talk to them of the coming of their king with this awful shadow across their path. The Thessalonians were taught of God "to wait for His Son from Heaven", to expect the Lord Himself, because it was, so to speak, the next thing to happen on the heavenly programme.

THE GREAT TRIBULATION THEORY

It is true that Peter was warned (in John 21) that he would glorify God by a certain form of death, but it is doubtful whether the words of our Lord, couched as they were in metaphorical language, were necessarily clear in their meaning, at the time, to the apostles. They did not, in any case, prevent Peter himself from speaking of the immediate return of the Lord Jesus as a possibility contingent on Israel's national repentance (Acts 3:20-21, RV).

A Modern Fiction

In 2 Thessalonians we gather that the Thessalonians were called to pass through persecutions at the hand of man so severe in character that they could only suppose they were in the last days. Now, were "the Tribulation Theory" correct, it is easy to perceive the particular form of error they would have fallen into. They would have imagined "the Great Tribulation" was upon them, for this period is supposed by the Tribulationists to precede "the day of the Lord". But what did they think? "The day of the Lord is present" (2 Thess 2:2, RV). Why does the apostle not put them right at once by quoting "the order of events" laid down by the Tribulation theorists, and remind them that they could not be in the day of the Lord, because the "Great Tribulation" and the "heavenly signs" had not yet taken place? Why does he not even refer to these two last-named events? Because he knew nothing of this modern fiction of a "day of the Lord", preceded by a Great Tribulation and heavenly signs.

Now, it is true that the simple and direct way of correcting their error would have been to remind them that "the coming of the Lord" had not yet taken place, and that therefore "the day of the Lord," which all are agreed must follow it, could not be in progress. But the apostle does do this indirectly, by appealing in v. 1 to "the coming of the Lord and our gathering together to Him", as a motive for not being "soon shaken in mind" by the novel theory they had received; but, as in other places, guided by the Spirit, he not only wishes to correct their mistake, but to take advantage of it in order to bring out further light for the saints of God in all time.

He therefore starts with "the day of the Lord" (RV) and works backward, and says, simply, you cannot be in the day of the Lord, for before that day can come there must be a great falling away, and the man of sin, borne along on the wave of apostasy, must be revealed. It is generally affirmed that "that which withholdeth" is the Church, and "He who withholdeth" is the Holy Spirit.

Some however have suggested that this hindering cause is rather the breaking down of law and order going on around us today, and that it is only when that is complete that Satan's man will appear. In a previous edition I adopted this view, but feel obliged now to return to the older interpretation. One special point seems to me to show the fallacy of above. It is true we live in anarchical days, but the Man of Sin will be himself the last Governmental head of the Roman Empire, and himself the very representative of autocratic rule – certainly conferred and supported by Satan, but none the less one of the powers that be that are ordained of God. So great will be the energy of Satan in these days that nothing but special divine power will restrain him. When we speak of the Holy Spirit being taken away we do not mean, as our critics insist on supposing, that He will cease to work on the earth. He worked all through Old Testament times, before He came at Pentecost. But when He is taken away it will only be in the sense of ceasing to do the work He is doing today of baptising all believers into one body. Probably when the Church is gone and the indwelling Spirit also is gone, He will work on the earth in the conversion of sinners in a way never before realized, and that through Israel restored to the place of testimony for God on the earth.

Let it be said in conclusion that though the revelation of Christ with His saints is often spoken of in connection with the Church as an incentive to faithfulness, because that appearing will be the moment of the manifestation of the saints in their position of reward and their place in the kingdom, it is none the less true that it is the coming of the Lord for His saints which is set before us in the epistles as the hope of the Church.

May we, then, be "waiting for His Son from heaven", and have our hopes so fixed on Him, that we may purify ourselves, even as He is pure; "giving thanks unto the Father, who hath made us meet to be partakers of the inheritance of the saints in light" (Col 1:12).

THE GREAT TRIBULATION THEORY

DIAGRAM

RAPTURE OF THE CHURCH (1 Thess 4)

Interval not defined in Scripture

A.	Beginning of Day of the Lord, probably Rev 6:1	
B.	Seven Years' Covenant made between the Man of Sin and the nation of Israel under Antichrist (Dan 9:27)	
C.	Ministry of Two Witnesses, lasting $3^1/_2$ years (Rev 11:3-6)	
D.	Breaking of the Covenant in the midst of the week; Sacrifices cease (Dan 9:27; 11:31). Death of Two Witnesses (Rev 11:7). Full manifestation of the Man of Sin and of Antichrist	
E.	Great Tribulation (Matt 24:21); and "the time of Jacob's trouble" (Jer 30:7); Heavenly Signs (Matt 24:29)	THE DAY OF THE LORD
F.	The Great and Notable Day of the Lord, or in other words the Appearing in Glory of the Son of Man (Matt 24:30; Acts 2:20)	
G.	The destruction of the enemy and the deliverance of Israel (Dan 12:1, Zech 14:3, Rev 19:11-21) Judgment of the Nations (Matt 25). First resurrection completed (Rev 20:4,5)	
H.	Satan bound (Rev 20:2). Millennial Reign	
I.	Satan unloosed. Last revolt of man and demons at close of Millennium (Rev 20:7,8)	
J.	Revolt suppressed. Satan doomed. Final judgment of wicked dead (Rev 20:9-15)	
K.	Eternal State	

Mysteries of the New Testament

1. INTRODUCTION

The subject of the 'Mysteries' of the New Testament is one of the highest importance and interest. We touch here some of "the deep things of God". Here are "waters to swim in". We need, therefore, in a special manner, the Spirit's teaching. "The things of God knoweth no man, but the Spirit of God" (1 Cor 2:11). But we may surely with expectant faith claim the promise of our Lord: "He shall teach you all things" – "He will guide you into all truth" (John 14:26;16:13).

The word 'mystery' does not occur in the Old Testament, but seems to correspond to the expression, "dark sayings of old" (Psa 78:2, see also Psa 49:4 and Prov 1:6); that is, sayings which have been kept dark, but which the Psalmist was inspired prophetically to reveal. I think this correspondence is shown by the way this passage is quoted by the Lord in Matthew 13:35, "I will open My mouth in parables, I will utter things which have been kept secret from the foundation of the world." The last phrase, "things which have been kept secret from (or even before) the foundation of the world" may serve well to explain the meaning of the word 'mystery'.

In modern speech, a mystery is something unintelligible and incomprehensible, something baffling and even uncanny. But it does not bear this sense in the New Testament, any more than in classical Greek, from which it is derived. The word comes from the ancient mysteries – the Eleusinian, for instance – which were religious ceremonies or rites practised among the Greeks. They consisted of purifications, sacrificial offerings and processions, songs and dances. These rites were kept secret from all except the initiated, but initiation was open to all who had the heart to seek it. In the New Testament, the word has the same general sense: not something kept secret, but a secret revealed for all, but only to the initiated.

The word is derived from a verb *muein* – 'to initiate' – closely connected with another verb, 'to close the lips, or eyes'. The initiate

MYSTERIES OF THE NEW TESTAMENT

was under obligation not to divulge the secrets learnt, and to close his eyes to all else.

This verb, 'to initiate' only occurs once in the New Testament. "I have learned in whatsoever state I am, to be content" (Phil 4:11). The word is, "I have learned the secret". Paul had been initiated into the mysteries of His Father's love and wisdom. He was assured that all was well. The word 'therewith' is in italics, and may well be omitted. He had learned to be content in – not with – his state of things. This is true christian experience. The believer finds out what God is, as he passes through circumstances and learns contentment.

A 'mystery', then, is not something that baffles solution, but a secret made known. There are mysteries which are "hard to be understood" (e.g. the mystery of 1 Cor 15:51), but this is incidental. That all living believers will be transformed when the Lord returns, is a truth revealed to faith, but how such an event is to take place is not explained. The fact that the word is usually linked with some such phrase as 'made known' or 'revealed', proves that the idea of a mystery is not of something which we may not know, but rather what has been made known by God Himself, for our instruction and edification.

But are not spiritual truths known only by the revelation of the Spirit of God? And yet all are not mysteries. How shall we then distinguish between truths which are 'mysteries' and those that are not?

I believe that a 'mystery' is a new and unexpected development of the purposes of God, in relation to some spiritual truth which may or may not have been revealed before – a surprise revelation, constituting something entirely new in the ways of God, though known to Him from the beginning. On the other hand, Creation, Redemption, Resurrection are all revealed truths, but they have not this feature of novel development. We may illustrate what is meant from a well known case in the Old Testament. That Joseph was in Egypt, could scarcely be a 'mystery' to his brothers. They had sold him to merchants travelling thither, and he might well be there. But that Joseph had been raised by God to be the Governor of all the land of Egypt, and that for their deliverance and preservation, was something they could have no conception of whatever, until Joseph made himself known, and revealed to them the purpose of God.

The infant Moses is another case in point. That he would be providentially delivered from death was, I would judge, real to the faith of Amram and Jochebed, and for that Miriam was set to watch, "to wit what would be done to him" (Exod 2:4). She did not expect to see him devoured by evil beasts or drowned in the Nile, but delivered in some way or other by El-Shaddai, the All-sufficient God. But that the babe should be rescued by Pharaoh's daughter, confided to his own mother to nurse, and brought up in the palace of the very man who sought his life, was something worthy of God, a totally unexpected development, 'exceeding abundant' above all that was asked or thought.

The same principle might be illustrated in the history of David, Esther, Daniel, and other saints of God. And so the apostle says, "We speak the wisdom of God in a mystery, the hidden wisdom, which God ordained before the world, unto our glory. But as it is written, Eye hath not seen, nor ear heard, neither hath entered into the heart of man, the things which God hath prepared for them that love Him. But God hath revealed them unto us by His Spirit, for the Spirit searcheth all things, yea, the deep things of God" (1 Cor 2:7-10).

2. SEVEN GREAT MYSTERIES

The Divine mysteries are the secrets of God made known to His people 'in due time'. They come as the answer of God to the consistent failure of man, and to the apparent victories of Satan, to his confusion and to the praise of the saints, who with one voice exclaim, "How unsearchable are His judgments, and His ways past finding out!" (Rom 11:33).

The Satanic mysteries are the counterfeits of the Divine – the bitter Dead Sea fruit of the creature's rebellion come to full maturity. In them will be clearly proved, what was shown at Calvary, the fearful and hopeless character of sin. They will be something novel, something startling, something more deliberately wicked than anything known before.

But when men have betrayed their trust and Satan has done his worst, God brings out of His treasury something new, something unexpected, something better than was before, because containing a fuller revelation of Christ. For all is summed up in Him, "in whom are hid all the treasures of wisdom and knowledge" (Col 2:3).

His atonement is the fulcrum on which the eternal counsels turn; His glory the supreme object of all the purposes of God; His Person the grand centre around which all else revolves. Of Him Jehovah says, "I have laid help upon One that is mighty; I have exalted One chosen out of the people. I have found David my servant; with my holy oil have I anointed Him" (Psa 89:19,20). And faith rejoins, "Let Thy hand be upon the man of Thy right hand, upon the Son of Man whom Thou madest strong for Thyself" (Psa 80:17).

It is a vast relief to remember, in view of sad corporate as well as personal failure, that all God's purposes and our eternal blessings are in the pierced hands of Him, "who His own self bear our sins, in His own body on the tree" (1 Pet 2:24), whom now God has glorified at His own right hand in Heaven, and whose presence is assured to us through His Spirit "all the days, even to the end of the age" (Matt 28:20, RV).

Early in the first Epistle to the Corinthians, the apostle disclaims the place of a denominational leader. It was indeed a signal honour put upon the apostles, that none of them founded sects. But later on in the Epistle, he indicates what he does claim to be. "Let a man so account of us as stewards of the mysteries of God. But it is required in stewards, that a man be found faithful" (1 Cor 4:2).

Stewardship involves responsibility. A steward must give account of his stewardship. In this matter, the apostle "knew nothing against (not by) himself". He who knew himself as "the chief of sinners" certainly lays no claim here to impeccability or infallibility. But he was not conscious of having betrayed his trust as "a steward of the mysteries". He had not tampered with one of them, but as far as he knew, had declared "the whole counsel of God". Let it be our ambition by grace, to do likewise.

Only three of the apostles, Matthew, John, and Paul, and two others, Mark and Luke, probably possessed of the prophetic gift, were commissioned to record the revelation of Divine Mysteries. But we need not suppose they alone had the understanding of them. We know at least concerning the great Mystery of Christ, that it was in general "revealed to His holy apostles and prophets by the Spirit" (Eph 3:5), though Paul was the chosen instrument for its official revelation to the churches. It had no doubt been widely preached long before the Epistle to the Ephesians was written (see Rom 16:25,26).

The Divine Mysteries are, as I judge, seven in number:—
1. The Mystery of the Kingdom   (Matt 13; Mark 4; Luke 8)
2. The Mystery of Israel's Fall   (Rom 11:25)
3. The Mystery of the Rapture   (1 Cor 15:51)
4. The Mystery of Christ   (Rom 16:25; Eph 3-5)
5. The Mystery of Godliness   (1 Tim 3:16)
6. The Mystery of God   (Rev 10:7)
7. The Mystery of Universal Headship (Eph 1:9-10).

Numbers four and five are called "Great Mysteries".

The Satanic Mysteries are twain :—
1. The Mystery of Iniquity   (1 Thess 2:7)
2. The Mystery of Babylon   (Rev 17:5).

It may be well to add here that the word 'mystery' is sometimes used in a secondary sense in the New Testament for a hidden spiritual truth, or for something figurative, as in 1 Cor 14:2, "but in spirit he speaketh mysteries", which can hardly mean that whenever a man spoke with tongues, he uttered the great Mysteries of God, but simply truths hidden till interpreted. In the same way are the words, "the mystery of the seven stars", interpreted as meaning the angels of the seven churches (Rev 1:20), the word standing for a hidden figure needing explanation. 'Angel' here, should be taken, I judge, literally, not figuratively, for how explain a figure by a figure? The candlesticks mean literal churches; and 'the angels' I submit, mean angelic beings. We know that such share in the government of the world (see Dan 10:13,20,21), and are also "sent forth to minister for them who shall be heirs of salvation" (Heb 1:14). The words we are considering would go to show that this is not only to saints in their individual but in their corporate capacity. Knowing how natural "the worshipping of angels" is to the heart of man (see Col 2:18; Rev 19:10; 22:8), the almost complete silence of Scripture as to the nature of their 'deacon work' is explained.

How serious to God must be the sin so prevalent in Christendom, of dedicating to angels, religious feast days and buildings!

3. THE MYSTERY OF THE KINGDOM (Matt 13:11)

We will consider this mystery first for the following reasons: it stands first in order in the New Testament; it was the only one revealed by the Lord when on earth; and it illustrates clearly the special character of a Mystery as already noted – a surprise development of a truth previously known in part.

"The Kingdom of God" was not a mystery. It was a frequent theme with Psalmists and prophets. The mention of Jehovah's 'King' occurs again and again in the Old Testament as a title of the Messiah. As such, He was the "Hope of Israel", not only in His sufferings, but in the glory that should follow. Psalm 2 speaks of His appointment: "Yet have I set My King upon My holy hill of Zion" (v. 6). Psalm 24:8 answers the question, "Who is the King of glory? The Lord strong and mighty, the Lord mighty in battle". In Psalm 72 we have an attractive and comprehensive picture of the extent and characteristics of the coming Kingdom. Isaiah 9:6 unfolds some of the glories of the King's name: "Wonderful, Counsellor, the Mighty God, the Everlasting Father, the Prince of Peace". Chapter 11 describes the effects of His rule: righteousness, peace, universal knowledge of God, and blessing to Israel. Daniel dwells on its all-embracing and eternal character, "a Kingdom which shall never be destroyed and shall be given to the people of the saints of the Most High, whose Kingdom is an everlasting Kingdom, and all dominions shall serve and obey Him" (2:44;7:27).

These are only a few out of numberless passages where the Kingdom is foretold in the Old Testament. Later on, it was the Kingdom which John the Baptist and the Lord Himself heralded. And when Christ taught His disciples to pray "Thy Kingdom come", it was no mere spiritual blessing they were to ask for, but that the literal Kingdom of God should be set up on the earth. This idea of the Kingdom, therefore, was perfectly well understood. But the Kingdom in Mystery was a new revelation, not once breathed before its mention in Matthew 13. This chapter (see also Mark 4 and Luke 8) marked a new departure in our Lord's testimony. He now begins to speak in parables of the Mystery or Mysteries of the Kingdom,[1] and why? Because 'the Kingdom' in the hitherto known sense was rejected. Each of these three chapters in the Synoptic Gospels is immediately preceded by a clear indication of this rejection. What else did the imprisonment of John mean? (Luke 7) What else the blasphemous imputation that the very mighty works which proved that the King was in their midst, were done in league with Beelzebub (Matt 12:24)? The Kingdom had "come unto them", but they had wilfully rejected it, in the person of their leaders. This was the first act in the rejection of the King. What, then, must happen? Clearly the literal Kingdom could not be then set up, for how could it exist in the absence of the rejected King? That it was to be set up in a new, undreamed of character, was a fresh revelation by Christ to His own. This is the Kingdom in Mystery. Its special characteristics are illustrated in the seven parables of Matthew 13.

The Seven Parables of The Kingdom

These parables do not present a consecutive panorama of the Kingdom in Mystery, but are separate tableaux of it in its moral aspects as seen by God; this one covering the whole period, that one showing a special development, others again running on contemporaneously. The special characteristics of the Kingdom in Mystery are as follows.

1. It is the realm of a rejected King. It extends over the period of Christ's rejection, and ends with His return to establish the earthly kingdom; as the words twice repeated in verses 48 and 49 show: "So shall it be in the end of the world" (or age). The Church is not seen as such in this chapter. The Kingdom begins before and extends beyond the Church period. Believers in this dispensation are seen here as "children of the Kingdom". But though the Lord is absent in body, He is present by His Spirit. To bow to His authority even now is incumbent on all, for "He is Lord of all" (Acts 10:36).

2. It is hidden from the eyes of men. For this reason the Lord speaks here in parables. "The kingdom of God is not meat and drink

---

[1] In Matt 13 the Lord gives seven parables of the Kingdom. In Mark 4 we have the first and third–the sower and the mustard tree, and an eighth, not found in Matthew, the parable of the growing seed (v. 26-29), all three, indeed, 'seed' parables. In Luke 8 we find the first, and in ch. 13 the third and fourth.

(does not consist of outward, tangible rites), but righteousness, peace, and joy in the Holy Ghost" (Rom 14:17) – fruits of His Lordship obeyed in the heart. "The Kingdom of God cometh not with observation", it is within (Luke 17:20). The figures used speak of its hidden character. Seed germinating, leaven permeating, treasure hid in a field, a drag-net operating unseen beneath the waves.

3. In it, the good appears to fail. The Sower sows the Divine Word, but the ground is hard and unprepared, so that much good seed is lost. In the second parable, the influence of that good seed – the children of the Kingdom, is met by the presence of the tares – Satan's counterfeit witnesses.

4. In it, the false seems to prevail. Multitudes with only a name to live, take their place in the Kingdom. They name the Name of Christ, but do not depart from iniquity. The mustard seed, instead of remaining a humble annual, becomes an abnormal perennial–a great growth, rivalling Nebuchadnezzar's tree (Dan 4). The big attracts. Hence the success of the bad in the third parable. In the fourth, the success of the bad seems guaranteed, because it is in its very nature to spread, except where, through grace, sight enables the evil to be put away. The three measures of fine flour, representing the pure, unsullied doctrine of Christ, are permeated with that which has but one meaning in the Scriptures – evil, doctrinal, moral, political.

5. God's purposes are ripening fast. This is taught in the parables of the Treasure and the Pearl, and in the eighth parable of Mark 4, the seed which "springs up, he knoweth not how", in the power of resurrection life. At least, in the first two, we see the Lord at work purchasing and manifesting His own. The Treasure, be it noted, is not a bag of specie or precious stones, detachable from the field, but something bound up with the field, like a mine of precious metal. Why else must the field be bought? The Treasure thus, I believe, represents the elect of Israel. Jehovah's "special treasure" (Mal 3:17, marg.), inseparably connected with the earth, by the promises made unto the fathers. The spot where the treasure is found is Palestine, but its possession necessitates the purchase of the whole earth. The Pearl cannot, properly speaking, be the Church as such, though it includes it, for how could the disciples understand that which was not yet revealed? That they were expected to understand the Lord's words, and did in fact do so, is evidenced by our Lord's question and their answer (see Matt 13:51). The Pearl is, I believe, the whole glorious aggregate of the children of the Kingdom. The purchase, both of the Treasure and the Pearl, entailed the sacrifice of all else. "Ye know the grace of our Lord Jesus Christ that though He was rich, yet for your sakes He became poor, that ye through His poverty might become rich" (2 Cor 8:9). And the same "precious blood" that redeemed our souls, has purchased this planet. He is now the lawful owner of the field by purchase, as well as creation, so that none but He can break the seven seals of the title-deeds of the 'inheritance' (Rev 5).

6. In it, His Spirit works on all. The mighty force of the drag-net in the last parable, symbolises this divine energy of His working on the hearts and consciences of men. God has never left Himself without a witness, much less will He do so in the last solemn days of the Spirit's testimony, when the time for such testimony is rapidly vanishing away.

7. It will need purging. All who come under the Spirit's sway and yield outward obedience to His influences, do not eventually prove to be true "children of the Kingdom". Bad and good are gathered in, and the testing day alone will reveal the character of each. We do not read that Christ will purge His Church at His return. He is doing so now. Then He will "present it to Himself a glorious Church, not having spot or wrinkle or any such thing". But when He comes again as the Son of Man He will purge His Kingdom. "He will send forth His angels and gather out of His Kingdom all things that offend, and they which work iniquity" (things and men, stumbling blocks and lawless persons). And "then shall the righteous shine forth as the sun, in the Kingdom of their Father" (v. 43). Then will be revealed also to the world the Mystery of the Kingdom – that through seeming defeat, the Lord was reigning. Yes, "the Lord reigneth" even in these dark and difficult times. Nor has He resigned either rod or sceptre into His people's hands. This surely ought to give confidence and comfort to those who are called to bear witness for His name in these last days of departure from the truth.

For a fuller treatment of this subject, see 'The Kingdom of God', earlier in this volume.

4. THE MYSTERY OF THE HEAVENLY REMNANT
(Rom 11:1-25)

This Mystery is the first referred to in the epistles, and is connected with God's present dealings with Israel. In this age they are cut off, as branches from their own olive tree – the similitude used in this chapter to describe their place of national privilege. The Gentile nations, though branches of a wild olive tree, are now grafted contrary to nature into the place of privilege. But "God hath not cast away His people which He foreknew". They will be grafted in again, and even now there are some branches left, for "Even at this present time, there is a remnant according to the election of grace" (v. 5). What then is the Mystery? It is not that blindness should happen to Israel. That was clearly foretold by Moses, if they disobeyed God, "The Lord shall smite thee with blindness" (Deut 28:28) and by Isaiah and David, as quoted here (Rom 11:8,9). But that this blindness should be partial, is now for the first time made known to us. "I would not, brethren, that ye should be ignorant of this Mystery, that blindness in part is happened to Israel, until the fullness of the Gentiles be come in" (Rom 11:25).

This Mystery then, is connected with the remnant of Israel in this dispensation, and especially with the peculiar character of that remnant. It is no new thing for God to reserve to Himself a remnant out of Israel. He did so, as we shall see, after the Babylonian captivity. He will do so in the last apostate days of Antichrist. But it is important to notice that in both these cases, the remnant is the representative of the nation in connection with earthly blessing and their national hope. The remnant we are now considering is to be distinguished from Israel nationally and religiously, and enters into blessing of quite another order.[2] It is a Heavenly Remnant. This was something unheard of in Old Testament times, and is one more unexpected and surprising development in the ways of God.

---

[2] We do not expect to find in Romans a full exposition of the Mystery of the Church, but it is clear that there could be no remnant of Israel recognised as an earthly remnant in the present Church period. An understanding of this would have saved people from the mistake of interpreting Matthew 24 in terms of the Church, when Israel is clearly in view as such, or of making the Church go through 'the time of Jacob's trouble' which is only another name for 'The Great Tribulation'.

The Epistle to the Romans falls naturally into three divisions. (1) Doctrinal, ch. 1-8; (2) Dispensational, ch. 9-11; (3) Practical, ch. 12-16. It is with the central division we have to do here. The word 'Dispensation' is from a Greek noun, which is sometimes translated 'stewardship' (Luke 16:2,3,4) and means a principle of God's dealing with His creatures.

These dispensations have been varied. From the Fall to the Flood, man was left without Law and Government, to the light of conscience. From the Flood to the call of the chosen Nation, he was placed under Government. Then followed God's dealings with Israel under Government and Law, with room for grace to act in virtue of the sacrifices. Now is the dispensation of Grace, in which is being unfolded the mystery of the Heavenly Remnant we are now considering.

But what is a remnant? It is that which God reserves to Himself in view of general failure. "What saith the answer of God to Elias? I have reserved to Myself seven thousand men, who have not bowed the knee to the image of Baal" (v. 4). This was the remnant of Israel in Ahab's wicked days, and there always has been such a remnant according to the "election of grace". We may note four remnants in the history of the Chosen Race, (1) Spiritual or Figurative, (2) Historical, (3) Prophetic, (4) Heavenly.

Romans 9 presents to us the first, "a remnant according to the election of grace". The passage from Romans 8 to 9 is as from July sun to Autumn chill. The apostle puts off the garment of praise for a spirit of heaviness as he turns from the contemplation of the glories of Christ to view the sad condition of "his kinsmen according to the flesh". He yearns over them with the affections of Christ. He would wish to be anathema[3] for them. Had ever a people such privileges? Had not the Saviour sprung from them, "Christ who is over all, God blessed for ever"? And yet they were not saved, for instead of receiving "Him, who is the end of the law for righteousness to every one that believeth", they were seeking by the works of the law "to establish their own righteousness". This did not show that God's

---

[3] Christ is never said to be 'Anathema'. The word in Gal 3:13, "being made a curse for us", is a distinct word (*katara*), which also occurs in Heb 6:8 and James 3:10. 'Anathema' is the word in 1 Cor 12:3, and Gal 1:8-9.

promise had failed. He had given no pledge that all Israelites should be saved; "for they are not all Israel which are of Israel". A man might be of the seed of Abraham, and not be a child of promise; a son of Isaac, and yet despise his birthright.

It will repay us to study carefully in their Old Testament settings the quotations throughout this chapter. The two quotations regarding Jacob and Esau are separated by the whole range of Old Testament Scripture. The first, "The elder shall serve the younger", was spoken before their birth, and was the sovereign decree of God, involving nothing but good to either brother: the other, "Jacob have I loved and Esau have I hated", was uttered through Malachi, fifteen centuries later, and marks the effect of the responsible choice of Esau and his race, in their persistent enmity to the people of God. None but the rebellious or the sentimentalist can dispute God's right to have mercy on whom He will have mercy, and to harden those who persist, like Pharaoh, in resisting His will.[4] These latter will become the "vessels of wrath fitted for destruction"; and the former "vessels of mercy prepared" by God "unto glory". In Israel, there were always two circles – an outer one of national privilege entered by birth and circumcision, and an inner one of grace, entered by repentance and faith in God. These latter always proved the spiritual remnant, corresponding to the 7000 in Elijah's day.

Later on, there was another remnant of a different character, the Historic Remnant that returned from Babylon. God had promised by Jeremiah, that after 70 years of captivity were accomplished, He would cause His people to return to Jerusalem. When the moment struck, Cyrus was stirred up to make a decree, that all who wished might return and build. It was an offer to all, but most preferred the quiet life in Babylon. About 42,000 responded, "whose spirit God had raised". They were spoken of by Ezra as a 'remnant': "And now for a little space, grace hath been showed from the Lord our God to leave us a remnant to escape" (9:8); and also by Nehemiah (1:3).

---

[4] Rom 9:15-18 should be studied in the light of the Old Testament history. It will be seen that had mercy depended on man's will, and on man's running after God, none would have received it. Pharaoh's life was prolonged (Exod 9:13-16, RV), when he might have been righteously cut off, that he might serve as an object lesson of God's wrath and power.

These met with great opposition, but became once more the representatives of the nation in their land. Later, in the days of Malachi, they had grievously declined, but even then there was a little living remnant, "who feared the Lord and thought upon His Name". These were the progenitors of the Simeons, the Annas, and the rest who "looked for redemption in Israel" and were ready to receive the Lord.

In the last days, there will be another Remnant – referred to frequently in the prophets – which we may call the Prophetic Remnant. Isaiah speaks of them. "Except the Lord of hosts had left unto us a very small remnant, we should have been as Sodom" (1:9). "The remnant shall return, even the remnant of Jacob, unto the mighty God, though Thy people Israel be as the sand of the sea, yet a remnant (and a remnant only) shall return" (10:22). These two verses are quoted in Romans 9 as teaching generally that God will have a spiritual seed from Israel in these days. But this is far from exhausting their meaning: in fact, it is an application rather than a fulfilment. Joel speaks undoubtedly of this latter day remnant. "In Mount Zion and in Jerusalem shall be deliverance, as the Lord hath said, and in the remnant whom the Lord shall call" (2:32). This remnant will play an important role in the closing days. When the "Prince that shall come", aided and abetted by Israel's false king, the Antichrist, breaks his covenant with Israel in the midst of "the week", and causes the sacrifice and the oblation of Jehovah to cease (Dan 9:27), the nation as a whole will apostatise. But the remnant will remain faithful, and will be sustained by God amid terrible persecution, called in Jeremiah "the time of Jacob's trouble" (30:7). Many of the Psalms, such as the 94th, 130th, 140th, describe the sufferings of these witnesses. Those who are spared till the return of the Messiah will be saved – according to Romans 11:26; "And so all Israel shall be saved", and will form the nucleus of the restored nation. They are, I believe, those whom the Lord refers to as "My brethren" at the judgement of the nations (Matt 25:40).

It remains for us now to consider briefly the calling and character of the Heavenly Remnant.

They are those who through the preaching of the gospel in this dispensation are brought to acknowledge Jesus as Lord and Saviour.

They are sometimes called today 'Hebrew Christians', but it is really a misnomer. They are Christians, members of that body in which there is "neither Jew nor Greek". Israel has rejected Christ, and He who might have been their corner-stone has become their stumbling stone. They were judged and scattered in 70 AD, and through their fall, salvation is come unto the Gentiles for to provoke them to jealousy. Not, of course, that all Gentiles are saved, but they are now in the olive tree. Instead of being in a less favoured position than Israel, it is they who are the favoured ones, and the gospel is sounded to them in every place. Thus the fall of Israel brings opportunity to the Gentiles, and they draw from the root and fatness of the olive tree. All of them who believe on Jesus Christ are brought into the Church, and with them all who believe from Israel. If, then, the fall of Israel is "the riches of the Gentiles, how much more (according to the blessed logic of Divine grace) their fullness?" If God blessed the Gentiles because of Israel's fall, He will not take away that blessing when Israel is restored. Through restored Israel will come a wider blessing than ever was known before. Now the Lord is gathering out a people, and the results seem sparse, but when Israel are grafted back into their own olive tree and become God's missionaries to every land, in the power of the great outpouring of the Spirit yet to come (see Joel 2:28,29), untold numbers will be gathered in, "a great multitude that no man can number". The Heavenly Remnant we are now considering is composed of Israelites who believe the gospel, and are baptised into one body in one Spirit, with all of every nation who receive Christ. Such lose their national standing and hopes, but enter into higher privileges and blessings, as members of Christ and temples of the Holy Ghost. This state of things will go on "until the fullness of the Gentiles is come in", that is, until the last Gentile destined to be a member of the church is saved. Then the church will be caught up, the Gentile branches who have abused their privileges broken off, and God will resume His relations with the nation of Israel. It was a very real test for a Jew who had believed in Christ to find himself cut off from his glorious historic past, shorn of his national hopes of the coming kingdom, and deprived of his traditional priesthood and religion, every part of which had been divinely ordained. It was for such the Epistle to the Hebrews was written. In it they might learn that all has been more than made up to them in Christ, who is the consummation of the prophetic testimony, the embodiment of the kingdom hope, and the substance of all the religious shadows of the past.

5. THE MYSTERY OF THE GREAT TRANSFORMATION
(1 Cor 15:51)

"Behold, I show you a mystery; we shall not all sleep, but we shall all be changed" (1 Cor 15:51.). The mysteries of God are undreamt of displays of His "manifold wisdom" and boundless reserves of grace and power; foretastes of those eternal revelations of Himself which will for ever be the joy of the redeemed. "This is life eternal, that they might know Thee the only true God, and Jesus Christ, whom Thou hast sent" (John 17:3). The knowledge of God in Christ not only communicates eternal life, but characterises it and that for ever. In the case before us, the revelation is made in full view of man's failure. The rejection of the Spirit's testimony to a crucified and glorified Saviour, must lead at length to the Apocalyptic judgements. Must the Church then pass through them? Had we only the Old Testament, it would appear inevitable. But would not a king, before attacking a rebellious city, seek first, if possible, to take out of it any faithful subjects within, as Saul called forth the Kenites before attacking Amalek? The 'mystery' we are about to consider is a way of escape for the Church, from "the hour of temptation that will come upon the whole world", or, in other words, from the Great Tribulation.

1 Corinthians 15 and 1 Thessalonians 4 are the passages which present us this deliverance in most detail, though it is referred to in many others. These two Scriptures are parallel, and should be carefully compared, for they emphasise different phases of the same truth[5]. In the Thessalonian Epistle, much is said of the actual coming of Christ, and of the meeting of the saints with Him. "The Lord Himself shall descend from heaven, we shall be caught up together,

---

[5] We may remind ourselves in passing that the Thessalonian Epistle was written from Corinth, according to the best authorities, during the apostle's stay referred to in Acts 18, and that addressed to the Corinthians during his stay in Ephesus, as narrated in Acts 19.

to meet the Lord in the air." In the Corinthian passage, neither of these events is mentioned specifically, but much attention is drawn to the processes which will take place in the sleeping and living saints – resurrection and transformation – at the moment of the coming. In the former church, the question seems to have been raised: "What will become of the sleeping saints when the Lord returns? Will they have no share in that event?" While in 1 Corinthians 15 the problem is: "If flesh and blood cannot inherit the Kingdom of God, what will become of the living saints? Must they be excluded?" The answer to the last difficulty forms the thesis of the passage before us. It may be called the "Mystery of the Great Transformation", and as such regarded from two points of view: (1) the Power that will produce the effect – the Coming of the Lord, and (2) the Character of the effect produced – Resurrection and Metamorphosis.

The coming of the Son of Man to judge was no mystery. The Old Testament prophecies are full of it (see Psa 50, 96, 97; Isa 58; Joel 2-3; Zech 12,14, etc.), but always in connection with antecedent tribulation. "When the Son of Man cometh, shall He find faith on the earth?" (Luke 18:8). No, but a world desolated by judgement, the faithful remnant of Israel under the heel of the oppressor, and man in open apostacy and rebellion against God – a condition of things closely analogous with that existing in Egypt before the Exodus of Israel. God will then be dealing once more in judgement with a greater than Pharaoh to deliver the same people from a worse oppression than that of Egypt. And they, too, will suffer as before from these same judgments. The coming of the Son of Man will be the supreme crisis in the long period called "the day of the Lord", intervening at the moment when Jacob's trouble will have reached its utmost intensity. "I beheld, and the same horn made war with the saints, and prevailed against them, until the Ancient of Days came" (Dan 7:22,25; see also Zech 14:2-4). This corresponds with the coming in vengeance spoken of in 2 Thess 1:7,8, and the appearing of the "Faithful and True" in Rev 19:11. This is the same phase that we have in the great prophetic discourses of our Lord in the Synoptic Gospels. The words in Matthew 24:40, "One shall be taken and the other left", are often interpreted as referring to the "catching up" of the saints as in 1 Thess 4:17, but I believe this to be erroneous. Surely the 'taking'[6] in Matthew 24:40-41, corresponds with what has just gone in v. 29, "the flood came and took them (i.e., the wicked) all away". Whereas in 1 Thess 4:17 the righteous will be taken away while the wicked are left for judgement. To sum up: the coming of the Son of Man was already well known, but that there should be a previous stage in His coming, to take away the saints "from the evil to come", was a Mystery unheard of by the prophets of old. Was not this in our Lord's mind (though He explains not the how and the wherefore), when to His sorrowing disciples He speaks of His speedy return, not now as "the Son of Man", but in the first person: "I will come again and receive you unto Myself, that where I am there ye may be also?" Here, there is no word of "heavenly signs" or "flaming fire", nor of "vengeance" or "mighty angels", but the calm, clear atmosphere of the joyful meeting, far above all the fogs and din of this dark scene. If the question be asked, whether or not the Old Testament will end before the New, it will suffice to read the closing chapter of each, and ask whether or not the "Morning Star" rises before the "Sun".

Then, again, we may consider the effect to be produced. The resurrection of the dead was not a mystery. The Sadducees, had they known the Scriptures, should have believed this much, and by the Scriptures, too, the religious world of our day might have been preserved from the idea which is so prevalent of a 'general resurrection'. The expression, "the resurrection of life", and the "resurrection of judgement", though occurring in the same verse (John 5:29), are sufficiently distinct, to save from this error.

At least a thousand years must elapse between the two resurrections (see Rev 20:5). We may notice first, that the resurrection spoken of in 1 Corinthians 15 is selective. The resurrection of the body is the great truth of the whole chapter. Properly speaking, resurrection always pertains to the body. It is quite certain that the wicked will have a resurrection body – "to every seed his own body" – prepared of God, according to His

---

[6] The words in the original for "taking away" and "take" are not the same. The context alone can determine the purport of the "taking" in v. 40 and 41, and also of the "leaving" which may well have the meaning "let go" (Mark 11:6). or "let alone" (Mark 14:6; Luke 13:8).

determinate purpose. But though the resurrection of the wicked may be incidentally included in such an expression as "the resurrection of the dead" (v. 13), the subject of the chapter practically all through, is the resurrection of sleeping saints. How could verses 42-49 refer to the ungodly? Their resurrection body could not be described as "glorious" or "heavenly". There is "a first resurrection" and there is a final resurrection. Only "the just" will share in the first. "Blessed and holy is he that hath part in the first resurrection" (Rev 20:6). Only the wicked will share in the last. They were judged, "every man according to their works". They had not therefore been justified by faith, but were still in their sins.

There is no thought in Scripture of a 'general judgment' of saints and sinners before the great white throne. If saints are there at all (as 1 Cor 6:2,3, would seem to indicate), they will be as assessors on the throne, not as prisoners before it. Those, then, who are said in 1 Cor 15:54, to "put on incorruption", are the sleeping saints; the rest[7] of the dead remaining in their graves till the final resurrection of "the dead, small and great".

So much for the saints who have died; now for the living. That there will be godly persons alive on the earth when the Son of Man returns, is abundantly clear from such passages as Zech 12:10. "They shall look on Me whom they have pierced", is spoken of the spared remnant of Israel. But that there should be a company of persons alive when the Lord returns, and instantly changed and fitted by "putting on immortality" to stand before Him and to enter His heavenly kingdom, was a truth hitherto unheard of. It is to this, therefore, that the words of the apostle – "We shall not all sleep, but we shall all be changed" – more directly apply. It is clear that none but believers will have part in this wonderful transformation scene. The hope of Israel is, to be carried through the great tribulation, as Noah was through the flood, and like him to enter on possession of a renovated earth. The hope of the Church is, to be taken away before the judgments fall, as Enoch was, by translation from earth to heaven. The exhortation in Luke 21:36, is not addressed to

---

[7] Those raised in Rev 20:4, are expressly said to have sealed their testimony with their blood in the great tribulation, at the hands of the Beast.

Christians, that they should pray to be caught away when Christ comes, inasmuch as this is part of their heritage as believers, but to pious Israelites that they may be preserved through the coming troubles, and be alive on the earth, when the Son of Man shall return in His glory. The truth of this coming could not but be associated in the minds of Israel with the thought of tribulation. The dread valley lay deep and dark between, and so it would be for the Church, but for the revelation of the rapture of the saints. And this is the hope of the Church, and the more we are walking with God in separation from the world, and suffering practically with and for Christ, this hope will become bright and sustaining.

One of the world's great texts is, "It is appointed unto all men to die", but the Scriptures say, "It is appointed unto men once to die, and after this the judgement" (Heb 9:27). "We shall not all sleep, but we shall all be changed." This is the 'sleep' of death, from which the word 'cemetery' is derived. None but true believers, strictly speaking, should be buried in a cemetery – i.e. a sleeping place – for they only 'fall asleep'. All others die. Now the "body is dead (exposed to death or mortality) because of sin, but the spirit is life, because of righteousness" (Rom 8:10). Then shall be fulfilled that quickening of which the apostle straightway speaks in v. 11: "He that raised up Christ from the dead, shall also quicken your mortal bodies by His Spirit which dwelleth in you." God is the Source of this great change, His Spirit the Power, and the Lord Jesus at His coming, the Agent. "When He shall appear we shall be like Him for we shall see Him as He is" (1 John 3:2). It is an unsound exegesis which interprets this verse as some present healing or strengthening of the body for service. The change referred to must be something commensurate with the mighty work of the resurrection of Christ – the great manifestation to the Church of the "exceeding greatness of His power" – just as the works of creation are to the heathen, and the deliverance from Egypt to Israel. What else then could be an adequate fulfilment of this promise, but that instantaneous and simultaneous transformation of myriads of living saints in a moment of time referred to here, the changing of the body of their humiliation into the likeness of His glorious body. The expression, "your mortal bodies", in Romans 8:11, points to the fact, that the apostle was not contemplating the resurrection of these saints in view of their death, but of their transformation, as in 2 Cor 5:4, "that mortality might be swallowed up of life". This will only apply to believers, for they only are waiting for the "adoption, to wit the redemption of the body". So that we may call this selective as regards the world in general.

But it will be universal as regards believers. I do not think we have Scripture for limiting the resurrection in 1 Corinthians 15 and 1 Thessalonians 4, to believers of this dispensation alone. Of course, if the phrase, "those who sleep in Jesus" in 1 Thess 4, were accurate, we must do so. But the Greek is confessedly 'through ' (see RV margin) not 'in'. Is not the thought here, rather, how the sleeping ones will be restored to those they love, 'by' or 'through Jesus', rather than how they were taken away from them. The word 'sleep' is sufficient to limit the application to those who have died in the faith. As regards the 'changed' ones, we may safely affirm that they are all Christians, for there is no other kind of believer on the earth today. There is at any rate no authority for excluding any saint of this dispensation from either the resurrection or the change. The hope of the Lord's appearing is one of the seven privileges in which all believers now share. "There is one body and one Spirit, even as ye are called in one hope of your calling" (Eph 4:5). There ought not indeed to be room for doubt on this point in the mind of any believer subject to the Word of God, for the affirmation could not be plainer. "We shall all be changed." "The dead (not some of them) shall be raised incorruptible." No hint is given that some of the saints will be excluded.

Again, the change will be instantaneous. "In a moment, in the twinkling of an eye": both of which words are used in the New Testament only in this place, serving thus to mark the absolutely unique character of the event.

The Lord 's coming for His own will take place at a special signal: "at the last trump". To the world, this expression speaks of the great final judgment "at the end of the world", as it is termed. But we read of no trumpet blast at the Great White Throne. Nor can there be any reference here to the Seven Apocalyptic Trumpets. "The seventh", which sounds (see Rev 11:15), is not called "the last trumpet", nor is it accompanied by the miraculous transformation of the living saints, but rather by judgement and wrath against the nations. And in any case, it will not sound until much later than the events of our chapter. May we not find help in Numbers 10 in the use of both silver trumpets for the convocation of the assembly? "When they (the priests) shall blow with them, all the assembly shall assemble themselves to thee." In the summoning of this solemn assembly of the heavenly people, it may be that the first trump will wake the dead and the last will change the living. Certainly the words, "at the last trump", seem to belong to what has just gone before, the change of the living. And may not the other phrase, "for the trumpet shall sound", describe the first blast which summons the sleepers from their graves? In Thessalonians we simply read, "The Lord Himself shall descend from heaven with a shout, with the voice of the archangel, and with the trump of God", but there is no differentiation as to first or last blast.

The change will be a radical one. The bodies of the sleeping saints are viewed here in their corruption. They will put on what is essential to them – incorruptibility. But this is not said of the living. In their case the body is not said to be 'corruptible' but 'mortal' and they will therefore "put on immortality". In either case, the change will be essential, and will mean for both dead and living, the possession of a glorified body, "like unto His glorious body" (Phil 3:21), spiritual, powerful, heavenly. The soul is not in question here, but "this mortal", that is the body. The soul is never once said to be 'mortal' in the whole range of Scripture, and could not properly be said to put on what it has never lost. Death is not a ceasing to exist, any more than life means merely 'to exist'. The eternal existence of man is a fundamental truth of God's Word, ever since God breathed into man's nostrils the breath of life (a thing He never did to the beasts of the fields), and man "became a living soul". This truth is bound up with man's responsibility and God's sovereign right to judge. The Christian receives pardon, justification, adoption, eternal life, union with Christ, the Holy Spirit, and many other blessings. Why is he never said to receive the gift of eternal existence? Because he has it already, by the fact of his creation. The phrase, 'Conditional Immortality', is a figment of man's brain, without any corresponding reality in God's Word. But is it not said in 1 Tim 6:16, that "God only hath immortality?" Yes, but this is not the same as saying "God only is immortal", as the passage before us proves. For here are persons spoken of as "putting on immortality". Without controversy, the angels are immortal. Whoever heard of an angel receiving immortality as a special gift? They are created so. God only has it in the essential sense in Himself, and He alone bestows it. The word 'immortality' (*athanasia*) only occurs in 1 Tim 6:16, and in our passage in 1 Corinthians 15. In other places it ought to be 'incorruptibility', as the Greek (*aptharsia*) shows.

The change will also be an abiding one. That this should be called in question may seem incredible, yet some are teaching that certain 'faithful' Christians, who have shared in this great resurrection scene, will later on, as a punishment for their sins, "temporarily return to corruption"! Such a statement is as senseless as it is subversive. To say that that which has "put on incorruption" will be corrupted, is a contradiction in terms. Were it possible, by what power, we may ask, would the unhappy Christian be transformed again? No, let us be sure that "whatsoever God doeth it shall be for ever, nothing can be put to it, neither can anything be taken from it, and God doeth it, that men may fear before Him" (Eccl 3:14).

This great transformation will be a seal of victory. "Then shall be brought to pass the saying which is written, Death is swallowed up in victory". The death of every Christian is a victory, for of each it can be said, "he is not dead, but sleepeth", for the sting of death pierced the heart of Christ, and there is none left for the believer. But the scene we are now considering is a victory manifest, and now on a grander scale than ever before, for He who died rose again, triumphant over death and the grave. Millions will then be delivered from the grave. Myriads will escape from dying. It is to be noted that this is not the fulfilment of the Old Testament prophecy (Isa 25:8). It does not say 'fulfilled' here, but only "brought to pass", an important difference, as may be noted in other places (e.g. Acts 2:16): "This is that which hath been spoken." The fulfilment will come later in Israel's history, as will also the fulfilment of the quotation before us, when "the first resurrection" will stand complete, in the resurrection of the martyred witnesses of the last days.

The hope of this change is the basis of present endeavour. "Wherefore, my beloved brethren, be ye steadfast, unmoveable, always abounding in the work of the Lord; forasmuch as ye know that your labour is not in vain in the Lord" (1 Cor 15:58). "The night cometh when no man can work" (John 9:4).

6. THE MYSTERY OF GODLINESS (1Tim 3:16)

Of the mysteries revealed in the Word of God, two are specially designated as "great" by the Holy Spirit–the "Mystery of Christ and the Church," and the "Mystery of Godliness" in the passage before us. And confessedly great they are, both being closely linked with Him who is "the great God and our Saviour Jesus Christ".

"The Mystery of Godliness" is often expounded as though it were equivalent to the "Mystery of God"; but godliness is not an attribute of God, but an attitude of man toward God. The word occurs in eight other places in 1 Timothy, and always as describing a certain character of life and conduct: e.g., "exercise thyself rather unto godliness", "godliness is profitable unto all things", "show godliness at home". Surely here, in the remaining occurrence, the word must bear the meaning. The godly man is the Godfearing man, who takes God into account, and lives subject to Him. The "Mystery of godliness" must reveal a life of perfect submission to God, in contrast with "the mystery of lawlessness", to be manifested later in the "son of perdition" who will "exalt himself above all that is called God" (2 Thess 2:4).

The apostle has been laying down from the beginning of 1 Timothy 2 the godly ordering of the assembly in their gatherings for prayer, scriptural relations of the sexes, oversight and ministry, in order that Timothy – and through him others – might know how to behave "in the house of God, which is the church of the living God". Any other order would be disorder; any other behaviour, misbehaviour. To emphasise this, he adds that the church is "the pillar and ground of the truth"; not the truth itself, nor the originator of it, but responsible to uphold it. How this responsibility is increased by the greatness of the truth to be

MYSTERIES OF THE NEW TESTAMENT

upheld! "Without controversy, great is the mystery of godliness: God[8] was manifest in the flesh."

Now, godliness in itself was not a 'mystery'. It had characterised the lives of the saints of God from Abel onwards. The word, *khaseed* is often found in the law and the prophets, and translated "godly, or holy one". "Let Thy Urim be with Thy holy one" (Deut 33:8). "He will keep the feet of His saints" (1 Sam 2:9). "The Lord hath set apart him that is godly for Himself" (Psa 4:3). But no saint ever exhibited perfect godliness. Yet there are foreshadowings in the Old Testament of One who could be a perfect Servant, and righteously able to claim blessing on the ground of personal worth. In Isaiah 50, the One who can "dry up the sea and clothe the heavens with blackness", is revealed as the fully obedient One, whose ear was opened, who was not rebellious, but who gave His back to the smiters and hid not His face from shame and spitting. In Psalm 24 also, we read of One who can claim to "ascend into the hill of the Lord" on the ground of "clean hands and a pure heart", and this One is "the King of Glory".

How this could be, remained a hidden mystery, until the One declared to be the eternal God, the Creator of all things, in infinite grace became flesh, and dwelt among us (John 1:1-3,14). This was indeed an unlooked for solution. That God should dwell on the earth in the Shekinah glory, was a marvel to Solomon (1 Kings 1:17), how much more when He was manifested in the person of the meek and lowly One. It was in Him that "godliness" was fully

---

[8] It would not be in place here to argue this much disputed reading, which a prince of scholars–Dr. Scrivener–has called the "crux of the cities". Whether the passage ought to read as above, or simply "Who was manifested in the flesh", does not so profoundly affect the sense as might at first appear. The truth embodied in "God" is implied in "who", for the pre-existence of the Person referred to is contained in the verb "manifested". This could not be said of any mere man. Men are born, not manifested. Nor could it refer to the birth of an angel, for such a thing has never occurred. Be that as it may, the fact that much, very much, can be said for the AV rendering, might well have sufficed to hinder the Revisers meddling with it. They were only authorised to correct 'plain and clear errors', and a matter which has left so many scholars in doubt, can hardly be 'plain and clear'. The subject is fully discussed in that valuable work, Dean Burgon's 'Revision Revised' (pp. 98-106. 424-501), a study of which convinced the well-known commentator, Dr. Christopher Wordsworth, who had previously championed "who", that "God" was indeed the true reading.

exhibited; as has been well said, "He was the source, power, and pattern of what is practically acceptable to God". His life in this scene was symbolised by the meat offering baked in the oven – spotless humanity passing through every fiery test and trial. A handful of this, with its oil and "all the frankincense" upon it, was burnt upon the Brazen Altar "for a sweet savour, even the memorial of it unto the Lord" (Lev 6:15) – fit figure of that precious memorial which the earthly life of the Lord Jesus is to God. This manifestation of the Word was very real. "He became flesh, and dwelt among us." His body was real flesh and blood, not a spiritual body, but a true human body. And He Himself was a true manifestation of the moral glory of God. He was the image of the invisible God. He that saw Him saw the Father. Seeing Him, we see the heart of God. Divine holiness, grace, love, compassion shine out brightly in all His ways.

None but God can fully know all that Christ's manifestation entailed. We have it presented to us very fully in Philippians 2:6-8: He who was in "the form of God", whose mode of existence was that of God, and who therefore was God, determined in the fulfilment of the Divine counsels not to insist on what had ever been His undisputed right, to be equal and no less than equal with God, but "made Himself of no reputation". This last phrase does not mean that He ceased to be a Divine Person. He always and ever was that. Nor yet that He divested Himself of His Divine attributes, His omnipotence and omniscience for instance, for then He must have ceased to be God. But He held them in abeyance, retaining them to the full, but never using them independently. That this is the true sense seems clear from the explanatory words which follow: "but took upon Him the form of a servant": a new mode of existence which He superadded to the former, without relinquishing it.

The special condition He assumed in order to carry out this service was not that of an archangel – that would have been infinite condescension – but that of man. He was "made in the likeness of men", yet only "in the likeness of sinful flesh" (Rom 8:3). Because, though truly man, He was morally and intrinsically unlike fallen man. "And being found in fashion as a man (that is, in outward semblance

MYSTERIES OF THE NEW TESTAMENT

in the 'accidents'[9] of His being seeming merely a man among men), He humbled Himself and became obedient unto death, even the death of the cross."

The path of perfect godliness meant the sacrifice of all, and He made the sacrifice, but to the apparent prejudice of all His claims. He died as one "numbered with the transgressors", forsaken of man and of God. Was ever apparent failure writ so large on any mission? Certainly His manifestation in the flesh and His atoning work had exposed Him to misunderstanding and misapprehension. He needed Divine vindication. "God raised Him up, having loosed the pains of death, because it was not possible that He should be holden of it" (Acts 2:24). It is with this vindication, I would submit, that the remainder of the verse is concerned. He was "justified in the Spirit". Some interpret "Spirit", of the Lord's human spirit or 'higher being', in order to make an antithesis between "in the flesh" and "in the Spirit", but the interpretation seems farfetched and hard of application.

The resurrection by the power of the Holy Ghost (see Romans 1: 4; 8:11), was God's answer to a Christ-rejecting world. He who was disapproved of men was approved by God as righteous[10].

Not only so, but in resurrection He was vindicated before angelic hosts, "He was seen of angels". They had seen Him made for a little "lower" than themselves, done to death, and engulfed in the tomb. They were the first to see Him on resurrection ground, as Conqueror of death and the grave.

Moreover, the very men who had at His death acknowledged themselves mistaken as to His Messianic claim, were so convinced by "many infallible proofs" of the reality of His resurrection, that they became His heralds, not only, as up till then, to the lost sheep of Israel, but to the uttermost ends of the earth He was "preached

---

[9] The 'accidents' of a thing are the visible, tangible, ponderable qualities of the thing. Thus the 'accidents of the bread and wine' mean the colour, appearance, and weight of the elements.

[10] "Justified" is used here in its usual tense in NT (see Luke 7:29), a passage which shows that the meaning sometimes attributed to justified as "made righteous" is wholly inadmissible and erroneous. Justification is being proved righteous or acquitted. The justified man leaves the court, without a stain upon his character.

among the Gentiles". These heard with their ears what the angels had looked upon, and received the testimony, for He was "believed on in the world"; not, it is true, universally, for not yet does the knowledge of the Lord cover the earth as the waters cover the sea – that will only be at His return in power – but selectively, for there are already some who hear the call and acknowledge Him as Saviour and Lord, during His rejection.

The crowning vindication is reserved to the last,[11] not because last in order of time, but because greatest in order of value. He was "received up into glory". Then the Lord's prayer was granted. He was glorified with the Father with the glory He had with Him, before the world was, awaiting the last supreme vindication when He shall be "revealed from heaven with His mighty angels, taking vengeance on them that know not God and that obey not the gospel of our Lord Jesus Christ".

7. THE MYSTERY OF CHRIST (Eph 3:4; Col 4:3)

The mystery now before us stamps a special character on the present dispensation, marking it off in the clearest manner from all that preceded or may follow it. It is designated in various ways in the Epistles. Paul calls it "The Mystery", as though to distinguish it from all the rest, as the Mystery par excellence. "If ye have heard of the dispensation of the grace of God which is given me to you-ward, how that by revelation He made known unto me the Mystery" (Eph 3:3). It was by a special revelation that the apostle had become initiated unto this Mystery, in the same way, indeed, that he had also had communicated to him the great truths of the gospel (1 Cor 15:3), the Lord's return for His saints (1 Thess 4:15), and the order of Lord's supper (1 Cor 11:23). And he tells us that, like the Mystery of Godliness, this also is a great Mystery. "This Mystery is great, but I speak concerning Christ and the Church" (Eph 5: 32). As far as we are directly concerned, it is of supreme importance, for it unfolds the deepest secret of the Divine counsels toward man. It is not

---

[11] The fact that the 'preaching to the Gentiles' precedes in this verse 'the ascension', surely shows that Alford's dictum that Paul is here following the 'historical order of events', etc., is erroneous.

surprising, when we discern its scope, that the apostle should count it a special grace to be the chosen instrument of its revelation. "Unto me who am less than the least of the saints is this grace given, that I should preach among the Gentiles the unsearchable riches of Christ"; and not only so, but "to make all men see what is the fellowship of the Mystery". And then to a still wider range, "to the intent that now unto principalities and powers in heavenly places might be known by the church the manifold wisdom of God" (Eph 3:8-10).

This Mystery is also termed the "Mystery of Christ" (Eph 3:4; Col 4:3), for though it deals with the body, the members cannot be separated from the Head, "from which all the body – having nourishment ministered – increaseth with the increase of God" (Col 2:19). And redemption is the base of it, for He who is the Head, the Centre, and Source of every blessing can only be so, because He was first the Redeemer. Then, again, this Mystery is called "the Mystery of the Gospel": "that I may open my mouth boldly to make known the Mystery of the Gospel" (Eph 6:19), for it is included in the gospel and is its legitimate outcome. Any gospel that does not eventually initiate souls into the enjoyment of the Mystery, is a defective gospel. How often the horizon of believers is limited, not seldom because the horizon of preachers is so too, by forgiveness of sins, justification by faith (but little understood), a certain striving "to become better", and "do something for God", and a hope of "going to heaven when they die"! But is this all that is meant by "the unsearchable riches of Christ"? Does this exhaust the blessing of being "in Christ"?

Had not the Old Testament saints forgiveness of sins and justification by faith? (Gen 15:6; Psa 32:1). Certainly they had, and knew the blessedness of them too, and we may truly say "there were giants in those days", compared with many of whom we are but pigmies. But still, our privileges are vastly greater. Not one in that great gallery of worthies whose names are given to us in Hebrews 11 had the most distant idea of the "Mystery of Christ", nor indeed had any share in it. The Spirit of God is careful to note that the Mystery was a new thing, "which in other ages was not made known unto the sons of men, as it is now revealed unto His holy apostles and prophets by the Spirit". The force of the word "as" is important.

It marks, not a comparison of degree, as some have thought, but of fact. That is, it does not compare between a greater and less revelation, but between a full revelation in the Epistles and none at all in the Old Testament. This is clear from Ephesians 3:9, "the Mystery that from the beginning of the world had been hid in God", or from Romans 15:25, where we learn that it was "kept secret since the world began" or, as in Colossians 1:26, "hid from ages and from generations", and unrevealed[12] in the Old Testament. It is true there are incidents therein, such as the formation of Eve, the call of Rebecca, the marriage of Joseph, which serve to illustrate what the Spirit of God is doing today in "calling out of the Gentiles a people for His name". But the Church was non-existent till Pentecost, and the purpose of God regarding it was a secret.

The revelation of this Mystery was God's resource for man's failure. Man at his best, surrounded by every advantage, had been manifested in his true colours at the Cross. The Jews, and by inference, all men, were seen to be utterly ruined and irremediable. Man "under law" and man "without law" are total bankrupts. Blessing to Israel, and through her to the nations, must necessarily be postponed in view of this national rejection of the Messiah. But must, therefore, God's purposes be altogether arrested? Nay, a divine counsel, more glorious than had ever been conceived, is now revealed in a new and altogether unexpected way of blessing to Jew and Gentile – the Church, the Body and the Bride of Christ. It was not, however, till the kingdom testimony had been definitely rejected by the elders of the nation, in imputing the signs of the kingdom to Beelzebub (Matt 11 and 12) that the Lord uttered the first hint of this in the memorable words, "On this rock I will build My church[13]."

It is really quite arbitrary to assert, as some do, that "church" here means, not the christian church, but the Jewish assembly. Why should

---

[12] 'The Song of Solomon' might seem to contradict this, but there it is the earthly bride, Israel, regarded as the married wife of Jehovah, whereas the Church is "betrothed to Christ". When this is seen, the 'Song of Songs' remains as a beautiful expression of the affection of the individual believer to the Lord, in all dispensations.

[13] The word for church *ecclesia* means 'a called-out assembly'. Thus Israel is called in one passage (Acts 7:38), "the church in the wilderness", a suitable description, in that they had been called out of Egypt. But this must be carefully distinguished from the technical use of the word, as used in the Gospels, Acts, and Epistles.

the Lord speak of building in the future what was already in existence? It is also quite illogical to affirm that "church" in the Acts is not the same as in the Epistles, on the ground, forsooth, that there is admittedly a "transitional" character in part of the Acts. Believers from Judaism were gradually weaned from their Jewish line of things to take up their heavenly character. Why should that alter the meaning of the "church", which was the very occasion of this transition?

No, the church the Lord spoke of was to be built at a later date ("I will build"), upon the foundation of the apostles and prophets (of New Testament times), Jesus Christ Himself – the Rock spoken of in Matthew 16 – being the chief Corner Stone. In the Acts we see it historically, in its local and earthly aspect. It is not permissible to argue that because full church truth, as revealed in what some term "the Prison Epistles" (that is Ephesians, Philippians and Colossians, written at the very close of the Acts period), was not fully revealed before, that therefore the church did not exist. Great Britain existed before 'Magna Charta'. The church was born at the beginning of the Acts, church truth at its close. The birth of the church, like that of Moses, was not fully revealed at first for obvious reasons, but even before Paul wrote Ephesians (Acts 28:30), he speaks at least four years before, in Romans 16: 26, of the Mystery being "made known to all nations". Nor did Paul claim to be the only initiate, for he associates with himself "the holy apostles and prophets" (Eph 3:5).

What then is the "Mystery of Christ?" Certainly not merely that blessing should come to Israel and through them to the Gentile nations. Of this the prophets are full, as such passages as Psalm 67, Isaiah 66, Amos 9 witness, the distinction between Israel and the nations being maintained. Israel was thus to be the head and the channel of blessing, the Gentiles the tail and recipient thereof. The Mystery is something quite different. It reveals that those called out of Israel and the Nations should be blessed together in one body and on equal terms. It has a threefold aspect as regards first the Gentiles, then the church as a whole, and lastly, individual believers.

First, the apostle Paul explains the Mystery in perhaps the most unexpected aspect – as regards the Gentiles. "That the Gentiles should be fellow-heirs and of the same body, and partakers of His promise in Christ by the gospel" (Eph 3:6). Nowadays, the conversion of Jews presents the greatest difficulty to our minds, but in the early days, when Israel at any rate still seemed to be the favoured nation, the idea of Gentiles being blessed on equal terms with her appeared a thing indeed hard to conceive. To accomplish this, four great barriers had first to be removed. The high middle wall of partition between Jew and Gentile had to be broken down. The world was like a great semi-detached house, inhabited by two lots of tenants, Jew and Gentile, separated from one another, at enmity with one another, and only united in one point, their hatred of the Owner. First, then, that which divided Jew from Gentile, and which constituted the former '"nigh" and the latter "afar off", was to be removed, for it must be remembered that the Jew had hitherto occupied the place of privilege. They were "a people near unto Him", whereas the Gentile was in a position of complete distance from God. The blood of Christ made the far-off Gentile nigh, without any intermediary stage of ceremonial nearness like the Jew. "Ye who once were far off (ye Gentiles), are made nigh by the blood of Christ." And the same blood availed for believing Israel. So that we read, "He is our peace who hath made both one, (Both what? Not peoples, that comes later; but here the word is neuter, and refers to their positions Godward) and hath broken down the middle wall of partition"[14] (Eph 2:14).

But there is a second barrier to be considered. Not only were the two peoples positionally divided, but they were at "enmity", on account of "the law of commandments contained in ordinances". How could a Jew be reconciled to a Gentile whom he despised as uncircumcised, or a Gentile to a Jew, when he found himself shut out like a dog from the Passover and the other privileges of Israel? Such a barrier could only be abolished by Christ, and He could only do it by His death: "having abolished in His flesh the enmity, the law of commandments." Those who share in that death by faith, die to

---

[14] This 'wall of partition' was of God, and should suffice to show that the Church position, where there is neither Jew nor Gentile, could not possibly have existed in Old Testament times.

the law, and are reconciled on resurrection ground, where the law has no claim.

But a yet more insurmountable barrier would still remain – the enmity of Jew and Gentile to God. What could remove this barrier, but the supreme manifestation of the love of God in the Cross? "That He might reconcile both (here it is both peoples, i.e., believers from both) unto God in one body by the Cross, having slain the enmity thereby." "Reconciled to God by the death of His Son." "We love Him, because He first loved us."

But was nothing else required but that the sinner should be reconciled to God? This might have satisfied man, but the Father's heart needed something more. He desired that the sinner should be brought as a purged worshipper to Himself. This too, is brought about by Christ. He "suffered once for sins, the Just for the unjust, that He might bring us to God" (1 Pet 3:18). And He, too, is the Way of the worshipper to the Father. "No man cometh unto the Father but by Me" (John 14:6). "Through Him we both (Jew and Gentile) have access by one Spirit unto the Father" (Eph 2:18). Thus we see that in order that the purpose of "the Mystery" might be realised, peace must be proclaimed to Jew and Gentile, peace made between the two peoples, and then between them and God "by the blood of His Cross". We might call the Mystery from this point of view, "the Mystery of the Broken Barriers".

The second view of the Mystery is that presented in ch.5 where it is not Jew or Gentile as such, but the whole church which is brought before us: "Christ loved the church and gave Himself for it" (v.25). This is the love of election. God loved that mass of corruption – the world. That was His universal love. Christ saw a pearl in that mass, loved it and gave Himself for it, that having cleansed it by the washing of water, that is by the once for all act of regeneration – (the word for washing here is the root employed by our Lord in John 13, "He that is bathed") – He might sanctify it – nourishing and cherishing it, while awaiting the day when He shall present it to Himself "a glorious church, not having a spot or wrinkle or any such thing". This is a great Mystery, the apostle adds, "but I speak concerning Christ and the Church".

The last aspect of the Mystery to which reference must be made is the personal and experimental side. "To whom God would make known what is the riches of the glory of this Mystery among the Gentiles, which is Christ in you the hope of glory" (Col 1:27). Grammatically we might read "Christ among you", but this would be no mystery. But that the saints should enter into such intimate spiritual union with Christ, as to become part of Himself, and have Him in the abundance of His resurrection life permeating their very beings – a pledge of future glory, that was indeed a mystery, worthy to be revealed to all saints as a great fact, and to be enjoyed by each (in a walk of holy separation from the flesh and the world by simple faith). This Mystery then unfolds the eternal purpose of God (Eph 5:32), the everlasting love of Christ (v.25), the present privileges and responsibilities of the believer (vv.27,29), and his future glory and service (3:21).

8. THE MYSTERY OF GOD (Rev 10:7)

Of all the Divine Mysteries, none can be greater than this, for it is "the Mystery of God, even Christ[15]", He who "in these last days" is the final revelation of God to man; not that the Mystery is yet fully consummated. That will not be till the seventh trumpet of the Apocalypse has sounded, and the kingdoms of this world are transferred to their rightful King. "In the days of the voice of the seventh angel, the Mystery of God should be finished, as He hath declared to His servants the prophets" (Rev 10:7). That this declaration had been concerning the kingdom glory of Christ is clear from 11:15. "And the seventh angel sounded, and there were great voices in heaven saying, The kingdoms of this world are become the kingdoms of our Lord and of His Christ, and He shall reign for ever and ever." When Christ returns, as the Son of Man, in the clouds, "every eye shall see Him", for His coming will be as the lightning, and His glory will fill the earth; but now to those who have eyes to see, "the Mystery of God" is revealed, "even Christ, in whom are hid all the treasures of wisdom and

---

[15] Of the many divergent readings in the MSS. of this passage, that adopted here is favoured by such scholars as Drs. Scrivener and Lightfoot, and seems to correspond best with the rest of Scripture. It is important to note that Christ is not in opposition to 'God', but to "Mystery"; and the meaning is the Mystery of God, which mystery is Christ.

knowledge[16]". Some translate 'in which', but 'in whom' is better, for only a Divine Person can contain all fullness.

The circumstances of the Epistle to the Colossians are noteworthy. The condition of the saints, their faith and love (1:4), and their order and steadfastness (2:5), called forth the thanksgiving of the apostle. But Satan was attacking their good condition, not openly by tempting to gross sin, but by side-tracking their faith. Moral evil is sure to follow doctrinal error. Doctrine is not human opinion, but the revelation of God's thoughts concerning Christ, man, sin, and atonement. The Colossians were in danger of being beguiled by philosophy and vain deceit and by the earthly principles of worldly religion. "Meat and drink, and holy-days, and new moons, and sabbaths" – the shadows were obscuring Christ, the reality. They were "not holding the Head". What a body is without a head, so is a Christian or a church, out of touch with Christ. What was the remedy? The only one that can ever set a Christian or a church right – Christ Himself. A serious feature of Satan's attack was that his agents (like their successors today, who quote much Hebrew and Greek while often knowing but little) lay claim to a special wisdom and an intuitive knowledge in Divine things. They could talk of the "assured results of the Higher Criticism", or of "the agreement of all scholars" with their own conclusions, or what was the equivalent of these boasts in their day. These pretensions beguiled the simple then, as now. The apostle accordingly, in his deep concern for them, prays that their hearts "might be comforted, being knit together in love, and unto all riches of the full assurance of understanding (for how much lack of comfort and spiritual understanding are breaches of fellowship responsible?) to the acknowledgment of the Mystery of God, even Christ, in whom are hid all the treasures of wisdom and knowledge". Why should they "compass themselves about with the

---

[16] As to the difference between "wisdom" and "knowledge", considered as human attributes, we may say, speaking generally, that the latter is acquired in the schools of learning, the former in the school of experience. Knowledge without wisdom is pedantry. Knowledge stores up facts; wisdom turns them to profit. Wise men lay up knowledge and know how to use it aright (Prov 10:17; 15:2). Knowledge is theory; wisdom practice. Knowledge tabulates diseases and remedies; wisdom diagnoses and prescribes. Knowledge puffeth up; wisdom humbleth. As has been said, "We know that we all have knowledge; would that we knew that we have not all wisdom".

sparks" of human philosophy, when they had such resources of Divine wisdom and knowledge in Christ, in whom the Mystery of God is revealed.

God had in times past made partial revelations of Himself. In creation, His eternal power and Godhead, as Elohim, were clearly seen. To the patriarchs in their pilgrim journeys, He had made Himself known as El-Shaddai[17], the all-providing God; to Israel as Jehovah, the unchanging covenant-keeping God. That there was a fuller revelation still to come was an open secret. Prophets spoke of a Child to be born who should bear the unheard of name of "God with us" (Isa 7:14), of a Son who should receive the undreamt of titles, "Wonderful, Counsellor, the Mighty God, the Everlasting Father, the Prince of Peace" (9:6); of a coming ruler of Israel "whose goings forth had been from of old, from everlasting" (Mic 5:2). Such words could only mean a revelation of God in human form. Surely there would be no room for doubt in face of such a manifestation. The godly of the nation waited down the centuries for the fulfilment of the promise. And in "the fullness of the time, God sent forth His Son" (Gal 4:4). And when He came, there were some who were waiting for redemption in Israel. Can it be that the long expected promise is fulfilled in the babe of Bethlehem, in the homeless Stranger of Galilee, in the meek and lowly Jesus, the Man of Sorrows and acquainted with grief, in the lonely rejected Man of Calvary–crying out in the darkness, "My God, My God! why hast Thou forsaken Me"? Yes, this is "the Mystery of God, even Christ". And God has attested it by raising Him from the dead and "giving Him glory", that our faith and hope might be in God. And "in Him are hid all the treasures of wisdom and knowledge" (Col 2:3). He is at once the Treasury, the Owner of the Treasure, and the Treasurer.

1. Christ is the Treasury. He is the repository of all the treasures of wisdom and knowledge, "in Him they are hid" – hid, that is, from the wise and prudent, and also in the sense that they are inexhaustible. There will always be more to know than has ever been revealed.

---

[17] Derived, as some believe, from Hebrew *shad*, a breast. It is in this sense that I take it here. This interpretation enables us to distinguish between Elohim and El-Shaddai, which is otherwise difficult.

2. He is also the Owner of the Treasure, for He possesses what He contains. He was omniscient in incarnation, as before, being "the wisdom of God". The words in Philippians 2:7, "He made Himself of no reputation", are literally "He emptied Himself[18]", and are explained by the words that immediately follow, "taking upon Him the form – or the mode of existence – of a servant". He did not divest Himself of His Divine attributes, but held them in abeyance: that is, He did not make independent use of them. He did not speak, act, or judge "from Himself" or on His own initiative. To continue to do so would have been manifestly inconsistent with the position of a servant (Greek, *doulos* – a slave), which He had voluntarily entered upon.

That our Lord possessed nothing short of omniscience during "the days of His flesh" is clear to all who bow to the Scriptures. He claimed it in word, and proved it in deed. He knew from the beginning who they were that believed not, and who should betray Him. "One of you is a devil," He said to the twelve, at an early point in His ministry (John 6:64,70; 13:11), but He acted as though He did not know. He took men on their profession and reputation, and allowed them to manifest themselves in their own time. Judas was chosen as apostle, no doubt, on his public record as a disciple. Had

---

[18] On these words, or rather on a misunderstanding of them, the Higher Critics have built up their theory of the Kenosis (the emptying), according to which our Lord entered into a condition down here in which he knew less of the Hebrew Scriptures and language and also of matters of fact than the Critics. But it may be questioned whether they really know as much as they claim. Has anyone who knows them been impressed to say to them, "Now we know that ye know all things"? The words of our Lord in Mark 13:32, are the solitary proof adduced to the Kenosis theory. The words are omitted in some MSS., but their admitted difficulty favours their genuineness. We may be sure there is no contradiction in Scripture, and we must not allow one obscure verse to annul the general positive teaching of Scripture. The verse does not, as a matter of fact, limit the knowledge of Christ as "the Son of Man", but as the Son, and so goes further than the Kenosis theory. In the next verse, the Lord says, "Watch and pray for ye know not when the time is," so that His "not knowing the day" had nothing in common with their human ignorance. The statement, moreover, does not read like an admission of instrinsic limitation on our Lord's knowledge. Why was it that He "who knew the Father as the Father knew Him", was unaware of a day known to the Father, seems beyond our understanding. Clearly, it did not lead the apostles to doubt His omniscience when they said, "Now we are sure that Thou knowest all things", nor oblige the Lord to correct them with the proviso, "except the day of My coming".

he been omitted, the other disciples, it may be, would have thought an injustice had been done. This omniscience of our Lord in incarnation resulted naturally from what He had been before incarnation. He was the same personality as He had ever been. He claimed to know God in a way enjoyed by no one else. "No man knoweth the Father save the Son" (Matt 11:27), and with the same absolute knowledge with which the Father knew Him. "As the Father knoweth Me, even so know I the Father" (John 10:15), and the word used here implies "accurate knowledge". To know the infinite God accurately includes all other knowledge, as the greater includes the less, and implies omniscience. The Lord enjoyed conscious knowledge not only of past time, "Before Abraham was I am" (John 8:58), but of a past eternity. "Father glorify Thou Me with the glory which I had with Thee before the world was" (John 17:21). If He had forgotten nothing of a past eternity, surely His memory of past history was as good as that of the critics who impugn Him!

In the Book of Isaiah, Jehovah attests His superiority over the idols of the heathen by His power to forecast the future. He challenges them to do the same. "I have declared the former things from the beginning – let them bring them forth and show us what shall happen; let them show the former things – and show the things that are to come hereafter, that we may know that ye are gods. Remember the former things of old, for I am God, and there is none else; I am God, and there is none like Me, declaring the end from the beginning and from ancient times the things that are not yet done" (48:3; 41:22; 46:9,10). This is the prerogative of God alone, and this power Christ claimed. He knew the future, not merely as a prophet by inspiration of God, but in Himself. He did not prelude His words with a "Thus saith the Lord", but with "Verily, verily, I say unto you", "My words shall never pass away". He knew He would come in glory (Matt 26:64), that all would stand before Him to be judged (7:22; 25:31; John 5:22). He knew what the judged would say, and what He would reply (Luke 13:23). He knew all things that should come upon Him (John 18:4), and He knew He would reign in this scene of His rejection (Matt 19:28).

Again, in the Old Testament Scriptures, to read the heart is declared to be the prerogative of Jehovah. "I the Lord search the heart" (Jer 17:10). "The Lord searcheth all hearts and understandeth all the imaginations of the thoughts" (1 Chron 28:9). "The Lord looketh on the heart" (1 Sam 16:7).

To claim such knowledge is to claim omniscience, and nothing short of this was claimed for and by Christ. "He knew all men, and needed not that any should testify of man, for He knew what was in man" (John 2:24,25). "I know you, that ye have not the love of God in you" (5: 42). "He knew in Himself that His disciples murmured" (6:61). "He knew their thoughts" (Matt 12:15; Luke 6:8). "He knew they were desirous to ask Him" (John 16:19). One day "God will judge the secrets of men by Jesus Christ" (Rom 2:16), for all secrets are known to Him. In relation to His Manhood, the Lord could be said to be "full of wisdom", and yet to "increase in wisdom" (not knowledge) (Luke 2:40,52). In the presence of the elder men, He acted as was seemly for a boy of twelve: "He heard them and asked them questions". But they soon made the discovery that they needed to ask Him questions, for we read, "All that heard were astonished at His understanding and answers".

The reply of our Lord to Mary, shows that even at the early age of twelve, He had full consciousness of His Divine mission and of His heavenly relationships. This need not surprise us, as the same was true from conception (Psa. 22:9.10). He was the 'wisdom of God', but His wisdom was manifested along natural[19] lines.

The Lord's omniscience shines out in the records of His ministry. He knew Zaccheus and Peter by name before He met them. He knew of the death of Lazarus before the news reached Him. He knew the past history of the Bethesda cripple and of the man born blind. Numberless instances could be adduced. He was acquainted with Nathaniel before Philip brought him to Him. The answer to his enquiry, "Whence knowest Thou me?" convinced Nathaniel that He who had seen him when hidden from the eyes of man, could only be the Son of God. And guileless souls will never doubt the Deity of

---

[19] It is mere trifling, to adduce our Lord's silence as to the facts of astronomy and modern discovery, as a proof of His non-acquaintance with these facts. The mere pedant loves to display his knowledge to all, but "The prudent man concealeth knowledge" (Prov 12:23). The Lord's mission was not to hypnotise men with His knowledge of science, but to impart to them the knowledge of sin and of God.

Him who knows them through and through. Could omniscience go further than our Lord's knowledge in the episode of the tribute money (Matt 17:27)? He knew a certain fish had swallowed a piece of money. He left Peter free to go to the sea and cast his hook where he would. He knew that no other fish would take the hook, but that this very fish would be the first taken up. He knew the piece of money would be a stater, the very sum required, two didrachma, to pay the temple tax. One instance more may suffice: the incident of the search for a room where to observe the Passover. The Lord, in sending forth His disciples into the city, left them quite free to take their own road, but knew that by the way they would meet a man bearing a pitcher of water – a most unusual sight in an eastern city, where it is the woman's work to carry water – that the man would be going to the very house in which the owner had furnished and prepared a large upper room, and that he would willingly place it at their disposal. Again we may ask, could omniscience go further?

3. He is also Himself the Treasure, "For it pleased the Father that in Him should all fullness dwell' (Col 1:19). He was God's treasure, in whom His soul delighted. He is the wisdom of God, through whom all God's wisdom and knowledge are revealed, in Creation, Providence, and Redemption. "The Lord by wisdom hath founded the earth" (Prov 3:19). He was the wise Architect who prepared the heavens; He is the Creator of "all things that are in heaven and in earth, visible and invisible". Angelic hosts, the stellar universe, the spirit of man, the "springs of the sea" (Job 38:16), the "goodly wings of the peacocks" (39:13), the "flower of the field", the bones of the behemoth (40:15,18), are but examples of His creative wisdom. The beneficent laws of Nature, the gifts of sun and rain, fruitful seasons, harvests, display His providential wisdom. Above all, the depths both of the riches of the wisdom and knowledge of God are seen, in His ways in redemption and grace, in "reconciling the world unto Himself". "Christ crucified" is unto them which are called, "the power of God and the wisdom of God", and proves that "the foolishness of God is wiser than man". "God hath concluded them all (both Jew and Gentile) in unbelief that He might have mercy upon all", and it is His purpose that "now, unto principalities and powers in heavenly places, might be known by the Church the manifold wisdom of God".

4. The Lord, too, is the Treasurer. He is the antitype of the treasurer, Eliakim (Isa 22:22) – the man whom God raised up, who was to bear on his shoulder the key of the House of David, "who openeth[20] and no man shutteth" not to the self-satisfied Laodiceans, but to the Philadelphians of "little strength", who had "kept His Word and had not denied His Name" (Rev 3:8). It is the function of the Holy Spirit to unfold "the unsearchable riches of Christ" by means of the written Word. Christ does not so much give us wisdom but "is made unto us wisdom, even righteousness, sanctification, and redemption". As a ray of light may be split up into light, heat, and chemical energy, so Divine wisdom is here seen resolved into its three constituents, by each of which is solved an otherwise insoluble problem. Is the question, "How can a guilty sinner be justified before a righteous God?" Christ is made unto us "righteousness". Is it, "How can an unclean sinner be made fit for a Holy God?" Christ is made unto us "sanctification". Or is it, "How can a helpless sinner be delivered from the thraldom of sin and Satan?" Christ is made unto us "redemption". Christ does not give us stores of blessing and strength and wisdom, but He becomes to us moment by moment all that we need and trust Him to be, and becomes in very deed the provision of God to our souls.

9. MYSTERY, BABYLON THE GREAT (Rev 17:5)

Leaving for later consideration the last of the Divine Mysteries, that of "Universal Headship" (Eph 1:9,10), let us turn to the solemn subject of what we may call the "Mysteries of Satan", namely "Mystery, Babylon the Great" and the "Mystery of Iniquity". These two consummations of evil, though sometimes confused, are really distinct, one being on the religious, the other on the worldly plane.

The Mysteries of God are, as we have seen, the unfoldings of His infinite resources in view of man's failures: the Mysteries of Satan are those failures in full development. The *ecclesia*, at the beginning

---

[20] A comparison of Isaiah 22:22 and Rev 3:7, seems to show that the opening referred to is primarily an opening of the treasury of God, revealing Christ in the Word to His humble people. To learn of the meek and lowly Teacher, the disciple should be meek and lowly.

of the present dispensation, in the first springtide of her love and devotion, "betrothed as a chaste virgin to Christ", continued "steadfastly in the apostles' doctrine and fellowship, and in breaking of bread, and prayers", and bore a bright testimony to her absent and returning Lord. If someone had seen this and then had fallen asleep, not for the twenty years of the legend, but for the whole course of the present age, what would be his horror on awakening to see in the place of professed testimony for God, no longer "a chaste virgin" but an abandoned woman, bearing on her brazen forehead the name of infamy – "Mystery, Babylon the Great, mother of harlots, and of abominations of the earth"? What means this horrible portent, and why is she called after Babylon, rather than after Sodom, Tyre, or any other place prominent in Old Testament history? Because of the relation which historical Babylon bore to Israel, and the spiritual significance of that relation. The countries brought into contact with Israel in old time seem to represent the world in its various phases of evil. Thus Egypt would stand for the world in its ungodliness and self-sufficiency. "The river is mine, and I have made it" (Ezek 29:9). Israel in Egypt corresponds with man in his unregenerate state. Tyre would represent the world in its commercial rivalries and race for wealth (Ezek 26; 2). (What was it but the spirit of Tyre that was behind the world wars?) Edom is the world in its hatred of God's people (Amos 1:4); Sodom, the world in its fleshy corruption; and Babylon, in its religious corruption and persecution of the saints. Israel was never again to return to Egypt as a nation, but might and did fall under the power of Babylon.

It is remarkable that the very king, through whom God granted deliverance from the open hostility of the Assyrian, was the first to fall under the basilisk spell of Babylon, presenting herself as friend and sympathiser, but how soon to rob his treasury and lead his people captive. Babylon was, in fact, the first great Gentile power to subjugate the people of God, and is regarded as their greatest enemy. Satan always makes his most deadly attack first, and at the last goes back to it again.

Babylon was the beginning of the kingdom of Nimrod, the grandson of Ham, "the mighty hunter before the Lord" (Gen 10:9), a hunter, surely, of nobler quarry than mere beasts, of "the bodies and souls of men" (see Rev 18:13, marg.). From the words, "He began to be mighty on the earth", we may gather that he was a successful conqueror. Not only so, but he was a mighty leader against God, for comparing this passage with the account of the building of Babel and its tower in Genesis 11, we see that he was the great initiator,[21] the brain of that tremendous undertaking which marked the first confederate departure from God since the flood; but the confederation ended in confusion and dispersion, as all man-made associations must. "Associate yourselves, and ye shall be broken to pieces". "Union is strength" only when it is a union which is of God and with God. 'United we fall' may serve as a motto for world-leaguers and alliance-mongers.

Nothing is said of the destruction of the tower of Babel, and there seems no doubt it became later the great temple of Belus, or Belá, the mighty lord, rival of the Lord of lords. This temple was half a mile in circumference and 660 feet in height, loftier than the Great Pyramid. It was constructed in eight successive towers, gradually decreasing in width, and surmounted by a golden statue, 40 feet high.

It is remarkable that Arabs call the immense mound which today marks the ruin of the tower, Birs Nimroud, thus marking its identity with its founder. Even if it cannot be proved that Nimrod claimed divine honours in his lifetime, he certainly was deified[22] after his death. Babylon was a centre of idolatry, and "Satan's seat" in a special degree. Thus it posed as the rival and opponent of Jerusalem, where was Jehovah's throne, "between the cherubim". The judgment of God fell on Babylon, not only because of the evil she had worked against Jerusalem (Jer 51:34), but first and foremost on account of her shameless idolatries. "Babylon is fallen, is fallen; and all the graven images of her gods He hath broken unto the ground" (Isa 21:9).

---

[21] Nimrod is represented by tradition as a black man with an enormous head, very ugly, and lame. He was evidently the archetype of the fire gods of Greek and Roman Mythology, Hephaistos and Vulcan, who were deformed monsters and lame to boot, and is no doubt the forerunner of the last great leader against God, that is to be, the Man of Sin. It is remarkable that Bel was a title attached to his name, Satan thus associating with himself this evil man. Babel, from a Hebrew root, signifying, 'to confound'. Our Lord recognised Beelzebub (the lord of flies of Ekron) as none other than Satan.

[22] 'The Two Babylons', by Hyslop.

"Two things shall come to thee in a moment – the loss of children and widowhood – for the multitude of thy sorceries and for the great abundance of thine enchantments" (Isa 47:9). "A sword is upon the inhabitants of Babylon for it is the land of graven images, they are mad upon their idols" (Jer 50:25,38). All idolatry is addressed to some demon, "for the things which the Gentiles sacrifice they sacrifice to demons and not to God"; and that of Babylon was to Bel, the prince of the demons.

Israel, by her departure from God to Baal, made it necessary for God in righteousness to hand them over to Babylon. It was fitting that their bodies should be carried where their hearts had already wandered. Today, when we see the feet of professed believers turned again to Babylon, we know that they have trod the path in heart before.

Babylon was built on both sides of the Euphrates in an immense square, of at the lowest computation, 34 miles in circumference (Herodotus made it 60 miles), of $8\frac{1}{2}$ miles to each side. The river was spanned by a great bridge of stone, clamped with iron and roofed over, which connected the two parts of the city, but of which no trace remains today. The temple of Belus was in the western city; the Hanging Gardens, built by Queen Semiramis on successive tiers of arches, up to the height of the walls, were on the eastern side of the river. There was a moat of running water around the city, and the walls, pierced for a hundred gates of solid brass, were at least 300 feet high and 70 feet broad, surmounted by a street on which a chariot of four horses could easily turn. Of all these enormous walls, the greatest known in the history of the world, nothing is seen today, though when the prophecies were uttered foretelling her utter ruin, nothing could have seemed less probable than such a catastrophe. But no word of God can fall to the ground. Isaiah prophesied more than 165 years prior to the taking of Babylon and 200 before Herodotus, "the father of history" as the world calls him, and yet the prophet not only names the man destined by God to be the first to humble Babylon, but describes the manner of its capture. Cyrus accomplished this in 538 BC, after more than two years' siege, by turning aside, as is well known, the course of the Euphrates. It was taken a second time by Darius Hystaspes in 516 BC, and later on by Alexander the Great. Through centuries, the great city declined, until the prophecies were literally fulfilled, the broad walls of Babylon were "utterly broken" and she herself "became heaps".

Some students of prophecy believe that Babylon must be rebuilt, on the ground that two or three specific details named in the prophecies have not been fulfilled in the destruction that has already taken place. I think a more careful reading of the prophecies goes to show that such an idea is mistaken.

Let us examine the supposed discrepancies. Does it not say, it is objected, that the judgment of Babylon should come upon her suddenly, which she should not know? (Isa 47:11). How reconcile this with centuries of decline and decay? The words of the prophet may quite well mean that she should be taken by surprise, as indeed she was. Her judgment was to come upon her suddenly, but it does not say it was to be finished suddenly. But then does not Isaiah 13:19 distinctly say that "Babylon...shall be as when God overthrew Sodom and Gomorrah: it shall never be inhabited, neither shall it be dwelt in from generation to generation"? Yes, the result would be the same in both cases. Babylon, like Sodom and Gomorrah, should not be inhabited, but it does not say that the manner of their judgment should be the same (see also Jer 50:40).

That Hillah, an Arab town of some importance, exists today in the neighbourhood, does not negative this, as it remains to be proved that this place is within the site of the ancient Babylon. The fact that in its gardens there are said to be no traces of ruins would rather point to the contrary. But again does it not say that no stone shall be taken from Babylon to build with, and is it not well known that neighbouring cities were built from her bricks? This last fact is so, but it is not accurate to apply the words of Jer 51:25,26, to Babylon as a whole. They are addressed to "the destroying mountain", now named "Birs Nimroud". "They shall not take of thee a stone for a corner nor a stone for a foundation." This has been literally fulfilled. The great mound of ruins is truly a "burnt mountain"–vitrified by a judgment of fire, and is thus quite unfit to produce either corner or foundation stones.

The idea that Babylon must be rebuilt is not only far-fetched and mistaken,[23] but introduces confusion into the description of the woman's seat in Revelation 17:9,18. The city on which she rests is built, we are told, on several mountains, and was, when the apostle wrote, "reigning over the kings of the earth". This was certainly not true then of Babylon, nor do seven hills exist in the plain of Shinar, on which the literal city of Babylon could be rebuilt. We have one city which corresponds with this twofold description, and we need no other.

But when it is affirmed that the prophecies against Babylon have been so literally fulfilled as to render needless any further rebuilding of the historical city, it is not meant that these prophecies have been exhausted. There is a "fulfilment" still to come, as we shall now see.

For centuries, Babylon had only been an immense historical reminiscence and nothing more,[24] a title to be conferred half in flattery, half in reprobation on one or another of the great modern capitals of Christendom, when suddenly the Prophetic Word presents her to us as an actual reality. "Great Babylon", we read, "came in remembrance before God to give unto her the fierceness of His wrath" (Rev 16:19). "Babylon the great is fallen, is fallen" (Rev 18:7). But how can that fall which has already fallen, or that be judged which has been destroyed? Only by having once more come into existence under a new guise. Satan will end where he began. It was, indeed, a crushing, personal reverse for him when Babylon was razed to the ground. "Bel was confounded." He found himself without a seat, and obliged to seek a new sphere, wherein to carry out the old policy. Here we see the malignant subtlety of Satan toward the Eve of the New Creation. Persecution had but fanned her faith, might not favour quench it? We know too well how he succeeded in his effort, and what the result has been.

Literal Babylon represents a city, the capital of the first great Gentile power, the centre of an idolatrous system centred in a city, the capital of the last great Gentile power. One of the seven angels, who had

---

[23] The reader is recommended to read 'Keith on Prophecy' (to which the present writer owes much information) if he would be convinced that the prophecies against Babylon have been literally and adequately fulfilled.

[24] The Babylon where Peter wrote his First Epistle, was probably a small town in Egypt.

just poured out the vials of God's wrath, is commissioned, in Revelation 17, to show John the judgment of the great whore, just as later to display the glory of the Bride. The "great whore" is referred to in v.1 as "seated upon many waters", explained in v.15 to mean "peoples and multitudes and nations and tongues". This describes her characteristic position for centuries past, the world-wide scope of her spiritual empire. But the special position in which the angel displays her to John is as "seated upon a scarlet-coloured beast". The preposition "upon" is the same in both places, but in v.3 it governs a case, denoting motion on to. She has clambered up on to the beast. At last she has realised her secular ambitions, and is seen in the zenith of her power – prelude to her everlasting abasement. A rider not only rides, but guides his steed. So the woman is seated on the beast and "reigns over the kings of the earth". It matters nothing that the beast is "full of the names of blasphemy". Ecclesiastical corruption is profoundly indifferent to christian principle. Spiritual life and separation from the world are immaterial; position, wealth, talent are indispensable. Does not she herself flaunt the shameless name – "Mystery, Babylon the Great, mother of harlots and of the abominations of the earth"? This sub-title "mother of harlots", is expressive of the true scope of Babylon. Just as "Babylon" of old days described often more than the city, so "Mystery Babylon" has daughters, harlots like herself, perhaps in externals diverse, in essentials certainly the same. The scarlet-coloured beast represents the Roman world in its last phase, but the fact that the ten horns are not crowned would show that the scene before us precedes the "hour" in which the ten kings will receive power as kings with "the beast" (17:12).

The woman is arrayed in purple and scarlet costume, thus rivalling by imitation the regal glory of the world, and is decked (lit. gilded) with gold and precious stones and pearls, in contrast with that which "becometh women professing godliness, good works" (1 Tim 2:9,10).

She holds a golden cup in her hand, travesty of the cup of salvation, and "full", not of joy and communion, but of abominations and filthiness. She is viewed, not as Israel of old as an adulteress, but as is proper for one who counterfeits the affianced bride, as an abandoned woman, committing fornication with the kings of the earth, and making the people drunk with the wine of her fornication. The great ones of the earth are not deceived, policy alone shapes their ends. But the vulgar crowd is deceived – intoxicated with her religious displays, art, music, oratory and millinery, as they are by operatic scenes or theatrical shows. And she is intoxicated herself. Instead of being "filled with the Spirit" she is "drunk with the blood of the saints, and with the blood of the martyrs of Jesus". But her triumph is short; her judgment lingereth not. It will fall first on the System by the hand of man (17:16), and later on the City from the hand of God (16:19).

10. THE MYSTERY OF INIQUITY (1 Thess 2:7)

The destruction of Babylon, the corrupt religious system, will make room for something even worse, the "Mystery of Iniquity". The same process is being enacted today in Papist countries, like France and Portugal, where a corrupted faith has practically given place to no faith. In such lands there is a certain liberty of indifference, which allows wide distribution of 'Gospels', but hearts open to the Gospel are but few. It will be when the Mystery of Iniquity is revealed, that "God shall send men a strong delusion that they may believe a (lit., the) lie". But this will not be till long after the coming of the Lord for His Church. Between that event and this delusion, will have occurred times of blessing, probably without parallel before in the history of the world. If Satan rises up against himself and destroys Babylon, it will be because she will have served his purpose long enough. He will have not a moment to lose "for he knoweth that he hath but a short time". "The Mystery of Iniquity" will be the climax of lawlessness[25] – when "iniquity shall have come to the full". The promise of Eden will then be consummated. It seemed such a trifling thing to take the forbidden fruit. Really, it was man setting up to be God on his own account, as every act of self-will is in principle today. "The Mystery of Iniquity" is the unexpected consummation of this. Lawlessness had been an age-long fruit of sin: there is nothing new in that.

---

[25] "Iniquity" in 2 Thess 2:7 ought to be translated "lawlessness". So also in v. 8, "that wicked" should be translated "that lawless".

Men like Nimrod, as we have seen, had been deified after their death. The "Mystery" was already working in the apostles' time. The Roman Emperors, some of them, were deified in their life time. The 'New Theology' pretends that man is divine, but who would have imagined that a man could claim to be the only God. We see things working up to a general revolt against all authority in the home, in the nation, and in the churches. Trade Unionism, Socialism, Syndicalism, and kindred godless movements will find an articulate cry in the words, "Let us break their bands asunder, and cast away their cords from us" (Psa 2:3). All is tending toward two great events, "The Mystery of Lawlessness" and then the "Mystery of His Will". But Israel must first be restored to the place of testimony. The true Pentecost of Joel will prepare her for this. Her testimony will be the Gospel of the Kingdom: "The King is coming!" Multitudes of all flesh will be saved, but it is easy to imagine how intolerable such a testimony will be to the ungodly world of those days, and Satan will prepare his counter-blast, "The King has come!" and the counterfeit God-man will be presented to an astonished world with the credentials of "all power and signs and lying wonders" in the person of the Man of Sin, the first beast of Revelation 13. His claims will be sustained with Satanic power by the second beast, the Antichrist, the false Messiah and King of Israel. These two supermen will form with the Dragon, who inspires them, the Satanic Triad of the last days, a counterfeit of the Trinity. The Dragon once had the highest place of any creature. "Perfect in beauty", "full of wisdom" he "sealed up the sum". He was "the anointed cherub that covered" (Ezek 28), but not content with this, he aimed at the throne of God. "I will exalt my throne above the stars – I will be like the Most High" (Isa 14:13,14). The greatest tragedy in the universe is a Cherub turned Dragon. The Man of Sin will arise out of the revived Roman Empire as the little horn of Daniel 7. Nebuchadnezzar, in his dream, saw four Gentile empires, to whom God intended to entrust the kingdom during the national dethronement of Israel – Babylon, Medo-Persia, Greece, and Rome – represented in their official glory by four metals – gold, silver, brass, and iron, decreasing in value as they recede from the Divine ideal of absolute monarchy. An element of weakness is introduced in the feet – the clay – the democratic socialistic element. In ch.7 the same empires are seen in their moral degradation as four wild beasts – a lion, a bear, a leopard, and a nameless monster, and these decrease in nobility and increase in ferocity. All attempts to form a fifth world empire have failed,[26] and must fail, for the fifth is "the Kingdom of God and of His Christ".

In his vision, Daniel saw the fourth empire as it will be under the ten horns, and therefore in its last stage of development. He describes the rise of "the little horn", which overthrows three of the ten. In Revelation 13 the beast is seen with seven heads as well as ten horns, of which one is wounded to death, is healed, and becomes eventually the eighth or last great ruler of the revived Roman Empire. The eighth head and the little horn are therefore identical, though in one extraordinary point they will not be. This we shall see later. Let us turn now for a moment to Revelation 13. The opening words, as is well known, ought to be, "And he (i.e., the dragon) stood upon the sand of the sea shore". Then follows the rise of the great beast, which we have little difficulty in recognising as the fourth beast of Daniel. It embodies traits of three previous empires – the leopard, the bear, and the lion; truly a monster "dreadful and terrible", having, as we have seen, "seven heads and ten horns, and upon his horns ten crowns, and upon his heads the name of blasphemy – and the dragon gave him his (i.e., his own) power and his seat and great authority", and then the apostle adds – "I saw one of his heads as it were wounded to death, and his deadly wound was healed" (Rev 13:1-3). The wounding and miraculous recovery of this head is well worth our close attention. In Revelation 1 the Lord describes Himself as "He that liveth and was dead and is alive for evermore". Throughout the Book, this is characteristic of the Lamb. He has been "slain" (e.g., see 5:6) but is now alive.

This word "slain" is the sacrificial word, and is identical with that used of the wounded head of the Beast "wounded to death" – the word "as it were" is simply the word translated in ch.5 "as it had been slain". The head will be truly slain and brought to life by satanic

---

[26] The Carthaginians, Moors, Turks, have all come near this, but have failed. The Germans made another attempt in the World Wars. If they had succeeded, a fifth world-empire, outside the old Roman Empire, would exist on the ruins of the British and French Empire, which form part of it.

power – a travesty of the resurrection. This marvel seems to be realised in a double way. The then ruler of the Roman Empire will be wounded to death and miraculously healed. But previously, perhaps centuries before, one of the seven heads of the beast will have been slain with a sword, and his spirit, instead of going to Hades, the usual abode of the wicked dead, will have been preserved in the bottomless pit or abyss – the very place Satan will be shut up in during the millennium. The first thing, indeed, we hear of the beast in his personal character is, that he will "ascend out of the bottomless pit", and make war against God's two witnesses, and will overcome them and kill them (11:7.) These two, the present and past rulers, will become in some way mysteriously combined. May it not be, I would suggest, that the wicked spirit of the past "head" will come out of the abyss and take possession of the body of the then present ruler, who had received the deadly wound. If this be so, the dead one will come to life again energised by the spirit of a past Roman Emperor, destined thus to play a second role in this world's affairs. The electrifying bulletin will circle the globe: "The deadly wound is healed." A miracle has been performed by the Dragon's power, and men will worship him as the Great Lifegiver. "The Man of Sin" will thus be a dual personality with superhuman powers, and he will be an object of almost universal worship.

The first beast of Revelation 13 is said to rise out of the sea, i.e., the Mediterranean, as the direct result of the presence of Satan on the earth. It is very important to notice that this beast represents first a system, the Roman Empire revived; then, after the wounding and healing of one of its seven heads, the system personified in that head, a Roman Emperor revived. This distinction has been overlooked, and confusion has been the result. The first beast is interpreted accordingly, meaning only the Roman Empire, and the second beast the human person, or the Man of Sin and the Antichrist rolled into one. That the first beast ends as a human person is clear from 11:7 and 17:8, where he is said to "ascend out of the bottomless pit". This could not be said of a system, whereas it is quite intelligible, if we allow that "the Man of Sin" will have already lived on the earth, died, and is brought back to this scene at a later date. Then, again, in ch.17 we read, "The beast that was and is not, even he is the eighth (head or king), and is of the seven, and goeth into perdition". Here the beast is personified in the eighth head, who will prove to be one of the previous seven raised to life again. 13:18 is even clearer, "Let him that hath understanding count the number of a man,[27] and his number is 666". This refers to the first beast, of whom the second beast makes an image.

The seven heads and ten horns are interpreted in either case as kings.[28] Thus we read in 17:10 of the heads, "There are seven kings, five are fallen, and one is, and the other is not yet come, and when he cometh he must continue a short space." This last phrase excludes the Papacy, for that has continued nearly 1500 years.

John was told, "The ten horns which thou sawest are ten kings, which have received no kingdom as yet, but receive power as kings one hour with the beast" (17:12). How then, if "heads" and "horns" both mean "kings", are we to distinguish them? The "heads" are successive (though not necessarily consecutive), the "horns" contemporaneous. The seven heads will have reigned during the first phase of the Roman Empire, the "horns" will reign after its revival, during its final phase. Not that the same geographical area will necessarily be rigidly adhered to, but the same parts of the earth will be represented, though the powers in question may have colonies and possessions outside the limits of the old empire.

Britain, France, Spain, Portugal, and Italy may prove to be the western horns, and Greece, Serbia, Romania, Montenegro, and some Syrian kingdom the eastern. Their reign will be brief, "one hour with the beast". We may connect this expression "one hour" with that in

---

[27] An attempt has been made to explain this number 666, as referring to the duration of the empires represented in Nebuchadnezzar's image. But is there any other instance in the New Testament of a period denoted by the values of the Greek letters?

[28] The heads also mean "seven mountains on which the woman sitteth" (17:9). The woman is therefore Rome, "the city of the seven hills", as she is known in history, "that great city which", when John was writing, "reigned over the kings of the earth". Whether Babylon be rebuilt or no, is not in my judgment a matter which touches this prophecy, for when John was writing, by no stretch of imagination could she be said to be built on seven mountains, or to be "reigning". The seven heads are sometimes interpreted as seven forms of government which have existed in the Roman State from its beginning, but this overlooks the fact that the beast represents Imperial Rome, in which only one form of Government is possible.

1 John 2:18, "the last hour, etc.", to be characterised by the presence of Antichrist. In Psalm 83:4-8 the subject is a confederacy against Jehovah and against Israel, "The tabernacles of Edom, and the Ishmaelites; of Moab, and the Hagarenes; Gebal and Ammon and Amalek; the Philistines with the inhabitants of Tyre; Asshur also is found with them". Ten peoples are enumerated here. May not these be the nations whose representatives are known today as the southern nations of Europe? Their object will be to cut them off (i.e., the hidden ones of Jehovah) from being a nation, that the name of Israel may be no more in remembrance (v. 4). And this will be the aim of the nations gathered together against Jerusalem in the last days (Joel 3:2; Zech 13:7,8; 14:2). But they will themselves be cut off, and then it will be true of their survivors, that "ten men shall take hold out of all languages of the nations (one from each) even shall take hold of the skirt of him that is a Jew, saying, We will go with you, for we have heard that God is with you" (Zech 8:23). Then, too, they will have to confess, "The Lord hath done great things for them."

The Man of Sin is not the Antichrist, though he too, will claim divine honour. God only recognises one building on earth as His temple, and that is the temple at Jerusalem. There, in the holy place, the Man of Sin will impiously take his seat as God. When not there personally, it seems likely that he will be replaced by the mysterious image – the synthetic man – which the Antichrist will produce by Satanic power. This will prove to be the "abomination of desolation spoken of by Daniel the prophet" (Matt 24:15) ("abomination" is a well-understood phrase in Scripture for an idol). That is to be the signal to all faithful Jews for their immediate flight to the mountains, from the tribulation which must then ensue. The "Man of Sin" will make extraordinary claims, but will also offer extraordinary credentials calculated to test the faith, even of the elect (Matt 24:24, RV). The first appearance of this terrible leader against God and His people, will be as "a little horn", arising among the ten horns of the fourth beast of Daniel (see ch.7). He will overthrow three of them, and the others will recognise the fait accompli and hail him as the Man of Destiny, qualified to lead the great confederacy.

Consummate Generalship, then will be the first credential of this

Man of Sin. The second will be his mysterious recovery from "the deadly wound" by satanic power, which will cause men to worship him. This effect will be heightened by his superhuman victory over the two witnesses. What greater proof of divine power than to slay the witnesses of God, who, till then, had slain all their foes? This victory will succeed his supernatural resurrection from the bottomless pit. It is as the beast that ascended "out of the bottomless pit" that he shall make war on the two witnesses and overcome them and kill them. He will further receive miraculous attestation. Not only will his coming be "after the working of Satan with all power and signs and lying wonders" (2 Thess 2:9), but his claims will be supported by the Antichrist, who will "exercise all the power of the first beast before him, and cause the earth...to worship the first beast whose deadly wound was healed...and do great wonders, so that he maketh fire come down from heaven on the earth in the sight of men".

Never will there have been such a being on the earth before, backed by all the power[29] of Satan, entrusted by men with all their powers, and having also power from God to continue forty and two months (Rev 13:4 7; 17:13). Then it will be, when the Man of Sin is fully manifested, that God shall send men a strong delusion, that they should believe THE lie, "that they all might be damned, who believed not the truth, but had pleasure in unrighteousness" (2 Thess 2:12). All will worship him, whose names are not written in the Book of Life of the Lamb slain, from the foundation of the world (Rev 13:8).

The coming of the Lord for His saints is not governed by dates, nor does it depend on historical or political events. With God's earthly people, it is different. Scripture shows that before a "covenant" with Israel as a nation is possible, they must not only have been restored, at least in part, to their own land, but their land must have been restored to them.

This covenant will be the recognition by the Powers of their national existence under their king – the one who will "come in his own name" (John 5:43), and whom Israel will receive. He must be a

---

[29] It is the same word *exousia* – authority – in all three cases.

Jew, for it is unthinkable that the nation would accept anyone else as their Messiah. This is the second beast of Revelation 13, who will arise out of the land – that is, the land of Palestine. He will in appearance be for God, having "two horns like a lamb", but will be possessed of Satan, for he will speak "like a dragon". He will doubtless further "the covenant" between Israel and the great Emperor of the Roman alliance – a covenant which will probably guarantee to the nation their national rights and religious freedom, but to the Spirit of God it will be "a covenant with death and an agreement with hell".

Two things will hold good during the first half of the week. The city, except certain portions, shall be "trodden down by the Gentiles" which means, I would suggest, that the city will be held in force by detachments of the troops of the ten kingdoms, to guarantee the inviolability of the holy places which could not be left in the hands of the Jews. During the same three and a half years, the two witnesses, probably Moses and Elias (not Enoch, for he was not of Israel, and could hardly take part in a Jewish testimony), will deliver their testimony, backed up by miraculous power. They, too, will be men brought back from the other world to live and act once more in this scene. When they shall have finished their testimony, "the beast that ascendeth out of the bottomless pit (the Man of Sin) shall make war against them, and shall overcome them and kill them". This will be the occasion for his full manifestation, and also for that of the Antichrist. "In the midst of the week", when the Roman Emperor, the Man of Sin, will tear up the covenant like another scrap of paper and cause "the sacrifice, the oblation, to cease" he will have the full support of the false King of Israel. Henceforth they will come forward as the avowed rivals and enemies of God and His Christ, for whose worship will be substituted that of the Beast and his image. The bulk of the nation will follow their king. The unclean spirit will come back to the nation and find it "empty, swept and garnished" (Matt 12:44), and they will plunge into an idolatry such as was never known before, and their last end will be worse than the first.

So Satan's false Christ will combine a claim to Messiahship with the office of False Prophet. The way "the false prophet" is introduced in Revelation 19 as "the false prophet that did miracles before the beast" clearly points us to the second beast of ch.13, and leaves no reasonable room for doubt as to their identity. The relation between the second beast and the first is that of prophet and god. Between them, the name of God will be banned in the earth. All open human testimony will be impossible. This will be the day of Jacob's trouble – the Great Tribulation of the Gospels. It will occupy the second half[30] of the 70th week.

The victory of Satan will appear complete. But his seeming victories are the times of his defeats. The two Arch-Rebels will be summarily dealt with. There will be no need that they should be judged before the Great White Throne. Their cup of iniquity will be not only full but overflowing, and their heinous guilt will be manifest to the universe. They will be cast alive into the lake of fire[31].

Two men in the Old Testament went to heaven without dying. Two in the New, will go to hell without seeing death. The first to enter that fearful place of everlasting torment, "prepared for the devil and his angels", will be two men, a Gentile and a Jew. Thus will the Mystery of Iniquity be unmasked and undone for ever, to make room for the manifestation of the "Mystery of His Will".

11. THE MYSTERY OF HIS WILL (Eph 1:9-10)

It is with relief that we turn once more from the Mysteries of Babylon and of Iniquity to the Mysteries of God. The former are the short-lived pseudo-triumphs of Satan; the latter will fill the eternal ages. God has revealed one more mystery, "the Mystery of His Will". "That in the dispensation of the fullness of times He might gather together

---

[30] The second half of the week will not, it would seem, reach its proper completion. "Except those days should be shortened, there should no flesh be saved: but for the elect's sake those days shall be shortened" (Matt 24:22). In Daniel 8:13, the question is asked, "How long shall be the vision concerning the daily sacrifice–to give both the sanctuary and the host to be trodden underfoot? and He said unto me, Unto 2300 days; then shall the sanctuary be cleansed." 2300 days is 220 days short of 7 years. The first half of "the week" will have run its full, the second will apparently be shortened by over 7 months.

[31] The question is sometimes asked, whether such and such a wicked ruler is the 'Antichrist' or the 'Man of Sin'? No doubt Satan has had his types of these men, like Nimrod, Rameses ii, Antiochus Epiphanes, Caligula, etc., but the Antitypes cannot be recognised until certain events referred to above occur, though it is not impossible that both these terrible men of destiny are alive on the earth today.

MYSTERIES OF THE NEW TESTAMENT

in one all things in Christ, both which are in heaven, and which are in earth, even in Him" (Eph 1:10). It is fitting to consider this last in the series of mysteries, for it is bound up with the eternal glories of Christ and nothing can supersede it. The word translated "gather-together-in-one" would be more accurately rendered "head up". It occurs in only one other place in the New Testament (Rom 13:9), and is there translated "briefly comprehended" or, as we say, "summed up". We may compare this with the word in Ezekiel 28:12, in the lamentation of Jehovah over the King of Tyre, who can be none other than Satan, "Thou sealest up the sum" or, as the French version has it, "Thou art the crown of the edifice". As Adam was the masterpiece and head of an earthly creation, so it would appear was Satan of the heavenly.

But it was God's purpose to take this place Himself in the person of the Son. Indications are not wanting (though it would be unwise to dogmatise) that the test of angelic obedience was the acknowledgment of the Headship of the Son to be manifested in a created form of a lower order than their own. This may be referred to in Hebrews 1:6, "And again when he bringeth (or in literal order 'when again he bringeth') the First-begotten into the world, He saith, And let all the angels of God worship[32] Him." This would account for the special hatred of Satan to Christ "the Firstborn" and to the "many sons" whom Christ is bringing to glory through Him, in whom they also have "obtained an inheritance" (Eph 1:11). When Satan fell, through exalting himself, the universe was, as it were, a pyramid without a headstone of the corner. This place is reserved for Him "who, being in the form of God...humbled Himself and became obedient unto death, even the death of the Cross" (Phil 2:6-8). As Satan's degradation is in stages (see Ezekiel 28:16-18), so is the elevation of Jesus Christ. Already has God "highly exalted Him, and given Him the Name which is above every name (that is the name of Lord in view of a future exaltation), that at the name of Jesus (not at the name Jesus, but His full title, the Lord Jesus) every knee should

---

[32] This is usually referred to as a quotation from Psa 97:7, "Worship Him all ye gods", but it is remarkable that the exact words, as quoted in Hebrews 1:6. are found in the Septuagint Version of Deuteronomy 32:43, from which it would seem clear that they existed in the Hebrew manuscript from which that translation was made.

bow, of things in heaven, of things in earth, and of things under the earth; and that every tongue should confess that Jesus Christ is Lord to the glory of God the Father" (Phil 2:9-11). In other words, there will be universal submission to His authority and universal admission of His claims. Then will the word of Jehovah in Isaiah 45:23 be fulfilled: "I have sworn by Myself, the word is gone out of My mouth in righteousness, and shall not return. That unto Me every knee shall bow, every tongue shall swear".[33] A king does not reveal, save to his nearest and dearest, his secret purposes concerning his son, and the fact that God is pleased thus to reveal the secret of His purpose is surely a supreme proof of His abounding toward us in grace – "having made known unto us the Mystery of His Will according to His good pleasure which He hath purposed in Himself" (Eph 1:9). How great, then must be this purpose!

The next verse tells us when it will be introduced, "in the dispensation of the Fullness of Times". God has not only His way but His time. He is never too early and never too late. It was in the "fullness of time" that He sent forth His Son (Gal 4:4). It was in "due time" that Christ died for the ungodly (Rom 5:6). He will come again, as Son of Man, in the day known to the Father (Mark 13:32). And so here, God has determined "the dispensation of the Fullness of Times" when all things shall be headed up in His beloved Son.

Divine Dispensations

It may be of help to us to here trace very briefly the Dispensations which have preceded this, the last and the eternal one. Dispensations are periods distinguished from one another by the special character of God's dealings with man. God knew from the beginning what was in man, but man must have opportunity to show what he is. He must also be revealed to himself, otherwise he might complain that he had never been properly tested. The Dispensations have been characterised by a complete breakdown on the part of man, and by mercy and judgment on the part of God. They have been varied and progressive, and in them God has revealed Himself in different ways and degrees.

---

[33] This quotation is specially noteworthy as one of that important group of passages which identify Jehovah of the Old Testament and the Lord Jesus of the New as the same Divine Person (see also Zech 12:1-10; Heb 11:26).

Conscience

When man fell, he started on his career of four thousand years probation, under the power of Satan, who had deceived him; with a corrupt nature within and a blighted creation without; with a knowledge of the eternal power and Godhead of the Creator from His works, and a knowledge of approach to God by sacrifice; with neither law nor government; but with a knowledge of good and evil, fruit of the fall, but unable to avoid the evil or attain the good, apart from the grace of God, but with that grace at His disposal. We may call this the Dispensation of Conscience. Men boast today that their conscience is sufficient. They were left to its guidance for two thousand years. The silver thread of grace ran throughout, but man's ways were marked with violence and corruption, and the flood at length swept the race away.

Government

The next Dispensation was that of Government, entrusted to man in the person of Noah. But Noah's early failure and the general revolt of mankind under Nimrod, proved Government as powerless to control man as Conscience had been. Judgment fell again at Babel in the confusion of tongues. The era of the nations began with conflicting ambitions and strife, as is witnessed until this day.

Law

From these nations, a special people was called out, in whom man might be submitted to a new test. Surrounded by every safeguard and many privileges, with Jehovah dwelling in their midst, they received the Law at His hand. Would not man with his conscience thus instructed and his conduct regulated by a holy Law, bring forth fruit to God? No, for we are told "they rebelled and vexed His Holy Spirit" (Isa 63:10). Instead of good fruit, they "brought forth wild grapes" (5:2). Instead of glorifying the Name of Jehovah, they caused that Name to be blasphemed among the Gentiles, and were judged accordingly. The kingdom was taken from them, and given to the Gentile powers.

Christ

A remnant returned later to their land to be put to a new test – the real presence of the Messiah. This was man's final test. The law had said, "Thou shalt love the Lord thy God with all thy heart – and thy neighbour as thyself". Christ presented Himself in this double character. "The Word became flesh, and tabernacled among us" (John 1:14, marg). "He went about doing good and healing all that were oppressed of the devil" (Acts 10:38). How did men respond to such grace? The Cross was the answer. Man at his best, in the person of the religious Jew, "crucified the Lord of glory" (1 Cor 2:8). After that, it is absurd, as well as unscriptural, to talk of man still being on "probation". The four Dispensations of Conscience, Government, Law, and Christ, have shown not only that there is something wrong with man, but that there is no good thing in him, and that no good thing can come from him. What must be done with him then? He must either be judged, or treated on terms of purest grace.

Grace

The descent of the Spirit initiated the Dispensation of Grace. Only in Christ, dead and risen, can any good be found. Christ is all in all for those who will receive Him. Most reject Him. Some respond and become a people to His Name, "the Church of the living God".

Mercy and Judgment

This Dispensation will end in the coming of Christ for His saints, and the great apostasy of Christendom, already ripening, will be followed by a short Dispensation of Mercy and Judgment, when God's judgments will be in the earth, and He will make them drink the mixed cup of Psalm 75:8. Of this period we have the prophetic outline in Revelation 6-18. Israel, restored to their land, will be blessed materially and spiritually (Joel 2:19-32), and, through the faithful ones among them, will issue to every nation a world-wide testimony of the coming King. The dispensation will close in the full manifestation of evil in the Man of Sin and Antichrist, who will be destroyed by Christ at His coming in judgment.

The Headship of Christ

The Headship of Christ is viewed in at least five different ways in Scripture.

(1) Headship in the Hierarchy of Rule: Christ is the "Head of all principality and power" (Col 2:10). This is His present relation to everything that God recognises in the universe as rule and authority. He is the Ruler of rulers. When He comes, He will bear the title, "King of kings and Lord of lords". God has placed Him "far above all

principality and power and might and dominion" (Eph 1:21), including the power of Satan's kingdom, which seems to be an imitation as far as may be of the Divine (see Eph 6:12). "Christ is over all, God blessed for ever" (Rom 9:5). To Him as Son of Man is this place granted. He could say, in resurrection, "All authority hath been given unto Me in heaven, and on earth" (Matt 28:18 RV). His authority is already recognised in heaven. Even now, He is there called "the Prince of the kings of the earth" (Rev 1:5), whether they will it or not. All are responsible to Him now, and to Him they will one day give an account of the way they have used their power.

(2) Headship in "the One Body": Christ is "Head of the Church" (Eph 5:23). There is no union between Christ and the "powers that be", but there is true spiritual union between His members and Himself. The body began to be fashioned at Pentecost after His death, resurrection, and ascension, and all who have believed in Him since have become members of that mystical body, united to the Head and to all the other members. The process by which this is brought about is the baptism in the Holy Spirit (1 Cor 12:13), and the moment at which this baptism takes place in the history of a saint is the moment he first believes in Christ[34]. The agent is Christ Himself. "The same is He which baptiseth with the Holy Ghost" (John 1:33). Writing to the Corinthians the apostle says, "For in one Spirit were we all baptised into one body, whether we be bond or free" (1 Cor 12:13). Christ holds the members for their final salvation. If one member were lacking, the Church might be "holy", but she could not be "without blemish". She must be both. The members hold the Head for communion and edification (Col 2:19).

(3) Headship in the hierarchy of Service: Christ is the Head of the Man: that is, of course, not of man in the sense of mankind, but of "the man" the male believer. "I would have you know", writes the apostle, "that the head of every man is Christ, and the head of the woman is man, and the head of Christ is God" (1 Cor 11:3). In "the

---

[34] It is quite erroneous to cite the twelve disciples of John at Ephesus (Acts 19), in order to prove that Christians may now be in the same state they were in then. They knew only the baptism of John. They were not "in Christ" at all. To them Christ was merely "One who should come after" John. No Christian can be in this state today. There are no disciples of John now.

Body", Christ is Head of the woman and of the man on equal ground; in fact, in this spiritual relation, "there is neither male nor female" (Gal 3:28). But in social, family, and church relationships, the difference is recognised and provided for. Here, there is a hierarchy of authority. Christ as the Servant is subject to God, so the man to Christ, and so in her service, whether in the home or in the church, is the woman to the man. Where this godly order prevails, how striking is the testimony to angels and men! Where it is reversed, how grave is the loss both here and hereafter! This authority is not autocratic, but transmitted. The man himself is 'under authority' to Christ. It is not a question of capacity or intelligence, but of godly order. While the woman's strength is in influence, man's is in administration, therefore the woman is "not to usurp authority" or "have dominion (RV) over the man" (1 Tim 2:12).

(4) Headship in the Place of Responsibility: Christ is the Head of the House of God. This is "the spiritual house" of 1 Peter 2:5. Christ is the Living Stone, and the Head Stone of a house formed of living stones. "The Stone which the builders disallowed, the same is made the Head of the corner" (v. 7). No other "house of God" is recognised in the Epistles as existing today. Christ is a Son "over His (God's) own house" (Heb 3:6, RV), and the proof of being living stones is continuance: "whose house are we, if we hold fast the confidence and the rejoicing of the hope firm unto the end" (Heb 3:6). The Lordship of Christ in the House of God is an intensely practical truth, yet too often ignored. "Why call ye Me Lord, Lord", He Himself asks us, "and do not the things which I say?" (Luke 6:46). To acknowledge Him as Lord, is to obey His Word (1 Cor 14:37).

(5) The last aspect of Christ's Headship is His *Headship of Universal Authority.* This is the side of truth we are now considering. "We see not yet all things put under Him" (Heb 2:8), but all things will be, for it is God's "good pleasure, which He hath purposed in Himself". Christ will yet become the Source of all blessing in a universe of bliss, the Centre of many and varied circles of the elect and redeemed of all ages, the Object of universal contemplation and worship.

Well may this be called "the Mystery of His Will", for such a glorious climax had never "entered into the heart of man". That one born as a babe in a village stable, and afterward a homeless stranger in a despised province, rejected by His own nation and handed over by them to a foreign power, who killed Him by the cruel and shameful death of crucifixion, should prove to be the long-expected Messiah, the heir to David's throne, the Saviour of the world, and "God manifest in the flesh"; all this is truly wonderful and utterly incredible to the carnal mind. Yet it was all foretold in the Old Testament Scriptures and confirmed by angels at His birth; that His kingdom should stretch from sea to sea and from the river to the ends of the earth, that it should last as long as the sun and moon endure (Psa 72:8-17); that not only Israel, but the Gentiles, should bow beneath His sway, had been sung by the psalmists and prophets of old. But that His kingdom should have height as well as breadth, and be heavenly as well as earthly, should include "all things that are in heaven and that are in the earth", and be coterminous with the infinite universe of God, were surely surprising and altogether unlooked for developments, which go far beyond the highest thoughts of the saints of the Old Testament times. This is, however, the purpose of God for Him whom He delighteth to honour, for "He hath put all things under His feet and gave Him to be the Head over all things to the Church which is His body, the fullness of Him that filleth all in all" (Eph 1:22).

"Head over all things to the Church". All these glories He possesses for the advantage of the Church, who shall share with Him the inheritance. This she will enter on in association with Him when He comes. He will come to set up His kingdom, not as the messenger of peace, but to make war, and as the Stone cut without hands to crush the Gentile power; not to sprinkle them with His atoning blood, but to sprinkle His garments with their blood, as He takes vengeance on them. Thus the air will be cleared as after a terrific thunderstorm for the establishment of the Kingdom, in which all will be "headed up" in Christ. What the characteristics of His kingdom are, we shall now consider. (A more detailed treatment of this great subject is given at the beginning of this volume.)

The Kingdom of the Lord Jesus Christ

There are four things we may notice about the Kingdom of the Lord Jesus Christ, as it is presented in the Word. They are (1) its

Progressivity, (2) its Stability, (3) its Eternity, and (4) its Universality.

(1) The Kingdom will be Progressive. The Millenium – the dispensation of the kingdom glory – will be only a first stage. Then the Lord will reign "in the midst of His enemies" (see Psa 110:2). This stage corresponds rather with David's reign than with Solomon's. Satan will be chained, but sin will be present. The powers of death will be limited, but death itself not yet destroyed. Righteousness will first 'reign', but later on it will 'dwell' among men. As David's reign ended in rebellion and judgment, so will the millennium, for multitudes will only have yielded a "feigned obedience". Before Solomon's reign was finally established, judgment was executed on the Adonijahs, the Joabs, and the Shimeis. It will be only when Satan has been finally dealt with, the wicked dead judged, and all hostile powers, including death and hades, cast into the lake of fire, that the Lord Jesus will deliver up the kingdom to God. And this is not, as has been often taught, in the sense of relinquishing the reins of government, but in the sense of restoring and presenting it to God, purged from every sin and freed from every foe. But "of the increase of His government and peace there shall be no end...to order it and to establish it with judgment and with justice, from henceforth even for ever" (Isa 9:7).

(2) The Kingdom will be Stable. Do not the names of Him, on whose shoulders the government shall be, assure us of this? "His Name shall be called Wonderful, Counsellor, the Mighty God, the Everlasting Father, the Prince of Peace" (Isa 9:6). The stability of the universe will be guaranteed by the fact that He who holds the sceptre of the universe is "God manifest in the flesh".

There are four kinds of equilibrium known to us. The first is what is termed by scientists labial equilibrium, that is the condition existing in an infinite fluid. This may be taken as corresponding to the ultimate equilibrium guaranteed to the universe by the fact of the omnipotence of God. Then there is what is called neutral equilibrium, that of a ball, which is always in equilibrium, but only by being never really so. This is the condition of the fallen creature – the prey to every impulse – powerless, hopeless. Then there is what is known as unstable equilibrium, that of an object balanced from below, like a stick on the hand. Such was the equilibrium of the heavenly and earthly creations under the hegemony of the highest created beings in their particular sphere, Lucifer and Adam. This balance once lost can never right itself. The creature in responsibility, unless in dependence upon God, has always failed, but God has ever had His resource in "the Man of His right hand, the Son of Man whom He made strong for Himself" (Psa 80:17). This is stable equilibrium, that of an object sustained from above, as is a pendulum. However great the free oscillation may be, stability is secured. The stability of the universe will be guaranteed by the pierced Hand that will sustain it from above. And by that same Hand we can be sustained now. Sin can never again appear in the universe of God. And yet God's creatures will not cease to be free moral agents, but they will delight to glorify Him and do His will of their own free choice.

Exactly how this will be brought about, may not be absolutely clear. It is certain that all traces of evil nature will be removed from the redeemed. They will be holy as God is holy. They will hate sin, as He hates it. But besides this, I believe there will be two great deterrents ever present to the universe, one an eternal proof that "God is Light": the awful reality of an eternal hell – perpetual monument of the fearful effects of rebellion against God, of the justice and necessity of which all will be convinced; and the other an eternal proof that "God is Love", the blessed reality of an exalted Redeemer – the Lamb upon the Throne. "Wherefore we receiving a kingdom which cannot be moved, let us have grace whereby we may serve God acceptably with reverence and godly fear: for our God is a consuming fire." (Heb 12:29)

(3) The Kingdom of Christ will be Eternal. This is an all-important truth, and yet, strangely, it has been overlooked and even denied by some. It was noticed first, and with perfect reason, that the kingdom prophecies of the Old Testament could not be exhausted in the millennium, with sin and death still present realities. Then the verse already referred to, 1 Corinthians 15:24, "Then cometh the end, when He shall have delivered up the kingdom to God", was explained as necessarily meaning that after that point, the reign of Christ would cease. To meet the difficulty, a period called the "dispensation of the ages" was imagined and inserted between the end of the

millennium and the beginning of the eternal state. But this whole theory, known as "after the thousand years", is founded on a mistaken premise. "Delivering up the kingdom" does not mean "handing it over" but "presenting it to God". The same word is used in v.3, "I delivered unto you first of all", where it is evident that the apostle did not relinquish the gospel, which he presented to others. This act of Christ will take place immediately after the Great White Throne judgment, when He shall have put down all rule and all authority and power – of which the last is death itself (vv.24 and 26). Then the Lord will present the kingdom back in all its pristine, nay, in enhanced beauty to God. The "till" of v.25, does not limit His reign to the putting down of His enemies, but guarantees His power finally to put down these enemies. The expression, "the dispensation of the ages of the ages" is quite a fanciful one, as descriptive of any period short of Eternity, for "the ages of the ages" is the Greek idiom for Eternity, and nothing short of it. Words are merely counters. Usage stamps them with their value. It is surely something worse than silly to translate such an idiomatic phrase as "ages of the ages" literally, and yet that is what the 'Revisers' have done in their margin, and are thereby, I doubt not, largely responsible for the generally loosened hold of the solemn truth of eternal punishment among professing Christians. In Gal 1:5; Phil 4:20; 1 Tim 1:17; 2 Tim 4:8; Heb 13:21; Rev 1:6; 5:13; 7:12, where honour, glory, and dominion are ascribed to God, the RV has this subtle marginal gloss: 'Greek – to the ages of the ages': suggesting, though not affirming, that the Greek does not really mean 'for ever and for ever'. But we may ask, is there a vestige of a hint in any one of these places, that the glory of God is to be limited to a certain period? The same phrase is used of the judgment of the Great Whore (Rev 19:3), of the torments of Satan, the Beast and the False Prophet (20:10). And in 1:18; 4:9; 10:6; 15:7, of the existence of God and of Christ, where the same marginal gloss is inserted, 'Greek – unto the ages of the ages'. Do the Revisers then suggest that God's existence is not everlasting? Is it not clear that Eternity is stamped on every occurrence of the phrase? To this let us hold fast, for it is the Word of God.

The Eternal character of the Kingdom of Christ is further shown in the following Scriptures. The expression is applied in Revelation

11:15 to the reigning Christ, by the voices from heaven. "The kingdoms of this world are become the kingdom of our Lord, and of His Christ; and He shall reign for ever." And to the same truth we will call three other witnesses: (i) King David, speaking of the kingdom of One greater than Solomon writes, "They shall fear Thee as long as the sun and moon endure throughout all generations – His name shall endure for ever" (Psa 72:8-17). It is clear that the idea of the reign ending is specifically rejected. (ii) The prophet Daniel is the next witness. "In the days of these things the God of heaven shall set up a kingdom which shall never be destroyed, and the kingdom shall not be left to other people…and it shall stand for ever" (Dan 2:44). "His dominion is an everlasting dominion, which shall not pass away, and His kingdom that which shall not be destroyed" (7:14). (iii) The angel Gabriel confirms this, for he affirmed to the virgin Mary of her Firstborn, "He shall reign over the house of Jacob for ever, and of His kingdom there shall be no end" (Luke 1:33). There can, therefore, be no doubt of the everlasting character of the kingdom of Jesus Christ.

(4) The Kingdom will be Universal. It will include "all things that are in heaven and that are in earth" – that is, the whole moral universe of God. When it is a question of submission, "things under the earth" are added, for the infernal powers, the lost of angels and of men will be included, but such will be forever excluded from the kingdom. Those who teach that some Christians will be excluded too, on account of a lack of faithfulness, really shut them out from salvation for ever, for the kingdom is only another term for the heavenly state. All believers will by grace enter into that kingdom "which God hath prepared for them that love Him", but their place in that Kingdom will vary with the dispensation in which each has lived and with their individual faithfulness. But Christ in all things will have the pre-eminence. He will be crowned with many diadems, and without one discordant note, the whole universe of bliss will proclaim His worthiness and His praise. And this will continue for ever.

"And every creature which is in heaven and in earth, and under the earth,[35] and such as are in the sea, heard I saying, Blessing and

---

[35] Quite a distinct expression from that already referred to in Phil 2:10.

honour and glory and power be unto Him that sitteth upon the throne, and unto the Lamb for ever and ever. And the four living creatures said Amen! And the four and twenty elders fell down and worshipped Him that liveth for ever and ever." (Rev 5:13-14)

"Now unto Him that is able to do exceeding abundantly above all that we ask or think, according to the power that worketh in us, unto Him be glory in the Church by Christ Jesus, throughout all ages, world without end. Amen." (Eph 3:20-21)

The Seven Covenants of Holy Scripture

INTRODUCTION

Human covenants are mutual compacts, between two or more parties, in which certain conditions are agreed upon and recorded. They are solemn enough matters, for "though it be but a man's covenant, yet if it be confirmed, no man disannulleth or addeth thereto" (Gal 3:15). How much more solemn and binding are Divine Covenants! It is no light matter to make a covenant with God, for, given man's inherent weakness and sinfulness, he can never keep his side of the compact. Covenants of works lead to inevitable disaster. But the true covenants of God are covenants of grace, which will stand for ever "ordered in all things and sure", for they rest on the work of the Messiah.

1. THE NOAHIC COVENANT

"The Lord thy God He is God, the faithful God, which keepeth covenant and mercy" (Deut 7:9).

The first covenant we read of in the Scriptures is the NOAHIC (Gen 7 and 9). The patriarch had just come forth from the ark. He had not been preserved from "the evil to come", like Enoch, figure of the Church, but had been brought through it in safety by Divine power as the remnant of Israel will be brought through the Tribulation of the last days (Luke 21:36). Now God makes a covenant with him, yet not with him or his seed alone, but with the whole earth.

Noah's first act was no doubt inspired of God. He built an altar to Jehovah and offered up burnt offerings of every kind; perfect expression of the sacrifice of Christ, to be offered 2,000 years later. The burnt offering speaks of the death of the Lord Jesus in its voluntary character and perfect acceptability to God. And "the Lord smelled a sweet savour", for He knew the meaning of Noah's sacrifice, and whatever men or demons may make of it, the offering of Christ at Calvary is always to Him "a sweet-smelling savour" (Eph 5:2).

This formed the basis of two things, blessing to Noah and his family, and a covenant which has been the ground ever since of providential mercies to the whole creation. Never again would the ground be cursed for man's sake or every living thing smitten by a flood. This covenant was one of pure grace, that is, no condition was attached to it; for the Lord knew that the imagination of man's heart was "the same as before, evil from his youth".

Now God controls the whole realm of nature for the benefit of His creatures. The orderly sequences of times and seasons; sunshine, rain, the fruits of the earth may be enjoyed alike by the just and the unjust, by the thankful and the evil. The very breath with which men deny the work of Christ or blaspheme His holy name is a fruit of the covenant of grace.

Another result was the restoration to man of effective control over the animal kingdom. Their flesh, too, was given him to eat, after 2,000 years of vegetarian diet. More important still the responsibilities of government, with powers of life and death, were placed in his hand, so that the violence of antediluvian days might be restrained. Three marks attach to this covenant.

1. Its Universal Character
It was with mankind as such, and the animal kingdom had their share in it. It was a covenant between "God and the whole earth" (Gen 9:13).

2. Its Enduring Character
It is termed an everlasting covenant and is said to be "for perpetual generations". It holds good today in all its essential features.

3. Its Ratification by an Outward Token
Possibly rain had never fallen before the flood (see Gen 2:5, 6). Now the rainbow appears as a token of the covenant. Millions have admired that beautiful sight, who have failed to appreciate its significance, but we are sure it has never failed to speak to God of His covenant.

We read of the rainbow in Ezekiel 1:28, and again in the closing book of Holy Scripture – it adorns God's throne in Revelation 4 and the mighty angel's brow in ch.10. Is not this intended to show that, even in those terrible days when all nature will seem out of joint and the very powers of heaven will be shaken, the Noahic covenant will stand, and God in wrath will remember mercy?

2. THE ABRAHAMIC COVENANT
"The Lord was gracious unto them ... because of His covenant with Abraham, Isaac and Jacob" (2 Kings 13:23).

The next covenant was the ABRAHAMIC. It was a covenant of pure grace, based on sacrifice, and everlasting, but differing materially from the previous one in being made, not with mankind as a whole, but with a chosen family.

Man under government after the Flood proved no less a failure than when left to his conscience before the Flood. When he knew God (as the descendants of Noah did) he "glorified Him not as God ...but became vain in his imaginations" (Rom 1:21). Two of the vainest of these ideas were to unite the race and get themselves a name apart from God, which led to their being broken in fragments, and another was to make gods like themselves and the beasts (see Joshua 24:14; Romans1:21,23), which led to the calling out of Abraham from the surrounding corruption to be the depository of the promises, and the father of a chosen nation and of that Seed, through whom all the families of the earth should be blessed, even Jesus Christ our Lord, son of David and of Abraham.

The promises of Jehovah to Abraham were certainly attractive to faith. "I will make of thee a great nation, and I will bless thee, and make thy name great; and thou shalt be a blessing: and I will bless them that bless thee, and curse him that curseth thee; and in thee shall all families of the earth be blessed" (Gen 12:2-3). Certain of these principles have been illustrated in the Great Wars. Those two arch-oppressors of the seed of Abraham, Russia and Romania, have been greatly humbled, and Great Britain, who, with all her faults, has in the main befriended Israel, has been chosen to deliver "the land" from the ghoulish rule of the Sublime Porte.

When Abraham reached his goal, yet another promise was added: "Unto thy seed I will give this land". This was again enlarged when Lot had 'picked the best' of the land, as men would say, and had gone his way. "Look from the place where thou art, northward and southward and eastward and westward: for all the land which thou seest, to thee will I give it and to thy seed for ever. And I will make thy seed as the dust of the earth" (Gen 13:14-16).

> "God always gives the best to those
> Who leave the choice with Him."

As God's covenant with Noah has formed the basis since of His providential dealings with the human race, so His covenant with Abraham has been the determining factor in His dealings in grace with the chosen nation.

To it His eye reverts and His word recurs. Centuries might leave it in abeyance; the Sinaitic covenant, four hundred and thirty years after, might seem to supersede it; ages of failure, culminating in the rejection of Messiah, might succeed one another, followed by ages of dispersion and tribulation; but nothing can disannul the Abrahamic covenant or "make the promise of none effect". The reason is, it was typically sealed by the blood of Christ, or to use the words of Galatians 3:17, "It was confirmed before of God in Christ". This expression is worthy of earnest pondering. How eloquently it sets forth the sanctity of that covenant in the eyes of God! Israel was loved for the fathers' sake. But on what ground were the fathers loved? For Christ's sake; for the covenant was endorsed in His blood. The giving of this covenant is described in Genesis 15 and 17. They are not two covenants, though the chapters are separated by more than 14 years, but one in two stages. This covenant is referred to again and again in the Scriptures as one and indivisible; as for instance in 2 Kings 13:23, "The Lord was gracious unto them ... because of His covenant [not covenants] with Abraham". (See also 1 Chron 16:16.) Chapter 17 amplifies and confirms chapter 15.

The occasion of its promulgation was the renewal to Abraham of the promise of an heir. His future seed is compared no longer to the dust of the earth, as in 13:16, but to the stars of heaven. This goes farther than a literal seed and higher than earthly blessing.

Those who will have followed the faith-steps of Abraham, in a past or future dispensation and will have passed from this scene, will no doubt share in heavenly blessing. They will have a place and portion in the heavenly side of the Kingdom – the New Jerusalem, "the city which hath foundations, whose builder and maker is God", for which Abraham looked. No doubt the Church will have her place there too, but her portion will be distinct. The Church will be in the city, but she is not, I judge, the City. The faithful remnant of Israel, who survive "the day of Jacob's trouble", will enjoy earthly blessings in the millennial earth. They will form the nucleus of future generations of that Holy Kingdom of Priests which Israel will be for ever.

Abraham was, of course, the father of all his descendants according to the flesh, but not all were his true seed. He rejoiced to see the day of Christ and "he saw it and was glad". How could men like the unbelieving Jews of our Lord's day, who hated the One he loved, be the true children of Abraham? No, such "say they are Jews and are not", but are "the synagogue of Satan", for they reject their anointed King.

Abraham, however, "believed God and it was counted unto him for righteousness". Nor was this recorded for his sake alone, but "for us also to whom it shall be imputed, if we believe on Him that raised up Jesus our Lord from the dead; who was delivered for our offences, and was raised again for our justification" (Rom 4:24,25). Abraham is the father of the faithful, be they Israelite or Gentile.

This act of faith led on to the renewal of the promise of the inheritance and to its confirmation by a solemn covenant over slain victims. In the predatory assault on these by the fowls of the air we may see Satan opposing the dedication of the covenant, as later in Egypt he opposed its realisation. How gladly he would have snatched away by violence the Christ of God before the appointed hour, or bound Him in the grave after its expiration! In the darkest hour, symbol of that deepest trial which is yet to fall on Israel, the presence of Jehovah passed between the sacrifices, as a furnace to try and a lamp to guide. When man passes between the victims it is his covenant and he undertakes to keep it. Dire collapse can only result (see Jer 34:18). How indeed can man presume to make a covenant with God? and yet that is the essence of all man's religion. He has forfeited his right to live. He cannot meet God's claim for the past, nor His requirements for the future. But Christ, in His life, the perfectly obedient One, "pours out His soul unto death" (Isa 53:12) as the covenant victim. His blood meets all the delinquencies of His people; His life in resurrection guarantees to them every covenant blessing.

In Genesis 15:18-21, the blessings to the literal seed are rigidly limited to the possession of the land from the river of Egypt to the Euphrates, including the territories of ten peoples. It is remarkable how the number ten crops up in the last days in connection with Israel. Her last great foe will be a certain ten-kingdomed "league of nations" (Rev 17:12 ; Zech 8:23).

The tract of country described here, covers a vast triangle, larger than a slice of Southern India cut off from Bombay to Madras. 2 Chronicles 9:26 tells us that Solomon reigned over all this area, but this was probably more in the sense of suzerainty, than of effective occupation; a large proportion of the land then being desert, but one day "the desert shall blossom as the rose", and then "the house of Jacob shall possess their possessions" (Obad 17). In Genesis 17 we have the amplification of this. It might have come sooner had not Abraham, at the suggestion of Sarah, attempted to force God's promise in a fleshly way. We cannot hurry God's purposes by carnal devices, though we may delay our enjoyment of them.

Abram now becomes Abraham, for he is the father of many nations; kings would come out of him; the covenant is to be everlasting and the possession too; and best of all, El-Shaddai pledges Himself to be the God of Abraham and of his seed.

In Genesis 17 down to v. 9, God reveals to Abraham what He will do; "I will make My covenant"; "I will establish"; "I will give", etc. All this is of pure grace – God the Giver; man only the recipient. But at v. 9 there is an apparent break, "Thou shalt keep My covenant". Does this introduce the legal principle of earning blessing by works? Were it so, neither the covenant, nor the possession of the land could be everlasting.

How then had Abraham to keep the covenant? By submitting to a rite which would bring him within its scope and remind his seed, as the rainbow does mankind, of the promises. This was no token in the sky, but a sign in the flesh, the rite of circumcision.

Circumcision was not a legal ordinance, but a token of the national covenant of grace: "It shall be a token of the covenant betwixt Me and you" (v. 11), and a distinguishing mark between Israel and the nations around. As our Lord reminds His hearers (John 7:22), it was not of Moses (that is in direct connection with the Sinaitic covenant) but of the fathers.

In fact it rose above the requirements of the law, in that, if necessary to its administration, the Sabbath might be broken, without a violation of the commandment. Stephen indeed calls the Abrahamic covenant "the covenant of circumcision" (Acts 7:8). In apostolic days it is true the ordinance became the badge of Judaizing teachers, who desired to "make a fair show in the flesh", "avoid persecution for the cross of Christ", and allure Gentile converts into the fold of a Christ-rejecting Judaism, of which the corner stone was the strict observance of the Mosaic law (Acts 15; Gal 6:12,13). That being so, we can understand the apostle's words, "If ye be circumcised Christ shall profit you nothing"; "Every man that is circumcised is a debtor to do the whole law". The rite was for these teachers a legal ordinance, necessary for salvation, as baptism is for thousands in Christendom today, but in its institution it could have nothing to do with a law given 400 years later.

How then did circumcision affect the position of Abraham? Abraham was justified before circumcision, "that he might be the father of all them that believe, though they be not circumcised"; "and he received the sign of circumcision, a seal of the righteousness of the faith, which he had yet been uncircumcised ... that he might be the father of circumcision to them who are not of the circumcision only but who also walk in the steps of that faith of our father Abraham, which he had being yet uncircumcised" (Rom 4:11,12).

In Christ Jesus it is not circumcision which avails anything, or uncircumcision, but "faith which worketh by love", and a "new creature" (Gal 5:6; 6:15). Uncircumcision does not exclude from blessing, if faith be present; circumcision does not include for blessing, if faith be absent.

Some have sought to justify infant baptism by the analogy of circumcision, and they point to the phrase quoted above, "a seal of the righteousness, etc". They say if circumcision was administered to babes, why not also baptism, letting it be to them the seal of the new covenant, as circumcision was of the old? But circumcision was never called "the seal of the covenant", but of Abraham's righteousness.

Moreover, a child of Jewish parents was a true Jew, and God commanded him to be circumcised. But the child of christian parents must be "born again" to become a true Christian, and then, but not till then, is he qualified for baptism. Baptism is indeed for children, but of a different order – newborn babes in the family of God. And there is no command of God to baptise any other kind.

Circumcision for Abraham was indeed "the seal of the righteousness of the faith which he had yet being uncircumcised", but this was only true of him or of any "justified" members of his household, circumcised with him, as also of truly righteous proselytes since. How could such a phrase apply to Isaac or any other Jewish babe down the ages, who had neither faith nor righteousness when circumcised? Baptism is never called in the Bible a seal of anything. The seal of Christianity is not an outward ordinance, however spiritual, but the indwelling Spirit (Eph 1:13). Circumcision admitted to the privileges of the Covenant people, apart from moral condition. A Korah could eat the Passover, if ceremonially clean, equally with a Moses, but the rite was intended to be followed later by a circumcision of the heart, without which he was no true Israelite. "He is a Jew, which is one inwardly; and circumcision is that of the heart, in the spirit, and not in the letter; whose praise is not of men, but of God" (Rom 2:29). How many who bear the name of Jew are thus disqualified, for, "uncircumcised in hearts and ears", they reject their Messiah – the Lord Jesus. But someone may say, "In baptising a child we too look forward to something deeper, the baptism in the Spirit." But Peter tells us this was to precede water baptism, and that the essence of this latter is "the answer of a good conscience towards God". Clearly an infant, having no conscience, cannot have "the answer of a good one" (Acts 10:47; 1 Pet 3:21).

One point in conclusion. Christians are said to be "circumcised in Christ with the circumcision made without hands, in putting off the body of the flesh (RV) by the circumcision of Christ" (Col 2:11). This cannot refer to the Jewish rite, to which our Lord as an infant was subjected, for that affects us directly in no way, but to the Cross. There He was cut off, and we in Him. Circumcision seems to recognise something bad in man, the Cross proclaims there is nothing good in him. Baptism sets forth our share in that cutting-off, and our burial and resurrection with and in Christ.

3. THE SINAITIC COVENANT
"Cursed be the man that obeyeth not the words of this covenant" (Jer 11:3).

This covenant, though historically the third between God and Man, is called in the Hebrews, "the first" (e.g. 9:1), because it is the first made with Israel, constituted as a nation, and in contrast with the "new covenant" with them yet to come.

It is important to note that God's ways with Israel in Egypt and their deliverance therefrom, were on the ground of the Covenant of promise. Moses reminds them of this forty years later, "The Lord did not set His love upon you, nor choose you, because ye were more in number than any people; for ye were the fewest of any people: but because the Lord loved you, and because He would keep the oath, which He had sworn unto your fathers, hath the Lord brought you out with a mighty hand and redeemed you" (Deut 7:7,8). Be they by birth Jew or Briton, God's people today need reminding that His sovereign choice has found no reason in them personally or nationally for its exercise. Pride of race has no place in the Church of God. "For Christ's sake" is the password to blessing for all, and the only one. In the case of Israel, however, national position was a very real privilege for the earth. This is borne out by what happened in Egypt. When the time of the promise drew nigh, the people cried unto God in their affliction and "God heard their groaning, and God remembered His covenant with Abraham, with Isaac, and with Jacob, and God looked upon the children of Israel and God had respect unto them" (Exod 2:24,25).

And not only were they brought out of the house of bondage by grace, but by grace they were led from the brick-kilns of Egypt to the slopes of Sinai. Though they murmured against Jehovah at the Red Sea, Marah, Sin, and Rephidim, He withheld His judgements, provided for their wants and protected them from the Egyptians and from Amalek. This treatment again rested on the Abrahamic covenant, and we might have thought the same principle would have sufficed them for the whole wilderness journey. So it would for their worldly ease and comfort, but as for their spiritual advancement it would have left them where it found them. Mere grace spoils, but does not soften unrepentant sinners, they need a "schoolmaster[1] unto Christ". God knew from the first what was in man; they must learn it too.

At Sinai then a new principle is introduced – privilege as the reward of obedience. Moses conveys to the people a new message from Jehovah, "Ye have seen what I did unto the Egyptians, and how I bare you on eagles' wings and brought you unto Myself [so much for the past, now for the future], now therefore, if ye will, obey My voice indeed and keep My covenant, then shall ye be a peculiar treasure unto Me above all people for all the earth is Mine [that is, in choosing Israel as His peculiar people, Jehovah did not relinquish His claims over the nations, nor cease to exercise toward them His providential care], and ye shall be unto Me a kingdom of priests and an holy nation" (Exod 19:4-6).

Now here we must guard against a very serious misunderstanding: obedience for the people of God today – the Church – is the condition of blessing, if it is to be enjoyed in the soul. There is nothing legal about the word commandment. It is perfectly evangelical. Because we are not "under the law", we are "not without law to Christ". "His commandments are not grievous", but they are realities. But it is His life communicated to us by the Holy Spirit, which makes us capable of obedience. It is a most unhealthy principle and one, it is feared, far too common, to make the grace of God an excuse for self-will. Fancy the returned prodigal excusing himself from obedience to his father on the ground that all was of grace. Yes, but that grace had bound him hand and foot to his father. These are truths for men in the spirit – regenerated and indwelt by the Spirit, and are perfectly compatible with a covenant of grace. But Israel was a nation in flesh. No doubt there were many truly godly

---

[1] The word is Pedagogue–the Greek word has the sense of a severe tutor, not a "teacher", which is a quite distinct word.

men among them, but nationally they were upon the earth-plane, and what was really needed in them was "repentance from dead works and faith toward God".

But man in the flesh, religious man even, does not perceive this. He considers himself perfectly capable of obeying the commandments of God, as he is. So man is to have the opportunity of showing what he is worth. This is the meaning of Sinai. It is true that left to himself, to the light of nature and conscience, man had proved a bad failure and filled the earth with violence and corruption. It is true that, under the restraint of government, he had failed to glorify God and had given himself over to idolatry. But surely, could he receive a succinct compendium of the Divine will in the shape of a code of laws from heaven, he would be able to glorify his God. The people at any rate did not shrink from the test, without so much as waiting to hear the terms of the covenant, they all answered together and said, "All that the Lord hath spoken we will do." It may remind us of another scene in the history of the same people, when with one voice they all cried out, "Let Him be crucified." Unanimously they accepted the law; unamimously they rejected their Messiah.

At once a notable change takes place in the attitude of Jehovah to Israel. Instead of bearing them on eagles' wings, He sets for them bounds; instead of bringing them to Himself, He retires to a distance; instead of covering them with a protecting cloud, He covers Himself in thunders and lightnings and thick clouds; instead of the voice of their Saviour-God, the voice of the trumpet exceeding loud, speaking of divine demands, peals forth, "so that all the people that was in the camp trembled". All this clearly marked the eternal principle that "the law worketh wrath", and that by the deeds of the law can no flesh be justified nor draw near to God. "But what the law could not do in that it was weak through the flesh, God sending His own Son", did (Rom 8:3). "The law was given by Moses, but grace and truth came by Jesus Christ" (John 1:17).

That the ministry of the law was glorious was shown by the shining of Moses' face when he came down from Sinai; but that that glory was transitory ("for the law made nothing perfect") was evidenced by the fading away of the brightness. The glory of God in the face of Jesus Christ is no transient shining, for the glory of His ministry is perennial and permanent. Another thing marked the temporary character of the Sinaitic Covenant. It was made without an oath, and this in contrast with the Noahic, of which we read: "As I have sworn that the waters of Noah shall no more go over the earth" (Isa 54:9), and the Abrahamic, which was confirmed with an oath (Gen 22:16; Jer 9:8). Why this difference? God's oath marks the subject of it as immutable and lasting, and is intended to convey "strong consolation to the heirs of promise" (Heb 6:17). 'For God, whate'er our changes, for ever is the same', and "it is impossible for Him to lie".

But could a covenant, resting on the obedience of man, be permanent? It was powerless to bring into blessing: indeed the absence of oath might in such a case be a consolation, for that would leave room for the bringing in of a better covenant. The only oath to Israel in the wilderness was: "They shall not enter into My rest", and this was the outcome of a covenant of works. Now this covenant was a new departure in the ways of God, as Moses reminded Israel: "The Lord made not this covenant with our fathers, but with us, even us, who are all of us here alive this day" (Deut 5:3). Why, seeing it was so ineffective for blessing, was it allowed to supersede, even temporarily, the covenant of grace? In other words: "Wherefore then serveth the law? It was added because of transgressions, till the seed should come, to whom the promises were made" (Gal 3:19). "Because of transgressions" means "for the sake of transgressions". Law aggravates the character of sin. Sin against law becomes transgression, with an added heinousness of guilt. Not only so, but it actually multiplies offences: "The law entered that the offence might abound" (Rom 5:20). So evil is man that prohibition arouses dormant passion, "Sin, taking occasion by the commandment, wrought in me all manner of concupiscence. I had not known sin, but by the law. For without the law sin was dead" (Rom 7:7,8). The law reveals sins. "By the law is the knowledge of sin" (Rom 3:20). Its function is, like a standard, to reveal, not heal, shortcomings, or as a mirror to show, not cleanse, impurities. It exacts the penalty. It curses but never cures. How sad and futile a thing it is for man to put himself under law, either for forgiveness or holiness! Christ alone can avail; His precious blood to save from the penalty of sin; His risen life from its power.

Israel, however, knew nothing of their own inability, and promised all obedience, possibly quite sincerely; but broke down at once in the matter of the golden calf. And each renewal of the legal covenant in their subsequent history only led to fresh and deeper failure. The renewal of the covenant under Hezekiah (2 Chron 29:10) was followed by the abominations of Manasseh; that under Josiah (2 Chron 34:31) to three ungodly reigns and the Babylonish captivity; and that under Nehemiah (Neh 9:38) to the declension deplored by Malachi, and to the rejection of the Messiah. The law said: "Love the Lord thy God, and thy neighbour as thyself"; but when God came down in perfect grace in the person of the Lord Jesus, and dwelt as neighbour among men, they hated and slew Him. The breaking of the first tables of the covenant by Moses on the Mount was a symbolical act, significant of the fact that the law itself being broken in one point, was broken in all. The second tables were placed in the ark of shittim wood, and there they were safe, for that ark represented the Lord in His spotless humanity, "made under the law" as a true Israelite. "He magnified it and made it honourable" by a perfect obedience. He "loved God with all His heart and His neighbour as Himself" - so far He acted for Himself to the glory of God. Then He recognised the righteous claims of the law on all under it (none of whom had continued in all things written therein), by dying on the tree. "Christ hath redeemed us from the curse of the law", writes the apostle Paul, "by being made a curse for us" (Gal 3:13). The law is not responsible in any way for man's failure. It is holy. The first covenant was faulty, but the fault was in man. The law was weak through the flesh. Like a lever of steel on a fulcrum of sand, it found nothing in man to work upon. The effect of the legal covenant was, as we have seen, to repel Israel to a distance from Jehovah. "They removed and stood afar off." How could they be brought back into relation with Jehovah and enjoy the privilege of being "a people near unto Him"? (Psa 148:14). And how could He go on with them after their worship of the golden calf. Why were they not cut off as a nation? Exodus 24 contains the answer to the first of these questions. Here we have a wonderful transformation scene; a change of weather, a new attitude of Jehovah to the people; an altered behaviour of the people toward Jehovah.

In chapter 19 "there were thunders and lightnings and a thick cloud upon the Mount ... and Mount Sinai was altogether on a smoke, because the Lord descended upon it in fire ... and the whole mount quaked greatly". It was very bad weather that day; perhaps no worse was ever known. But in chapter 24 there is a change, the mists have rolled away; the thunders have ceased; all is calm and peaceful. "And they saw the God of Israel, and there was under His feet as it were a paved work of a sapphire stone, and as it were the body of heaven in his clearness" (v.10). The glory of God (though no similitude was seen) shone forth in a cloudless sky of sapphire blue. This remarkable change in weather conditions was the result of a still more wonderful change in the attitude of Jehovah. In ch. 19 bounds had been set by His command at the base of Sinai, and no one, on pain of death, might set foot on it. Now Moses and Aaron, Nadab and Abihu, and seventy of the elders went up that same mount, and instead of cutting them off in judgement, "upon the nobles of the children of Israel He laid not His hand", for they were His invited guests. A change in the behaviour of the people was the result here as before, "all the people that were in the camp (including Moses) trembled", the elders of Israel now had confidence, in the presence of Jehovah. "They saw God and did eat and drink." How account for all this?

A strange peculiarity, common to all Israel in the plain and to their representatives in the Mount, might be seen at a glance: their garments were all spotted with blood. That blood came from the covenant victims. Half had been sprinkled on the altar, there meeting Jehovah's righteous requirements, and the other half was sprinkled in part on the book of the covenant, signifying that the claims of its every sentence, crying for obedience or the death penalty, had been fully met. The antitype of this we have in Colossians 2:14, representing one aspect of the death of Christ, "Blotting out the handwriting of ordinances that was against us, which was contrary to us, and took it out of the way, nailing it to His cross". After this the rest of the blood was sprinkled on the people. Israel was thus linked with the sacrifice. Each bore on his person the mark of death; for if blood, coursing in the veins, is the life of the body, it always means death when shed. Moses' words, when he sprinkled it, were significant: "Behold the blood of the covenant, which the Lord hath made with you concerning these words". It was by that blood Israel entered into covenant relation with Jehovah. Though the covenant of works could never guarantee blessing, the blood of the covenant victim did. It is true that Christ died "to gather together in one the children of God which are scattered abroad", but He died also in a peculiar sense for Israel – the only nation, as such, that was ever in covenant relation with God (John 11:50-52). It was then the blood of the covenant which brought Israel ceremonially near to God.

The second question is, Why did not Jehovah cut off the people from being a nation, when they set up the golden calf? In Exodus 32:10, the Lord said unto Moses: "Let Me alone, that My wrath may wax hot against them, and I will make of thee a great nation." This was doubtless to test Moses, for He Himself knew what He would do. And Moses knew the ways of the Lord. Like the true Advocate, of whom he was the type, he alleged no merit in the offending people, no extenuating circumstances, no promise of future amendment, but reminded God of His glory and His covenant. His name would be dishonoured among the Egyptians, and what would become of His covenant to the fathers? "Remember Abraham, Isaac, and Israel, Thy servants to whom Thou swearest, etc." That was enough; for that covenant of grace had never been abrogated. It still held good, though in a modified and hidden way. Dispensationally and governmentally Israel was under a covenant of works, but the law could not disannul the covenant of grace, which had been confirmed of God in Christ with Abraham four hundred and thirty years before (Gal 3:17). But though the people were not cut off, they were chastened governmentally by a plague, and Jehovah withdrew "without the camp, afar off from the camp". He could not go on in their midst at the expense of His holiness (Exod 33:3,7).

This leads to our third question, How could Jehovah once more resume His place in the midst of His people? For that He did so is evident, when later His glory filled the Tabernacle (Exod 40:34). It was on the ground of sacrifice, which was at once instituted, and especially of the blood-stained mercy-seat. On that the eye of Jehovah could ever rest with satisfaction, for it spoke of Christ meeting all His holy claims in death. Beneath, in the ark, lay hidden the unbroken tables of the law and over it the Shekinah shone forth.

The covenant of works was solemnly renewed forty years later in the land of Moab. "These are the words of the covenant, which the Lord commanded Moses to make with the children of Israel in the land of Moab, besides the covenant which He made with them in Horeb" (Deut 29:1). This "besides" is remarkable, but cannot mean there were two covenants of works; but only that besides the giving of the law at Sinai, it was repeated and renewed for the new generation, just before they entered Canaan. There were no thunders and lightnings, but the occasion was a solemn one. Blessings were promised to obedience, but what bulked much more largely were the curses threatened to disobedience, with warnings of fearful judgements to come. But warnings proved as powerless as thunders to secure legal obedience. Israel under the law proved as great a failure in the land as in the wilderness. They that are in the flesh cannot please God. The new birth is necessary, that Christ may be "all and in all".

To the Sinaitic, as to the two former covenants, a sign was attached; not in the sky, nor in the flesh, but in the week–the Sabbath day. "Wherefore the children of Israel shall keep the sabbath...for a perpetual covenant. It is a sign between Me and the children of Israel for ever" (Exod 31:13). It was for them a weekly remembrance of the covenant and they were to remember to keep it holy. "Remember" cannot have here the retrospective sense of "continue to observe", for the Sabbath was instituted now for the first time. The words in Genesis 2:3, "God blessed the seventh day and hallowed it", were not addressed to Adam in the beginning, but through Moses 2,500 years later, primarily no doubt to Israel, for whom the Sabbath was instituted. No instance occurs of its observance by the patriarchs either before the deluge or up to Sinai. Such an institution as "the christian Sabbath" is also quite foreign to the New Testament.

When a Jew today becomes a member of the Church of God, he ceases to be of "the Jew's religion". He now knows Christ in resurrection and the first day of the week becomes his day of remembrance. Then it is he assembles with the Church to break bread in remembrance of Christ (Acts 20:7). The Sabbath rest was on the seventh day, the reward of six days of labour; the Lord's Day begins the week, and tells of rest in Christ, before one work can be done for God. To use the Lord's Day merely for pleasure or self-interest is "the straw which shows in what quarter the wind blows", a clear symptom of alienation from God, and marks the rebel. But to think to improve "a sinner of the Gentiles" by putting him under the Sabbath law, is like catching a straw to change the wind, or clipping a Upas tree to get grapes. Man needs repentance toward God and faith in our Lord Jesus Christ. He must be born again, then fruit for God will result.

4. THE LEVITICAL COVENANT
"My covenant was with him (Levi) of life and peace" (Mal 2:5).

This is a covenant within a covenant, made not with all Israel, but with a tribe. Two persons stand out pre-eminently in the sin of Baal Peor: the prophet Balaam and the priest Phinehas; the one, who brought down wrath on Israel, as a warning against covetousness; the other, who by his zeal turned away that wrath, as a monument of faithfulness. He did what others cared not or dared not do, and probably had scant recognition from man, but God approved (see Psa 106:31) and rewarded him too; "Behold, I give unto him My covenant of peace...even the covenant of an everlasting priesthood" (Num 25:12,13). This covenant had been already made with the tribe of Levi, as we learn from Malachi: "My covenant was with Levi of life and peace, and I gave them to him for the fear wherewith he feared Me" (2:5).

Here is a remarkable instance of sovereign grace. There was nothing in the beginnings of the tribe to justify such a hope. Indeed, the scathing words of Jacob seemed to preclude it: "Simeon and Levi are brethren. Instruments of cruelty are in their habitations... cursed be their anger, for it was fierce, and their wrath, for it was cruel. I will divide them in Jacob and scatter them in Israel" (Gen 49:5-7). Could prospect seem more hopeless? But God can turn cursings into blessings. The first hint of future blessing to Levi was the faith of Amram and Jochebed and the call of their sons, Moses and Aaron. Again at Rephidim, though in a hidden way, God had Levi specially in view: "Thy holy one, whom thou didst prove at Massah, and with whom thou didst strive at the waters of Meribah"

(Deut 33:8). But the episode of the golden calf was the vital crisis. Then they definitely turned to God. In answer to Moses' question: "Who is on the Lord's side? (not on my side), let him come unto me", the sons of Levi gathered themselves together unto him, and when commanded "to slay every man his brother and every man his companion", they obeyed. That brought Jehovah's blessing at once, and was remembered forty years later by Moses in his parting words: "Who said unto his father and to his mother I have not seen him, neither did he acknowledge his brethren...for they have observed Thy word and kept Thy covenant" (Deut 33:9). A similar condition of discipleship exists today (Luke 14:26). Happy they who love Christ first of all!

The blessing referred to in Exodus 32:29, seems to correspond to the covenant of Malachi 2, but God's purpose had already been revealed on Sinai. "Take thou unto thee Aaron thy brother and his sons...that he may minister unto Me in the priest's office" (Exod 28:1). The Levites were equally set apart: "At that time the Lord separated the tribe of Levi to bear the ark of the covenant of the Lord" (Deut 10:8).

This covenant was an everlasting covenant. The priesthood failed under Eli and his sons (1 Sam 2:27), and later on in the person of Abiathar; but though the priesthood was transferred to Zadok, of the younger branch, it never left the line of Phinehas. "The priests, the Levites, shall never want a man before Me to offer burnt-offerings ...Thus saith the Lord, if ye can break My covenant of the day, then may also My covenant be broken...with the Levites the priests, My ministers" (Jer 33:18-21). Though the tribe of Levi is merged in the Jewish people today, Jehovah's "Covenant of Salt" (Lev 2:13; Num 18:19) will not fail. He will know His true priests and Levites in the coming kingdom (Isa 56:6), and they will still be sons of Zadok, faithful while others turned to idolatry (Ezek 43:19; 44:15). The Levitical priesthood is for earthly places, the christian one for heavenly; that was the monopoly of a tribe, this the prerogative of all believers; that bestowed material privileges (e.g. Lev 24:8,9), this heavenly blessings. Aaron was called of God to a place of honour, but his sons might not enter the holy of holies; Christ "hath obtained a more excellent ministry", and His priests can draw nigh into the

Holiest by His blood. Aaron could not, by reason of death, continue his priesthood, but Christ can save to the uttermost ... seeing "He ever liveth to make intercession for us" (Heb 7:25).

5. THE DAVIDIC COVENANT

"I have made a covenant with My chosen, I have sworn unto David My servant" (Psa 89:3).

This is distinguished by the fact that it was not made with the nation, though the faithful portion will share in it (Isa 55:3), nor yet with a tribe, but with an individual – David and his seed after him. Jacob, in blessing his sons, had foretold: "The Sceptre shall not depart from Judah...until Shiloh come; and unto Him shall the gathering of the people be" (Gen 49:10). The birthright forfeited by Reuben passed by Judah; yet in one respect he prevailed over his brethren: "Of him came the chief ruler" (marg., prince) (1 Chron 5:2). This was a sure word of prophecy concerning the Messiah, but not a covenant.

The covenant was made later with David: "whom God had taken from the sheepcote...to be ruler over His people" (2 Sam 7:8). David had desired to build a house for Jehovah, but Jehovah covenanted to build him a house. "The Lord telleth thee that He will make thee an house...I will set up thy seed after thee...and I will establish his kingdom. He shall build a house for My name and I will establish the throne of his kingdom for ever...If he commit iniquity I will chasten him...but My mercy shall not depart from him" (v. 11-15). Here the seed is Solomon. In spite of his grievous departures, the dynasty never failed, as again and again in Israel. In the parallel passage in 1 Chronicles 17 the reference to possible failure is omitted, because here the seed is Christ, and it is from this chapter that the quotation is taken in Hebrews 1:5, proving the Lord to be higher than the angels.

These promises to David are referred to as a Covenant in Psalm 89:3: "I have made a covenant with My chosen. I have sworn unto David My servant"..."I will build up thy throne to all generations...I will make him My firstborn, higher than the kings of the earth. My mercy will I keep for him for evermore, and My word will I not break, nor alter the thing that is gone out of My lips. Once have I sworn by

My holiness that I will not lie unto David. His seed shall endure for ever, and his throne as the sun before Me. It shall be established for ever as the moon, and as a faithful witness in heaven" (v. 27-37). This is clearly Messianic.

Several important points in this covenant are emphasised: (a) Its *enduring character*. It will be "to all generations", "for evermore". Abijah reminds Jeroboam that "the Lord God of Israel gave the kingdom over Israel to David for ever; to him and his sons by a covenant of salt", and is granted the victory (1 Chron 13:5). (b) Its *unchangeableness*. Jehovah will not break His covenant, nor alter the thing that is gone out of His lips. (c) Its *certainty*. In spite of the failure of David's children, Jehovah will not utterly take His lovingkindness from his seed (v. 30,33). (d) It is *made with an oath* (v. 35), that the heirs "may have strong consolation" (Heb 6:17). (e) A *sign is given*: the orbs of day and night, on which the Noahic covenant depends (v. 36,37). "Thus saith the Lord, If ye can break my covenant of the day, and My covenant of the night...then may also My covenant be broken with David My servant, that he should not have a son to reign upon his throne" (Jer 33:21).

This has no doubt been true all down the centuries; the "sons" have not been lacking, but, owing to Judah's sins, the throne has been temporarily transferred to the four Gentile powers, and the words of Hosea have come to pass: "The children of Israel shall abide many days without a king and without a prince" (3:4). But when God's hour strikes, His King will appear, and one of His many crowns will be the long-lost diadem of the throne of David. This is no doubt the diadem spoken of in Ezekiel 31:26,27: "I will overturn, overturn, overturn, and it shall be no more (i.e., the diadem shall not be worn again) until He come whose right it is, and I will give it to Him". He will be the universal King, but there will be a prince of the House of David – the then representative of the royal line – who will act as His viceroy.

This prince is not the Lord Himself, for "he will eat before the Lord" (Ezek 44:3). "He will prepare for himself...a bullock for a sin-offering" (45:22,23). "He shall not take of the people's inheritance by oppression" (46:18). It is also clear that though his name will be David, he will be David the second, a man in the flesh, having sons

(46:16), not a resurrected man. But the Lord will be the King of kings; Heir to the promises, as the seed of Abraham; Heir to the throne, as the offspring of David, by His conception in the virgin's womb. Once in a humble guise He offered Himself to Israel as their King, but was rejected. Now, in the absence of the King, a spiritual kingdom has been set up in the hearts of believers, and the literal kingdom remains in the hands of the Gentile powers. But the sands of "the Times of the Gentiles" are sinking fast, and soon the King will return to take possession of the Kingdom by Divine power.

The last words of David emphasise the principle of grace underlying this covenant. He describes the character of the true King and His future glory. If the covenant depended on his house attaining such a standard, what hope could he entertain? But he falls back, as we must, on the grace and faithfulness of God. "Although my house be not so with God, yet He hath made with me an everlasting covenant, ordered in all things and sure ('the sure mercies of David'), for this is all my salvation and my desire, although He make it not to grow" (2 Sam 23: 3-5). To sight, all might look failure and barrenness, but faith could count on God for present deliverance, and hope look forward to His making "the horn of David to bud", and "his crown to flourish" (Psa 132:17,18).

6. THE COVENANT WITH DEATH
"Your covenant with death shall be disannulled" (Isa 27:18).

This covenant differs from the others we have considered in being between man and man, not between man and Jehovah. The parties to it will be Israel under their "king" on the one hand, and "the prince that shall come" of Daniel 9:26. "He (that is, the prince of the people who will have destroyed Jerusalem and the Sanctuary) will confirm a covenant with many for one week." "The people" referred to here were, of course, the Romans under Titus, so that "the prince of the covenant" will be the head of the Roman Empire.

This covenant is also distinguished by being a subject of prophecy, "the lamp shining in a dark place", here the darkest hour of Israel's history, "the time of Jacob's trouble, but he shall be saved out of it" (Jer 30: 7). The blackest night will give place to the "rising of the Sun of righteousness, with healing in His wings". The covenant will no doubt appear to the leaders of the nation to be a stroke of wisest policy. "When the overflowing scourge shall pass through it shall not come unto us." What indeed, humanly speaking, could make their national position so strong as an alliance with the great Roman Empire? But in Jehovah's estimate it will be only "a covenant with death and an agreement with hell" (Isa 28:15). In fact Jehovah had already warned them against such an alliance: "Associate yourselves, O ye people, and ye shall be broken in pieces...Say ye not, A confederacy, to all them to whom this people shall say, A confederacy; neither fear ye their fear, nor be afraid. Sanctify the Lord of hosts Himself, and let Him be your fear...and He shall be for a sanctuary" (Isa 8:9-4). So in chapter 28 the Lord encourages them to build on the Rock whom He had provided: "Behold I lay in Zion for a foundation stone, a tried stone, a precious corner stone, a sure foundation: he that believeth shall not make haste" (v. 16). That One indeed would never fail them, but "the arm of flesh would fail them". "The hail shall sweep away the refuge of lies, and the waters shall overflow the hiding place. And your covenant with death shall be disannulled, and your agreement with hell shall not stand; when the overflowing scourge shall pass through, then ye shall be trodden down by it." But though the cruel foe, "the King of Assyria, should come up over all his channels and go over all his banks, and should pass through Judah and should overflow and go over, and the stretching out of his wings should fill the breadth of Thy land, O Immanuel", yet at the very zenith of his pride and victory, "when he shall shake his hand against the mount of the daughter of Zion, the hill of Jerusalem", at that moment of man's extremity, the Lord, Jehovah of hosts, will intervene and "lop the bough with terror ... and Lebanon shall fall by a mighty One" - even the "Child born and the Son given – the Mighty God" Himself. (See Isa 8:7,8; 10:33,34; 9:6).

This covenant will mark the utmost limit of Israel's departure from God, as the Cross marked the lowest depth of their hatred to God. For the "Prince of the Covenant" will prove to be Satan's counterfeit of God, the devil's own, the "Man of Sin"; whereas the king of Israel, the mediator of the covenant, will stand forth as "the Antichrist", and in the sequel the nation will deliberately apostatise from Jehovah and choose the "Man of Sin" as their God and the Antichrist as their Messiah.

Much interest is naturally being aroused today in the future of Palestine. Some speak as though by the fact of its deliverance from the Turk, Jerusalem had ceased to be "trodden down of the Gentiles", and that therefore the era of blessing, spoken of by the prophets, had already begun. But Britain is no less a Gentile nation than Turkey, and though God is using her providentially to prepare the land for His people, yet, as a future member of the revived Roman Empire, she will herself be found among the nations gathered together for special judgement at the siege of Jerusalem. The return of the Jews to their land is no doubt a phenomenon of deep interest, for it not only testifies again to the fact that, however delayed, the Word of God shall never pass away, but it also bears witness to the solemn reality that we are in the very closing days of the present age. But let us not forget that those who return now to Palestine are going into the jaws of Antichrist either for apostacy or for the most fearful persecution the world has ever known.

In order to understand the closing scenes of Israel's history in this age, we must distinguish between the bulk of those who return to Jerusalem before the end – worldly, godless, and ready for any political combination, if only they can have a quiet time and secure national and material advantages, and on the other hand the God-fearing portion of the nation – sometimes spoken of as "the faithful remnant", who, though in a decided minority, will, by their spiritual power and earnestness, be a powerful factor in the trend of events. Some scriptures take special cognisance of the faithful portion of the nation. In Joel, for instance, the nation is regarded from this point of view, but in such passages as Isaiah 8 and Daniel 11 it is more the apostate nation in their self-will and attachment to their false king.

It is important, too, to distinguish between "the covenant with death" made with the Prince – a worldly expedient for political ends, and "the Holy Covenant" referred to in Daniel 11:7,8,30, which will be the renewal of the Levitical covenant, by the nation at large formally, and by the godly remnant with true purpose of heart. The former covenant will make the latter possible.

But Israel will soon experience the truth of the warning, "Cursed be the man that trusteth in man, and maketh flesh his arm, and whose heart departeth from the Lord" (Jer 17:5). In the midst of the week the Prince "shall cause the sacrifice and the oblation to cease", and "place the abomination that maketh desolate" (Dan 9:27; 11:31). Abomination is a frequent term in Scripture for an idol. The special idol here would seem to be the image of the Beast of Revelation 13: 14,15, which will breathe and speak. To this the Lord would refer in the words, "When ye shall see the abomination of desolation standing where it ought not" (Mark 13:14), or in the holy place (Matt 24:15). The Lawless One himself "will sit in the temple of God showing himself that he is God" (2 Thess 2:4), but when not there in person, he will, it would seem, be replaced by this image.

But this anticipates. The Jews must first be re-established in their own land. Zionism has brought the dry bones of Judaism together, and the British Protectorate of Palestine will no doubt open the way for a return to the land on an unprecedented scale. Then the choice of a ruler will be only a question of time. A "vile person" will obtain the kingdom by flatteries, and will prove to be the man of destiny–the Antichrist (Dan 11:21). He will develop into a successful leader, consolidate his power by gifts and bribery, and pose not only as the protector of the national interests, but as the champion of their religion and of the worship of Jehovah. Between the nation under this king and "the Prince" will a covenant, or as we call it today an alliance, be made for "one week", or period of seven years. This will complete the "70 weeks" or 490 years revealed through Gabriel to Daniel, as determined upon his people (Dan 9:24). Four hundred and eighty-three years of these were fulfilled when Messiah was cut off, and this covenant week will, after an interval of more than 1,900 years, complete the total.

Three remarkable happenings will follow the making of the covenant. First the destruction of the Northern army, by a miraculous intervention of God (see Ezek 38:22; Joel 2: 20; Dan 11:45); next a wonderful season of material prosperity. The former and the latter rains will once more fall in abundance and God will "restore the years that the locust hath eaten" (Joel 2:23-27). Then afterward a still more wonderful spiritual effusion will be vouchsafed. The Holy

THE SEVEN COVENANTS OF HOLY SCRIPTURE

Spirit will be poured out first on the chosen of Israel (Joel 2:28), the 144,000 of Revelation 6 and 14, to prepare them to be God's final witnesses, under the leadership of "the two witnesses", Moses and Elias, as I believe (see Rev 11). This testimony will be sustained by Divine power, in judging those who oppose it and in converting those who receive it. The blessing of Pentecost will prove to have been only a pale shadow of the world-wide blessing of these future days. The myriads converted in the Acts will be paralleled by millions then – "the great multitude which no man could number" of Revelation 7:9. In other words, "the harvest of the earth will be reaped" (Rev 14:15).

This testimony will last during the first half of the Covenant week, in spite of the deadly opposition of men and demons, "but when they (the two witnesses) shall have finished their testimony, the beast that ascendeth out of the bottomless pit shall make war against them and slay them" (Rev 11). Who is this "beast"? The very Prince of the Covenant, henceforth a dual personality, being indwelt by the spirit of a former Head of the Roman Empire, for "he is the eighth and is of the seven" (Rev 17:11). He will then be manifested as the Man of Sin, will denounce the Covenant and claim to be God, "opposing and exalting himself above all that is called God or that is worshipped (2 Thess 2:4). What part will the false king of Israel play at this juncture? He too will throw off his mask and appear in the new role of claimant to the Messiahship of Israel.

The Lord Jesus came in His Father's name and was rejected; he will come in his own name to be received (John 5:43). He too will claim Divine honours, for "he shall exalt himself ... above every God" (Dan 11:36); yet two gods he will recognise, for in his estate shall he "honour the god of forces and a god whom his father knew not shall he honour with gold and silver and with precious stones" (Dan 11:38). Can this "god of forces" be Satan and the other "god"–the Man of Sin, the two other members of the Infernal Triad? It is clear from Revelation 13 that just as our Lord, while accepting the acknowledgment of His own Deity, sought to glorify the Father, so the second beast – the Antichrist, will seek the glory of the first beast – the Man of Sin (see Rev 13). Like another Judas, he will betray the godly remnant of Israel, who will refuse to deny Jehovah. These in the fires of his persecutions, will remember how once they took sweet counsel together, and will sorrowfully acknowledge, "He hath put his hands against such as be at peace with him, he hath broken his covenant" (Psa 55:20; Isa 28:18).

But the nation as a whole will completely apostatise from Jehovah, and accept the Man of Sin as their God, and the Antichrist as their Messiah. The demon of idolatry left Israel at the captivity. Since then they have been for many days "without an image, and without an ephod, and without terraphim" (Hosea 3:4). But now the demon returns and finds them as a nation "empty, swept and garnished", and the last state shall be worse than the first (Matt 12:45). But while the nation will be plunged in the worst idolatry ever known – of man as the only god, the faithful remnant will be passing through persecutions such as the world has never seen. It will be "the time of Jacob's trouble, but he shall be saved out of it" (Jer 30:7), by the coming in glory of Him whom they pierced. They will mourn for Him as a man mourneth for his only son, and a fountain (which sprang at Calvary) will be opened out to them for sin and for uncleanness (Zech 12:10; 13:1).

7. THE NEW COVENANT

"I will make a covenant of peace with them ... and will set My sanctuary in the midst of them for evermore" (Ezek 37:26).

This covenant stands out doubly bright against the dark background of the "Covenant with Death". It is the last and, best of all – Jehovah's crowning covenant with His people. When Israel has drunk to the dregs the bitter cup of judgement for the rejection of Messiah, God will give them the valley of Achor for a door of hope (Hosea 2:15), and bring forth the best wine, bidding them make merry and be glad. He will make an everlasting covenant with them, even the sure mercies of David (Isa 4:1,3).

The terms of this new covenant are contained in Jeremiah 31:31-34. Space forbids quotation in full, but a careful reading is advised, as also the verses 37 to end of next chapter, where additional details are given, and of Ezekiel 37:21-23, where the re-union of the twelve tribes, to form one nation under David, is foretold. From a comparison of these passages it is clear that the covenant will only be made when God has restored His people as a whole to Himself and to their land. The present return to Palestine, providentially permitted, is merely a national and semi-political movement, not to be confounded with the final return, which will be the direct work of God. "I will plant them in the land assuredly with My whole heart and with My whole soul" (Jer 32:41). The present return is partial in unbelief and for judgement; that will be the fruit of repentance and faith, for blessing and complete.

But why should Jehovah make a new covenant? Why should it not be a renewal of the Sinaitic Covenant, as in the revivals of Josiah and Nehemiah? Because that would only be to court fresh failure. It is clearly stated "not according to the covenant that I made with their fathers in the day that I took them out of the land of Egypt, which My covenant they brake, although I was an husband unto them". "If that first covenant had been faultless, then should no place have been sought for the second" (Heb 8:7). The fault was this. It was too holy for faulty men; in other words it was "weak through the flesh". A perfect plumb line will never straighten the leaning tower of Pisa – a perfect law will never straighten out crooked man.

Who are the parties to the New Covenant? Jehovah and Israel. "I will make a new covenant with the house of Israel and with the house of Judah." These will be united once more and for ever in a single nation, according to the parabolic prophecy of the sticks in Ezekiel 37:20. Israel and Judah will return to the land divided; they will become one in the land. This seems to dispose of the idea some hold that the ten tribes are not lost, but only merged in the twelve million Jews scattered through the world. No doubt considerable numbers of the ten tribes were thus merged before the dispersion and are referred to in this prophecy, "the children of Israel Judah's companions", but the ten tribes, "all the house of Israel, Ephraim's companions", are distinct and will be known as such. Does anyone ask who and where are the lost tribes now? It may not be easy to answer. Of one thing we may be sure, they are not the mixed race, composed of ancient Britons, Danes, Saxons, Normans, etc., inhabiting the British Isles. When you lose a thing, it is not a bad idea to look for it where you lost it. The ten tribes disappeared in the environs of Assyria. Why not look for them thereabouts, say in the mountains of Armenia?

But have Christians no part in the New Covenant? The Epistle to the Hebrews clearly says they have, in so far as its blessings are applicable to a heavenly people. This epistle is addressed to believers in Christ from Israel and no doubt members of the Church. Why should they need a special epistle? Because things had changed much since the early days of our Lord's ministry and of the testimony of the Twelve in the Acts. Then a Jew did not lose his national privileges, hopes and blessings by receiving the Lord Jesus as Messiah. It would have been strange to lose national standing by accepting the national Hope.

It was only through Paul that the new order – the heavenly calling in one body of Jew and Gentile – was revealed. This entailed a break with the past and exclusion from present Levitical and national privileges. Tens of thousands, "myriads" the word is, were at once believers in Christ and zealous of the law (Acts 21:20). No better Jews could be found. What a day of bitter trial and testing it was, when they found themselves forced to choose between Christ and all they valued as men in the flesh, the institutions of God Himself. The pull back to Judaism was tremendous. Hence the Hebrew Epistle, with its warnings and encouragements.

One of these latter was the assurance of a present share in the spiritual blessings of the New Covenant. Else why dangle it before their eyes in ch. 8? Nay in 7:22 they were already taught that their Lord Jesus was the surety of a better covenant than the Levitical, and in 10:15,16, the perfection of their standing in Christ is proved by a quotation from the very words of the New Covenant, "Their sins and their iniquities will I remember no more". Still there is much in the promises to Israel under the New Covenant which do not apply to the Christian now.

Why is this covenant called "New"? Not because it is everlasting, of grace, and ratified by blood; nor because in it God promises to Israel possession of the land and to be their God. All that was also true of the Abrahamic Covenant. But for three reasons. It is ratified, not only by blood, but by the blood of Jesus Christ Himself – "the blood of the everlasting covenant" (Heb 13:20), He thus becoming its Surety. Secondly, the sins of His people are not only forgiven, but forgotten. "Their sins and iniquities will I remember no more." Thirdly, Jehovah, always faithful to His side of the covenant, now guarantees that His people shall fully respond to His desires. "I will put My law in their inward parts and write it in their hearts." They will remember and love it, and all (i.e. of the house of Israel) "shall know Me from the least to the greatest". But obedience will not be mechanical or enforced, but induced by adequate motive and power; "I will put My fear in their hearts, and they shall not depart from Me" (Jer 32:40).

Space forbids to dwell on the glories of the New Covenant. The greatest of all will be, Jehovah-Tzidkenu, the "Lord our Righteousness", in the midst of His people (Jer 23:6); and so vastly will this fact transcend every other, that not only will Judah have this His name upon them (Jer 33:13), and be called also "Jehovah-Tzidkenu"; but Jerusalem itself, the most celebrated city of history, will lose her secular name and be known as Jehovah-Shammah (Ezek 48:35).

Beyond the Grave
or
What saith the Scriptures
about the intermediate or final state?

1. INTRODUCTION

That death is not a terminus, but that there is another state of existence beyond the grave, are beliefs to which the universal conscience of mankind has testified in all ages. The history and religions of mankind, and the burial rites of primitive races revealed by the spade of the archaeologist, all bear witness to this. The Scriptures are very plain throughout: "The spirit shall return unto God, who gave it" (Eccl 12:7); "Many of them that sleep in the dust of the earth shall awake, some to everlasting life, and some to shame and everlasting contempt" (Dan 12:2); "At Thy right hand there are pleasures for evermore" (Psa 16:11); "After death the judgment" (Heb 9:27).

But not only do the Scriptures bear consistent testimony to a future existence, they testify with equal clearness to its everlasting[1] character whether at home with God, or banished from His presence. This is expressed in terms which are equally applied to God's being and glory (see, e.g., Dan 12:3; Matt 25:46; Rom 9:5; Gal 1:5; Heb 9:12; Jude 13; Rev 4:9, 14:11). Man's beginning, as described in Genesis, points to the same conclusion. When God created man, He did four things for him which He did for no beast. He formed his body first, then breathed into his nostrils the breath (*n'shamah*, only used of Himself and man) of life, and man became a living soul; thirdly, He

---

[1] This is loosely described as the 'immortality of the soul': a term which is based on a misapprehension, as to the meaning of death. If man had been created incapable of death, the Divine warning would have been meaningless: "In the day that thou eatest thereof, thou shalt surely die." Man is capable of death by his very constitution, but not of ending his being. He must exist eternally either in harmony with God, which is life, or out of harmony with him, which is death – "the second death."

made him capable of communion with Himself, as no beast ever was, and lastly, He put him under a moral test. Could such a being be created to perish like the beast? If the Divine breath be indestructible in the Creator, how conceive it as destructible in man, created in His image?

If this be true, the question as to what the future life will be becomes one of infinite importance to every man. Especially is this the case if it be realised that the present is always viewed in Scripture as the unique time of probation, on which the eternal state of each depends, "He that believeth (i.e. in the gospel) and is baptised shall be saved; he that believeth not shall be damned" (Mark 16:16); "These shall go away (i.e. from the earthly scene) into everlasting punishment, but the righteous into life everlasting" (Matt 25:46). "In the place where the tree falleth, there it shall be" (Eccl 11:3). The most acute minds have feverishly searched the Scriptures to find one clear promise of a future probation for the wicked dead, but without success. They have only two or three ambiguous texts, and made deductions therefrom, but the main drift of the Scriptures is against them.[2] In fact it cannot be shown that men who have wilfully refused to turn to God in this day of grace, would listen better, were a further probation granted. It is only too likely that they would always count on another chance, and yet another. There is nothing except the desire that it might be so to encourage what is called 'the Eternal Hope doctrine'. Men argue about the heathen to show that they must have another chance or God would be unrighteous, but it is not they who are going to the heathen with the gospel. They let

---

[2] Two verses are sometimes quoted to prove what is called 'the second chance', both in Peter's first epistle, 3:19,20; 4:6.

Whatever the first-named passage may mean, it cannot be, in any case, interpreted with any justice as anything but a proclamation or heralding to certain spirits in prison of what we are not told, with what object we are not told, with what effect we are not told. There is no reason why such an event as the death of the Son of God should not be made known in the nether world, or are they to be kept for ever in ignorance of it. Certainly such proclamations may be thus made to those who have died in their sins; but between this and the offer of a second chance there is a wide difference.

As for the second verse: "For this cause was the gospel preached also to them that are dead." I remember Dr. Handley Moule telling his students that as a matter of translation there was nothing in the Greek to show that the gospel was preached to the persons referred after they died, though they were dead when Peter wrote.

others do that; they stay at home and find fault with God. We may be sure that God has not left Himself without a witness in any single case, and the reality and sufficiency of such an appeal must not be minimised: "Shall not the Judge of all the earth do right?" and will He not be justified in all His ways, whether of judgment or of grace? Why, moreover, if anything could possibly be done, should He wait for a future eternity to pass, if we may say so, before doing it, and keep the lost waiting in 'eternal hope'? Indeed the two ideas of 'eternal' and 'hope' are incompatible. Such a hope is a hope that maketh ashamed. In reality the dogma of 'eternal hope' was invented, not for the heathen at all, but for the so-called christian world in the homelands, where the gospel can be heard, and the Scriptures procured at a minimum of pains and cost, and where men, if they ever do go to the place of the lost, have to "trample under foot the Son of God, count the blood of the covenant...an unholy thing, and do despite unto the Spirit of Grace". Nor is it for us to profess to scan the pages of the Book of Life or take for granted that the number of the lost will exceed the saved, nor indeed to pass sentence on any. God is the Judge and He alone.

It is true that the Lord, addressing the feeble remnant of His day, called them a "little flock", but when asked later, "Are there few that be saved?" He did not reply in the affirmative, but only urged His hearers to strive to enter in at the strait gate, as it would be too late when once the door was shut! When He was about to depart out of this world unto the Father, He promised His disciples to send the Holy Spirit, at whose advent they would be enabled to do even greater things than He Himself had done. Accordingly, Peter, on the day of Pentecost, in his one brief sermon, led six times as many souls to Christ, as had been drawn to Him during His whole earthly ministry, and at the close of the Acts we read of tens of thousands (Greek, myriads) of Jews who believed. We can form little idea of the number of Israel who were saved down the ages before Christ, nor of the immense aggregate gathered out from Jew and Gentile during the present dispensation to form the church; nor yet of that great multitude, which no man can number, of those who will be saved after the church has gone, "of all nations and kindreds, and peoples and tongues" (Rev 7:9).

Who, moreover, can estimate the millions who will be eternally saved during the long years of the Millennial reign of peace and glory? If we allow for all who have died before the age of responsibility (calculated as at least half of the whole total of the human race), and who, we believe on scriptural authority, will be saved without knowing it, on the ground of the atonement of Christ (as they were lost without knowing of it by the fall of Adam), we may well comfort ourselves with the thought that our Lord will have pre-eminence as in all else, in the numbers of those saved, as compared with the lost.

We propose to consider this subject under the following headings: The Intermediate State – its true character and reality, its denial, its travesty; The Millennial Reign and the Everlasting Kingdom; The Future State of the Saved, and of the Unsaved; and close with a consideration of the doctrines of Universalism and Conditionalism.

2. THE INTERMEDIATE STATE

Its Reality

The expression, "Intermediate State", denotes the condition of the departed between death and resurrection. The actual phrase is not found in Scripture, but describes what is referred to as the "unclothed" or "absent-from-the-body" condition. See for instance the Apostle's words in 2 Cor 5:4, "We that are in this tabernacle (i.e. our present body) do groan, being burdened: not for that we would be unclothed (i.e. die and exist without the body) but clothed upon (i.e. receive our resurrection body at the coming of the Lord) that mortality might be swallowed up of life". When the Lord comes, His people who are found alive on the earth will never know the experience of death, nor the ensuing experience of an unclothed condition, as verse 2 affirms, "If so be (the if here has not the sense of doubt, but of 'seeing that') that being clothed, we shall not be found naked." That is, they would be clothed upon at once with their resurrection and glorified body, and never be found in an unclothed or naked state. These are true believers (how else could they be thus clothed?). Consequently the idea that "naked" expresses here a manifestation of unreality and final perdition, as some have stated, cannot logically be upheld. Naturally the unclothed condition for a human spirit, created to inhabit a body, is not the ideal. It is an unnatural condition, and yet Paul, so great was his desire to be with Christ, was willing to enter into this disembodied and abnormal state, so as to be nearer his Lord than is possible here: "We are confident and willing," he writes, "rather to be absent from the body and to be present with the Lord" (v. 8). This cannot describe the resurrection day, as believers will not then be "absent from the body", but in the 'Intermediate State' – a blessed condition of communion with Christ, above anything known before, as the apostle says, "To depart and to be with Christ which is far better" (Phil 1:23). It cannot, however, equal the perfect blessedness to be experienced on the resurrection morning. Then the believer will find himself conformed, spirit, soul and body, to the image of Christ.

There is one expression in this passage which we must consider, as it has been used to support the contrary idea, that the full state of blessedness ensues at once after death. "For we know that if our earthly house of this tabernacle were dissolved we have a building of God, a house not made with hands eternal in the heavens" (v. 1). This is pressed to mean that – we have this house at once, but only as a temporary provision. But the following words rule out such an interpretation, for the house, whatever it be, will be eternal in the heavens. It represents a final, not a temporary, state of blessing. The context, moreover, shows that this does not describe a condition at once enjoyed by the believer at death, for then there would be no sense in speaking of an 'unclothed state' (e.g., v. 4, "not for that we would be unclothed"). The words only mean we have it promised or in prospect, as an Israelite might have said to his son who would have expressed regret on the Passover night, at the necessity of leaving their house in Egypt, "Well, if we leave this one we have one in Canaan we shall never have to leave," although an intermediate wilderness lay between. That there must be an intermediate state is clear from the fact that the resurrection of the body is not a present or merely an individual experience, but future and collective. The Lord said, "The hour is coming, that all that are in the graves shall hear His voice and shall come forth, they that have done good unto the resurrection of life, and they that have done evil unto the resurrection of judgment" (John 5:29). We know from Rev 20:5 that a thousand years will elapse between these two resurrections. "But the rest of the dead lived not again until the thousand years were finished. This (referring to the previous verse) is the first resurrection. Blessed and holy is he that hath part in the first resurrection: on such the second death hath no power." The second resurrection, that is of the wicked dead, occurs only when we reach verse 12, "And I saw the dead small and great stand before God". This will be the Judgment of the Great White Throne – the final assize, ending up with the terrible sentence, "And whosoever was not found written in the book of life was cast into the lake of fire." All this is future, so that there must be an intermediate state between death and resurrection, and that for both the just and the unjust.

What then is its character? Is it a prolongation of probation – a further opportunity for those who have died in their sins, of being purified from those sins and made fit for heaven? or is probation over, and the destiny of each settled, though its degree not yet assigned? In other words, are such to be compared to debtors working off their liabilities, or to condemned convicts awaiting in prison the execution of their sentence? The Lord Himself settles the matter once and for all, for any who are subject to His word, for in Luke 16 He lifts the veil of the unseen world – the place of departed spirits, as it was when He was on earth, and shows us two specimen men – one in Paradise, the other (not in Gehenna, the final place of the lost, but) in Hades,[3] the Unseen World, the place of departed spirits: the vestibule of hell, and of a similar character. That this does not represent the eternal state is evident from the fact that the lost rich man has five brethren still alive on the earth, living ungodly lives, as he had himself done, but still where he supposed a warning from Lazarus might arrest their downward course.

The reply of Abraham not only shows the futility of any such testimony from the grave as the lost rich man proposed, but also that his own condition was final, as the great gulf testified. Reading Luke 16:19-31 shows that the intermediate state is (1) a disembodied state, and (2) a state of real existence. The persons are real persons – Abraham, Lazarus, the nameless rich man; who, though dead to the world, are not dead to God, for "all live unto Him" (Luke 20:38).

---

[3] This is the word employed by the Lord. "In hell he lifted up his eyes being in torment."

(3) It is a conscious state, not one of soul-sleep or unconsciousness, as certain false teachers would have us believe, "He (that is Lazarus) is comforted and thou art tormented" (v. 25). (4) It is a state of recognition and remembrance: "Father Abraham", "Send Lazarus!" "I have five brethren", "Son remember!" (5) It is an immediate state: it is at once entered upon at death. "The rich man died, and was buried, and in hell (Gk., *Hades*) he lifted up his eyes being in torments." "It came to pass that the beggar died and was carried by the angels into Abraham's bosom." To this we may add the words of Christ to the repentant thief: "Verily, verily, I say unto thee, Today shalt thou be with Me in Paradise" (Luke 23:43). (6) A present experience of punishment has already begun, corresponding to the imprisonment of a condemned criminal, prior to the carrying out of his final sentence; for the ungodly, as it is said of the rich man, are already in torment. Indeed he calls his abode; not "this place of cleansing", but "this place of torment". Lazarus, on the other hand, is already comforted. We may compare with this again the words of the apostle Paul, "To depart and to be with Christ which is far better" (Phil 1:23); and this without prejudice to the fact that neither the full blessedness of the resurrection morn nor yet the full terrors of the lake of fire are yet experienced. (7) It is an irrevocable state – "between us and you, there is a great gulf fixed, so that they which would pass from hence to you cannot; neither can they pass to us, that would come from thence" (v. 26). Clearly any thought of a further probation is ruled out by such words.

Its Denial

All this is denied by most of the quasi-religious systems around us to-day, such as Spiritism, Theosophy, Christian Science, Seventh-day Adventism, Russellism, etc. It would be strange indeed if such systems, which deny all the fundamentals of the Christian faith – the fall of man, atonement by the blood-shedding of Christ, His deity, etc., – should be sound on the future state. They deny their need of a Saviour and so reject the Lord Jesus Christ, who is willing to be theirs.

Certainly for the spiritist, death is no crisis, for probation is not over. Spiritual development continues without interruption. They cannot deny death, but they do deny resurrection of the body, so that there can be no intermediate state. They make no claim to base their teaching on the Scriptures, but believe what their familiar spirits communicate to them.

Theosophy borrows widely from Hinduism, which like Spiritism is purely demoniacal (1 Cor 10:10-20). The spiritist affirms that after death souls enter into seven revolving spheres or stages of progress, corresponding closely to the seven planes of Theosophy. Only the two lowest are places of suffering, the third is a place of discomfort, much like the earth with its compensations, spiritual arm-chairs, cigars, whiskies, animal pets, debating-societies, lending-libraries; and then follow other stages of various degrees of happiness. But man is his own saviour, and very little is heard of God or Christ, nor does the spiritist seem to want to be brought nearer them. His ideal heaven is eventually merely a more comfortable worldly place. Spiritists do believe, they say, in a hell, as a great remedial agency (fire being apparently the only thing they know of which can cleanse away sin or improve the sinner), but "no great gulf is fixed between it and heaven", say these teachers, in flagrant contradiction to our Lord Himself. Can anyone doubt that such a system emanates directly from Satan, the great seducing spirit, who led our first parents to their fall with his lies. Truly Spiritism is no new thing, seeing that it began in Eden, and is condemned by the Spirit of God, throughout the Scriptures; thus "Thou shalt not suffer a witch live" (Exod 22:18); "Regard not them that have familiar spirits, neither seek after wizards, to be defiled by them" (Lev 19:31); "The soul that turneth after such as have familiar spirits, I will even set My face against that soul, and will cut him off from among his people" (20:6); "There shall not be found among you a consulter with familiar spirits, or a wizard or a necromancer; for all that do these things are an abomination unto the Lord" (Deut 18:10); "And when they shall say unto you, seek unto them that have familiar spirits and unto wizards that peep and mutter; should not a people seek unto their God? For the living to the dead? To the law and to the testimony; if they speak not according to this word, it is because there is no light in them" (Isa 8:19,20).

In closing I will cite one more solemn passage as to the eternal fate of those who yield to such practices, in which the Spirit of God affirms that "sorcerers" (another name for spiritists), classing them with "the abominable and murderers, and whoremongers, and idolaters and all liars", "shall have their part in the lake, which burneth with fire and brimstone, which is the second death" (Rev 21:8).

From all this we gather that Spiritism is deceptive, defiling, forbidden, abominable to God, punishable (under the Mosaic law) with death in this world, and leading its votaries straight to the lake of fire in the next. It is readily perceived that for Spiritism as a system and for kindred cults there is no intermediate state. But while such deny the truth, the Roman Catholic system travesties it.

The Travesty: Purgatory

Purgatory, from a Latin word, *purgare*, to cleanse, is a state of suffering after death in which the souls of those who die in venial sin, or who still owe some debt of temporal punishment for mortal sin, are rendered fit for heaven.

This is the Roman Doctrine [Infallibility (Salmon), p. 10], so that the Papal Church does hold an 'Intermediate State' in its own peculiar partial sense, that is, for all who are not bad enough to go to Hell, or good enough to go to Heaven; there is an Intermediate State filled up with Purgatory. This Purgatory is taught by the Roman hierarchy, and almost universally believed by the rank and file of Romanists, who, possibly because the doctrine is a great source of revenue to the priests, are left by them in this belief. But it has never been authoritatively laid down or localised by pope or council as an article of faith, binding on the conscience of every Romanist. If you believe current stories of Purgatory you are commended for your faith, if not, you do not incur official censure. At least, up to the time of Augustine of Hippo [*De Civitate Dei* xxx. 26] at the beginning of the fifth century, it was only held as a speculative belief, which might or might not be true. But what is this without the authority of the Scriptures? And high Romanist authorities, such as the late Cardinal Wiseman, admit that there is not a word about it in the Bible. It is in fact the merest speculation. It is certain that it was not arrived at even by tradition or Augustine would have known of it before.

According to Rome there are five possible locations in the future state: the lowest of all, Hell; above that, Purgatory; next, the limbo of unbaptized children; then the limbo of the Patriarchs; and over all, Heaven.

As for the first, Hell, it is supposed by these teachers to be at the centre of the earth, and is for all those who die in mortal sin, and theoretically for all who die outside the pale of the R.C. Church. Those who go there are definitely lost forever. That it is no empty place, the testimony of the well-known Bernard of Clairvaux among others is quoted. This 'saint' is said to have enjoyed the privilege on two successive days, of standing by the judgment throne of God, and hearing the sentences pronounced on all the souls that died on those two days. He was horrified to find that of 80,000 souls, only three of grown-up persons were saved on the first day, and only two on the second, and that of these five, not one went direct to heaven; all had to visit purgatory for an indefinite period. The testimony of Bernard is not a good advertisement for that salvation by human merit, on which the whole Romanist system relies. If, out of the 80,000 souls, 79,995 were lost for ever in Hell, and only five had any hope of Heaven, and that only after centuries in the fires of Purgatory, the Romish boast that outside the church there is no salvation, should be modified into, there is no salvation inside it.

What a contrast to all this is found in the Word of God, which tells us plainly of salvation sure and perfect for all through repentance and faith in the finished work of Christ, and of His precious blood which cleanses us from all sin, and of a great multitude which no man can number, who have washed their robes and made them white in the blood of the Lamb, and are therefore before the throne of God. Before considering Purgatory further, we might say in passing that the Limbo of the Patriarchs is now held to be empty since the resurrection of Christ who transferred them to be with Him in the Paradise above. The limbo of children is reserved, as they have stated, for the unbaptised. They do not suffer, but they are denied entrance into heaven, or the beatific vision. This is merely a pious belief, necessitated by the unscriptural practice of infant baptism and the doctrine that baptism cleanses from original sin. But the Lord Jesus expressly tells us, "In heaven their angels (i.e. of little ones, of whose baptism not a word is said) do always behold the face of My Father which is in heaven" (Matt 18:10). It would be strange that the little ones should enjoy a lower place than their ministering angels. In Luke 19:10, where the Lord is speaking of an adult, Zacchaeus, He says, "The Son of Man is come to seek and to save that which is lost". The adult, being of responsible age, can offer resistance to the appeal of Christ, but here in Matthew's Gospel the words run simply, "The Son of Man is come to save that which is lost", for infants have no responsibility, and are saved by the grace of God alone as we have already seen. They are lost without knowing it by the fall of Adam, and saved without knowing it by the atonement of Christ. We may safely hold then that all children dying before the age of responsibility are in heaven with Christ, and that for eternity; that not one such will be found in any other part of the universe of God.

The doctrine of Purgatory has been gradually built up on apparitions and visions, said to have been vouchsafed mostly to highly imaginative and hysterical females, on the authority or veracity of which even the Pope makes no pronouncement. Purgatory is supposed to be divided into three regions according to the severity of punishment due to its inmates. The lowest is principally occupied by Popes, Bishops, and other dignatories of the R.C. Church. The doctrine is not based on any Scriptural teaching, but on deductions from incidental passages as, e.g., 2 Maccabees 42 seq; an Apocryphal book never recognised by the Jews as part of their true Canon – which seems to indicate a common belief among them as to the efficacy of prayers for the dead. Our Lord's teaching and the apostles' then differed from the current belief, seeing that prayers for the dead are nowhere taught in the Scriptures. However, this practice is assumed as right and useful. Then for whom are such prayers to be offered? The saved in Heaven do not need them, the lost in Hell cannot benefit by them. There must be, it is argued, a third class, neither saved nor lost, for whom prayer is needed and effective. Purgatory then must exist!

It is one invention of man to justify another. There is only one Purgatory, or place of cleansing, as the word implies - the Cross of Christ; only one means of cleansing - His precious "Blood" that "cleanseth from all sin". Instead of these, Rome has instituted Purgatory and its flames, but as Cowper says:

"The dying thief rejoiced to see that fountain in his day,
And there may I, though vile as he, wash all my sins away."

In one moment that hell-deserving criminal became whiter than snow and fit for Paradise, through faith in the Lord Jesus, who at that very moment was "bearing his sins in His own body on the tree" (1 Pet 2:22). He ought, admittedly, according to the Roman doctrine, to have gone to Purgatory at least for a number of years, but this is got over by the theory that he made a perfect act of contrition at the last moment, from pure love of God, and so could dispense with the cleansing flames.

It is always something that man can do, according to the Romish theory, that can get him to Heaven: acts of merit; acts of religion; acts of contrition; acts of self-inflicted pain; or suffering in Purgatory. But how little place is given to "the offering of the body of Jesus Christ once for all" (Heb 10:10), that is, His atoning sufferings, of which the Scriptures speak so much. We are not surprised that so few Romanists are saved, if they trust in the things they do. But this explanation of the robber's sudden and complete transformation sounds as though invented for the occasion. He did acknowledge that he was suffering justly for his sins, but not a word do we find of any perfect act of contrition. He believed in the Lord as far as it was possible for him then to do, and that was enough. His sins were forgiven and cleansed away, because of the vicarious sufferings which Christ was enduring once for all on the cross, for him and for vast multitudes besides. It is there we must look, on Him we must trust. This has ever been the sole hope of the redeemed of all ages.

When John beholds the great multitude that no man could number, and is told whence and who they are, he learns that they have come out of the great tribulation and have washed their robes and made them white in the blood of the Lamb, and his heavenly mentor adds, "Therefore are they before the throne of God, and serve Him day and night in His temple" (Rev 7:14-15). They could not all have made 'perfect acts of contrition'; all we know is, they had accepted by faith the blood of Christ as their sufficient atonement. Nothing is added of purgatory or masses or money-payments, which seem to compose the essentials of salvation, according to the Roman Catholic Church. To say that believers need to be made fit for Heaven is a confusion between christian acceptance in Christ, His justification which is perfect, and the same for all believers, and christian attainment or sanctification, which comes subsequently and varies with each believer. Not even the Apostle Paul had attained to perfection (Phil 3:12), but he was not trusting in that for his salvation as the concluding verses of the chapter show (vv. 20,21). He was not seeking a place in Heaven; that he had received by grace. He was seeking a prize in Heaven, and that he had not attained to. The two things are quite distinct.

In writing to the Colossians, who were ordinary Christians like most believers today, he joins them with himself, "giving thanks unto the Father who hath made us meet to be partakers of the inheritance of the saints in light" (Col 1:12). But he expects them to "seek the things which are above, where Christ sitteth at the right hand of God" (3:1). In other words, since you are going to Heaven, be heavenly-minded. We see at once how sadly all the dark systems of men come short of the gospel of the grace of God. And where is Christ in it all? He might never have suffered and risen again, and the practical value attached to His work is, for all intents and purposes, nil. 1 Peter 3:18 tells us, "Christ once suffered for sins, the just for the unjust, that He might bring us to God" – not to Purgatory, which is the highest blessing anyone but 'a perfect saint' in the Romish Church can hope for – but to God.

The whole idea of being fitted for Heaven by suffering is based on a misunderstanding. It is to have the sinful nature, which is unchanged even in believers, made holy. It would be far easier to wash coal white or to make poison into wholesome food. When a man is brought to God and believes on His Son, not only does he receive forgiveness of his sins and cleansing from all defilement, but he is born again; that is he becomes a new man in Christ Jesus, the Holy Spirit indwells him, and he is henceforth possessed of a new nature, in which he is united to Christ and becomes holy in Him. It is this new man that is fit for Heaven, not the old which was condemned at the Cross. All that we had done as sinners (our sins), and all that we were as sinners (our sin) was dealt with there. The first was borne by Christ; the second was condemned in the person of Christ, and all now are forever put away from before a holy God.

What we are called to, is to "abide in Christ", to "stand fast in the liberty wherewith He hath made us free", to "walk in the Spirit and not to fulfil the lusts of the flesh". He who does this most will have most reward in the coming kingdom.

But when Christ comes, all that is of the flesh will disappear, the saint will no longer have in him an evil nature to humble and annoy, but will in all things be conformed to the image of Christ. No wonder the pious members of the Roman Catholic Church are in slavish bondage at the prospect of death, and at what will happen beyond it. In fact the more pious they are, the worse their fears, for they are under law, and can never enjoy settled peace with God. "They have a zeal of God but not according to knowledge, for they, being ignorant of God's righteousness, and going about to establish their own righteousness, have not submitted themselves unto the righteousness of God; for Christ is the end of the law for righteousness to everyone that believeth" (Rom 10:2,3).

How different the experience of the true believer! "To depart and to be with Christ, which is far better" (Phil 1:23). "For we know that if the earthly house of this tabernacle be dissolved, we have a building of God, a house not made with hands, eternal in the heavens" (2 Cor 5:1). "We look for the Saviour who shall change the body of our humiliation, that it may be fashioned like unto His glorious body" (Phil 3:21). This blessed prospect is for the most unworthy who will trust in Christ alone, for He declares, "Verily, verily, I say unto you, he that heareth My word, and believeth on Him that sent Me, hath everlasting life, and shall not come into judgment, but is passed from death to life" (John 5:24).

3. THE MILLENNIAL REIGN
AND THE EVERLASTING KINGDOM

Although this is not primarily a study of prophetic events, which are shortly to transpire on the earth, we must briefly touch on Christ's future reign, in its two phases – the heavenly, in which all saints, who will have quitted this world by death or translation, will have a share, and the earthly, which will last a thousand years on the earth, and eventually merge into "the everlasting Kingdom of our Lord and Saviour Jesus Christ".

God has a wonderful programme: not only has He glorified His

Son in Heaven, but He will also glorify Him in the very scene of His rejection. He must enjoy the fruits of His victory where He won it. He will be King of both the heavenly and earthly kingdoms. To set up this latter He will come with all His saints. The destruction of the armies of His enemies will be followed by the judgment of the living nations, who survive them. The judge will divide them, that is the individuals comprising them, as a shepherd divideth the sheep from the goats, and these (the reprobates) shall go into everlasting punishment, but the righteous into life eternal. This judgment will determine the eternal state of those judged. At the same epoch, the judgment of the twelve tribes of Israel will be carried out, and of this judgment the twelve apostles will be assessors with Him, to whom all judgment is committed, for both are to take place when the Son of Man shall sit on the throne of His glory (see Matt 19:28; 25:31). The saved, whether of the nations or Israel, will form the nucleus of the Millennial Kingdom.

The characteristics of the earthly kingdom

A state of things quite unprecedented will prevail on the earth during this period. It will be characterised by the following features[4].

(1) The Presence of the King

The personal revelation of the Son of Man in His glory will then be manifested to all, as it was revealed to a chosen few on the Mount of Transfiguration. Not that the Lord will, of necessity, be continuously on the earth. He will reign over it as well as on it. The Prince of Ezekiel's prophecy (e.g., 44:3) will act as His Viceroy in His eventual absence. Communication will then be established between heaven and earth. The true Jacob's ladder will be set up and the angels of God will be seen ascending and descending upon the Son of Man (see Gen 28:12 and John 1:51). He will be the connecting link between heaven and earth, and the centre and source of blessing. His glory, His mighty deeds, His wonderful words, will fill the earth. His dominions will "stretch from sea to sea, and from the river unto the ends of the earth". And "all kings shall fall before Him: all nations shall serve Him", and "daily shall He be praised" (Psa 72:8,11,15). His will be a righteous rule and based on atonement. This is why

---

[4] More details of this are given earlier in this volume, p.40-41.

our Lord would not accept the crown from an unrepentant nation: they did not acknowledge His righteous claims, which alone atonement upholds. If men rebel, then they will find that the rod that rules them is a rod of iron, lawlessness will be met with condign punishment. Then all wrongs will be righted; all abuses and monopolies swept away, and one great cause of sin will be banished from the scene.

(2) The Absence of the Usurper

The first thing that will occur at the return of the Son of Man, after the destruction of the armies of the revived Roman Empire confederacy, and the summary judgment of the two rebel leaders, the Beast and the false Prophet, will be the imprisonment of the Arch-rebel designated under his fourfold description of the dragon, the serpent, the devil and Satan. But it is to be noted that he is not sent to Hades, the place of departed human spirits, nor to the lake of fire, where the beast and the false prophet will be, but to another place called the Abyss or Bottomless Pit, there to be kept in durance vile for a thousand years.

Two questions seem naturally to arise from this fact, first, Why not to hell proper? Because he is to be allowed out again (and no one could ever emerge from the lake of fire) to show that a thousand years in that awful prison-house cannot change his character, nor a thousand years of the manifested glory of God, man's character, apart from the grace of God. The second question is, Why is no mention made of Satan's host of fallen angels? They are mentioned in chapter 12 as having been cast out with Satan from heaven to the earth, but from that point onwards no mention is made of them. It is quite unthinkable that they should be left free to roam about on the earth to trouble and tempt during the Millennium, and equally so that they should escape the final doom of their leader. In fact by the words of Christ, everlasting fire was prepared for them equally with him (Matt 25:41). The simple explanation is, I hold, that they are all included with their leader representatively. They are seen in him, they will be shut up with him in the pit, loosed with him from thence, and finally cast into the lake of fire with him (see also Isa 24:22 – "the host of the high ones that are on high"). The absence of Satan and his angels during the millennium will indeed be an immense relief to the troubled scene, freeing the world from the greatest source of temptation from without.

(3) Universal Blessing

This will be the natural outcome of the presence of the King: "The earth will be filled with the knowledge of the glory of God as the waters cover the sea", and a time of universal peace and prosperity will be enjoyed. The promise will at length be fulfilled, "They shall beat their swords into ploughshares, and their spears into pruning hooks; nation shall not lift up sword against nation, neither shall they learn war any more" (Isa 2:4). This will not be the result of conferences of the League of Nations or arbitration pacts. God alone will "make wars to cease". Then the groaning creation shall enter into rest. "The wolf also shall dwell with the lamb . . . and the lion shall eat straw like the ox" (11:6-7). Humanity will be relieved of its three most crushing burdens: sacerdotal religions, military organizations and extortionate business competition. The deserts of the earth will be turned to profit: they "shall be glad, and the desert shall rejoice and blossom as the rose" (35:1). These will indeed be "seasons (*kairoi*) of refreshing from the presence of the Lord" (Acts 3:19).

(4) The Kingdom will be the scene of rewards.

All the saints will share in it, but not all will have the same place, rank or reward therein. These will be allotted at the Judgment Seat of Christ. Some will have crowns – varying according to their service and faithfulness – incorruptible crowns, crowns of life, of glory, of righteousness. Each will have the place for which they have been fitted, and for which they have fitted themselves. All the tribes of Israel will be restored to their land, and Israel will be the head of the nations. It will be "the time (*chronos*) of the restitution of all things" (Acts 3:21). Jerusalem will be the metropolis of the world, and the centre of the earthly Kingdom and of Jehovah's worship (Zech 14:16,19). Then the earth will know universal prosperity, and from Israel will go forth a world-wide testimony to Jehovah (see, e.g., Isa 66:18-20), and no doubt untold millions will be gathered to the name of Christ and be eternally saved.

But all this must be tested. Satan and his angels will be set at liberty once more, and will go forth to deceive the nations and raise the standard of revolt. In numberless cases they will succeed, and great multitudes will be found ready to yield them allegiance. They will gather together against the Holy City, but the times of war are past: speedy vengeance will be meted out to them, "fire from heaven will devour them". Satan and, no doubt, his angels will then be summarily dealt with and cast into the lake of fire. Following on these tremendous events, the final assize – the judgment of the Great White Throne will be carried through by Him to whom all judgment is committed, and the wicked dead will receive their final doom, and death and Hades be cast into the lake of fire.

This is the complete victory of Christ, described as "the end". "Then cometh the end, when He shall have delivered up the Kingdom to God, even the Father; when He shall have put down all rule and all authority and power, for He must reign until He hath put all enemies under His feet. The last enemy that shall be destroyed is death" (1 Cor 15:24-26). The delivering up the Kingdom is usually, but I believe quite erroneously, interpreted as meaning that the Lord will transfer the Kingdom to the Father and cease to reign. But if this were so, what would become of the various passages where the never-endingness of the Kingdom is clearly asserted in different ways? Thus, "A Kingdom which shall never be destroyed" - nor "left to another people" (Dan 2:44); "Of the increase of His government of peace there shall be no end ... from henceforth, even for ever" (Isa 9:7); "He shall reign over the house of Jacob for ever, and of His Kingdom there shall be no end" (Luke 1:33); "And He shall reign for ever and ever" (Rev 11:13); and then later in describing a time subsequent to "the end" referred to in 1 Cor 15, we still see "the throne of God and of the Lamb" (Rev 22:1,3) and in v. 5 we read of the Lord's servants, "And they shall reign for ever and ever." Will servants reign for ever, and their Lord cease to reign? Impossible! Some under the bondage of this idea, recognising that the Millennial reign will not exhaust what is predicted of Christ's reign, have imagined a long period after the thousand years' reign which they call "the ages of the ages". But "the delivering up of the Kingdom" synchronizes with the final victory of Christ over His enemies and the destruction of death, the last enemy, which takes place as we have seen at the Great White Throne (Rev 20:11-14). The difficulty seems to arise from attaching a mistaken meaning to the words "deliver up", namely of handing back the Kingdom in the sense of relinquishing it and ceasing to reign, and neglecting the real meaning, that of restoring it to God purged of every stain, and freed from every foe in enhanced glory. The exact order of the following Greek words fits in exactly with this thought: "Then also (then in the moment of complete victory, no less than during the conflict of the ages and the mediatorial reign) will the Son be subject": that is, He will not even then claim independent rule, but will continue to reign as before as the Viceroy of God, the Father, that God may be (not become, for He is it now) all in all. The Millennial reign will be, as we have already seen, only the first stage of "the Everlasting Kingdom of our Lord and Saviour Jesus Christ" (2 Pet 1:11).

4. THE FUTURE STATE OF THE REDEEMED

In the Eternal State there will be not only a New Heaven, but also a New Earth, and if during the Millennium there will be, as we have seen, close connection between the two, we can hardly conceive that this will be less so in the Eternal State. No doubt the everlasting inheritance of the twelve tribes of Israel will be on the New Earth, as promised to Abraham (see Gen 13:15; 17:19).

There will also be inhabitants of the New Earth from saved Gentiles: "The nations of them that are saved shall walk in the light of it" (Rev 21:24). These will have survived the Millennium having proved themselves as truly of God. There is no reason why the heavenly kingdom should be eternal, and the earthly only temporal, though the conditions are difficult to grasp no less in one than the other. Indeed of the two, possibly the heavenly can be grasped the more easily than the other, owing to the fact that the tabernacle in the wilderness was constructed according to the pattern of heavenly things shown to Moses in the Mount (Heb 8:5). If this be so we learn the following things about heaven.

(1) Heaven is the place of God's Glory.

The first thing that would meet the eye of the High Priest on entering the Holiest would be the Shekinah glory, (from the Hebrew, *shah-chan* – 'to dwell': the glory marked God's presence) before which neither Moses nor the priests could stand at the first, and he only on the ground of the blood of atonement. This corresponds to the central object of heaven: "The glory of God in the face of Jesus Christ". There is "no need of the sun...the glory of God did lighten it, and the Lamb is the light thereof" (Rev 21:23).

(2) Heaven is the place of God's Holiness.

"God is light, and in Him is no darkness at all" (1 John 1:5). Clearly nothing inconsistent with that holiness can be permitted in heaven. "There shall in no wise enter into it anything that defileth ... but they which are written in the Lamb's book of life" (Rev 21:27).

(3) Heaven is the place of God's Righteousness.

Here all the divine claims will have been fully met and safeguarded, as testified by the fact that the One on the throne is the Lamb, bearing for ever in His glorified body the marks of His sacrificial work.

(4) Heaven is the place of God's Love.

"God is love." The love of the triune God was engaged and fully manifested in the work of redemption; the Father gave, the Son offered Himself and it was by the Eternal Spirit that He did so. In heaven this love will be fully enjoyed (see Eph 2:7).

(5) Heaven is the place of conformity to Christ.

To this the redeemed are predestinated "that He might be the firstborn among many brethren" (Rom 8:29). This perfect conformity to Him will extend to spirit, soul, and body. "As we have borne the image of the earthy, we shall also bear the image of the heavenly" (1 Cor 15:49). This complete transformation will take place in the Church on the day that she is caught up to meet the Lord in the air (1 Thess 4:17).

(6) Heaven is the place of companionship.

The saints will be for ever with the Lord and fit companions for Him, though as the only begotten, eternal Son, He will always be infinitely above the highest of the redeemed, or the most exalted of angelic beings. The redeemed will never lose the sense of His greatness, nor yet of His grace, or of their indebtedness to Him, for He will never lose His character of Redeemer. The blood of Christ will ever become to the redeemed more and more precious, for the throne of heaven will always be that of God and of the Lamb. Christ is now and ever will be Head of the Church and Saviour of the body, and the Church will always be subject to Him.

(7) Heaven is a place of employment.

The idea that heaven is a place of eternal rest must be qualified. It is based chiefly on two verses: "They 'rest' from their labours" (Rev 14:13), and "There remaineth therefore a rest (Gk. *sabbatismos*) to the people of God" (Heb 4:9). The first refers to earthly service, which is often uphill, and opposed by Satan and the world. The character of service in heaven will be different, but it will be real service. The rest referred to in the Hebrews passage is not a future heavenly rest, but present Christ-rest, in contrast with the Creation and Canaan rests, broken or never attained. The believer is called to cease from his own works now and so enter into his rest. There will be no unemployment in heaven. All will be suitably and happily employed: "His servants shall serve Him; they shall see His face and His name shall be in their foreheads." The service will be perfect, varied, and continuous, for "there shall be no night there". To judge from the scenes of Revelation 4 and 5, worship will be one constant employment of the redeemed, but as to the exact form service will take, little is said. There may be a form of testimony in the universe to angelic hosts, or to other created beings in the future ages which the redeemed of this fallen world, and not least the Church, will be specially qualified to render (see, e.g., Psa 22:31). There will be the response of love, there will be interest and a share in all the purposes of God, and a growth in acquaintance with Him, whom to know is eternal life, and that in and through an ever-increasing knowledge of His Word, which "He has magnified above all His Name, and which is for ever settled in heaven".

(8) Heaven is a place of perfect blessedness.

All the promises of God will be fully realised then: "He that overcometh shall inherit all things" (Rev 21:7), for Christ is Head over all things to the Church (Eph 1:22). That inheritance will be incorruptible (death will not mar it); undefiled (sin will not pollute it); fading not away (age will not spoil it) "reserved in heaven for you" (nothing can deprive the saints of it). To form an idea of the happiness of heaven we must remind ourselves that true happiness consists on the one hand of what is excluded: no sin, no enemy, no

Satan, no pain, no death, no curse; and then in what will be included, as one has well said, 'In the perfect adjustment between what we desire and what we possess; between what we are and what we ought to be.' It will also entail the perfect satisfaction of every legitimate need and aspiration in the presence of the God and Father of the redeemed, in whose house they will enjoy the eternal privileges of sonship, of union with Christ, their Lord and Bridegroom, and the fulness of the Spirit whose temple they are unto all the fulness of God. They will know, too, the society of the saved of all ages, of patriarchs, apostles, saints, and also of angels who have ministered here below "to those who shall be heirs of salvation". Above all they will "ever be with the Lord"; "they shall hunger no more, neither thirst any more, neither shall the sun light on them, nor any heat; for the Lamb that is in the midst of the throne shall feed them and shall lead them unto living foundations of waters: and God shall wipe away all tears from their eyes" (Rev 7:16-17).

The question has sometimes been asked, and it is one of the greatest importance: Will there be any possibility in a future eternity of another outbreak of sin and rebellion, when the memory of the present tragedy shall have passed away, if that were ever possible? The failure of the present rebellion under the highest leadership and the most favourable conditions will show its utter futility, and an eternal hell its infinite penalty. But the answer is perfectly plain from other considerations, and is given in two promises, depending on a great and unchangeable fact, which the Spirit of God has caused to be written in one verse for our learning. The two promises are, "There shall be no more curse", and "His servants shall reign for ever and ever", and between them the great fact which secures them for us: the throne is "the throne of God and the Lamb" (Rev 23:3), that is, God Himself and the Lamb will guarantee its stability. But there is another, and if possible more potent reason still: the hand that holds the universal sceptre is a pierced hand. Love will ever speak in the scars of Calvary, and will bind the universe together eternally in one: the Spirit of God sustaining it in willing obedience to God. Therefore we conclude that although God will for ever reign over a universe of free moral beings, its eternal and uninterrupted blessing is perfectly secured.

5. THE FUTURE OF THE WICKED

In these days of general declension, with Christendom worm-eaten with evil doctrine of every kind, it behoves us more than ever to cleave fast to the Scriptures and their unchanging testimony. This is especially necessary in the case of the doctrine of the eternal punishment of the wicked. The denial of this foundation truth (see Heb 6:2) opens the door to a general letting-go of fundamentals, such as the Divine Trinity, the Deity of Christ, His Eternal Sonship, the Personality of the Holy Spirit, the Atonement, the Inspiration of the Scriptures, etc.

The general belief of Christians from the beginning has been that the Bible certainly does teach the eternal punishment of the wicked, and, if the ordinary man of the world is acquainted at all with the Scriptures, nothing can persuade him that this is not so. This teaching is said to have made many infidels, but the statement is more than doubtful. The only way a man can at all consistently go on in sin is to profess not to believe in the warnings of Scripture as to future punishment; but no doubt the fear of hell has acted as a tremendous deterrent to multitudes.

Has a new Bible then been found in which no hell is taught? It is still left standing in the Revised Version, though the marginal notes tend in some places to obscure the issue. But the reality and finality of the truth we are considering does not rest on one or two words or phrases. The very resources of the language are exhausted, so to speak, to remove all doubt as to its fearful and enduring character–"for ever"; "for evermore"; "for ever and for ever"; "their worm dieth not and the fire is not quenched"; "everlasting destruction from the presence of the Lord"; "shall not see life, but the wrath of God abideth on him", etc.

This denial is a common feature of heretical sects. They all agree that the Scriptures do not teach eternal punishment, but their unanimity is discounted by the eloquent fact that they cannot agree as to what the Scriptures do teach. Some affirm that it is universal salvation or restoration; others with equal certainty that it is universal extinction of being. Some try to combine the two, but with indifferent success. One American heretical teacher holds that the wicked, after 'an unconscious slumber(!) in the lake of fire', will all be reconciled to God. But I understand he does provide for a few incorrigibles being left out of the arrangement. These will be annihilated, so that the epithet of 'universal reconciliation' is stultified. We may well leave these Satanic sects to devour one another, while we bow to the testimony of God's immutable Word.

The doctrine of Christ

Let us then apply the Scriptural test to this solemn truth. It is twofold but really one, and should be applied to all teaching today. It is not, What do children believe? as has been suggested, for they believe anything they are told; but, Is it according to "the doctrine of Christ"? that is, Did He teach it? and secondly, Is it according to "the doctrine of the apostles"? Did they confirm it? These doctrines are the same, for Christ taught by the Spirit, and the apostles were taught by the same Spirit. We know nothing of that dangerous conception which pits 'Jesus' against 'Paul', for it ignores the fact that the Spirit carried on in the apostles the teaching which the Lord had begun to communicate to them, but could not complete owing to their disabilities. It was not that this needed to be confirmed in the sense of proved true, but developed and enlarged: "He shall bring to your remembrance"; "He shall guide you into all truth." But I believe it is correct to say that all truth, subsequently fully revealed in the doctrine of the apostles, already existed, in embryo at least, in "the doctrine of Christ". [This expression has been taken by some to mean 'the doctrine concerning Christ', as though it were objective, whereas, as Alford points out, 'the doctrine taught by Christ' is much more likely. This certainly is the case by the analogy of such phrases as 'the doctrine of the Pharisees' (Matt 16:22), 'the doctrine of the apostles', etc., where the subjective meaning is clear.]

Now let us examine our Lord's own teaching, which really is fuller than that of the apostles on the subject before us. He loses no time, if we may so say, in setting His divine seal to the unequivocal testimony of the forerunner to Himself, "Whose fan is in His hand and He will thoroughly purge His floor, and gather His wheat into the garner, but He will burn up the chaff with unquenchable fire" (Matt 3:12). Then in ch. 5-7, in the very warp and woof of "the Sermon on the Mount", to many, who ignore its contents, the very symbol of 'Christianity freed from all dogma', He warns of "the danger of hell fire" (5:22); "of the whole body being cast into hell" (5:29,30); of "the broad way that leadeth to destruction, and of the many that go in thereat" (7:13); and of the ruin of the house built on the sand, when "the rain descended, and the floods came, and the wind blew" (7:27). What more complete, more irremediable spiritual ruin is pictured than by the ruin of a house, carried away with a flood, the materials themselves scattered and no longer available for their destined use, or in other words destroyed.

This is the very sense in which our Lord speaks in Matt 10:28, "Fear Him which is able to destroy both soul and body in hell": destroy, not merely kill, much less annihilate, but irremediably ruin. This root - *apollumi* - is used in 9:17, "The bottles will perish": such still exist but are useless for their original purpose. So that all the arguments for the annihilation of the wicked from these words, 'destroy', 'perish', 'lost', fall to the ground. The words represent a condition of total perdition. "None of them shall taste of My supper." They will have enjoyed the pleasures of sin; they will have had their portion of this life, but they will never drink of the river of His pleasures, for they refused the summons to the gospel feast. It will be a condition of separation from the source of all good. "Depart from Me," and there is no shadow of a hint that they will ever make the return journey, for in ch. 25 we are told by Christ Himself whereunto they depart: "Depart ye cursed into everlasting fire prepared for the devil and his angels." Could more vivid terrifying language be used to describe an endless, hopeless, fearful fate – separated from God, segregated with the devil and his angels? We must put alongside these, those earlier words of the same Gospel – "It is better for thee to enter into life halt, or maimed, rather than having two hands or two feet, to be cast into everlasting fire" (Matt 18:8) (lit., the fire, the everlasting). It will not suffice in that day to allege, as in 7:22-23, "Lord, Lord, have we not prophesied in Thy name? and in Thy name have cast out devils? and in Thy name done many wonderful works!" Nor yet as in Luke 13:26-28, as other professors, to tell of religious privileges: "We have eaten and drunk in Thy presence and Thou hast taught in our streets." But He shall say, "I tell you I know not whence ye are; depart from Me all ye workers of iniquity. There shall be weeping and gnashing of teeth," etc. The same solemn words occur in other places. But with all their external works and privileges and appearances nothing is said of their new birth, and we may be sure none of them had experienced it, nor had they trusted in the atoning work of Christ, and "washed their robes and made them white in the blood of the Lamb".

But how unlike these words are to an 'unconscious slumber', as the evil teacher above referred to pretends! They seem to be having fearful dreams! Are they "weeping and gnashing their teeth" in their sleep? How terribly these words accord with our Lord's own interpretation of the parable of the tares! "So shall it be at the end of this world. The Son of Man shall send forth His angels and they shall gather out of His Kingdom all things that offend, and them which do iniquity; and shall cast them into a furnace of fire; there shall be wailing and gnashing of teeth" (Matt 13:42). These are not the imaginations, as some would have men believe, of mere bigots, as they would term us, but the measured words of the omniscient, compassionate Son of God, the future Judge, but the present Saviour of mankind. How can it be said with even the appearance of truth that such words bespeak, as some affirm, a 'wondrously gracious reticence'? Indeed such would be cruel, not gracious, in face of such appalling perils. It is the Holy One Himself who knew what perdition would entail for the lost, and what atonement would entail for Himself, who uttered these words of solemn warning. Let us then consider afresh "the doctrine of Christ" on this subject.

Our Lord's closing words in Matthew 25, to which we will now return for further consideration, have long, and in vain, exercised the ingenuity of the opponents of the truth; some seeking to explain them away in one way, some in another. For anyone, however, subject to God's truth, the words are plain and simple and leave no loophole for misunderstanding: "These (i.e. on the left hand) shall go away into everlasting punishment, but the righteous into life everlasting"; the same word *aionios* in each case. To refuse to translate the word, and talk about aeonian this and aeonian that, may seem learned and may mystify some readers, but it does not really help to clarify the sense. There really is no shadow of excuse for raising difficulties as to the meaning of this adjective, making allowance for a figurative use of the word, which is perfectly understood in our own language, as when we read of the "everlasting hills", or of a person making everlasting complaints. What we have to do is to find out the general usage of the word in the New Testament. Thus the word is applied to the "covenant" between God and His people (Heb 13:20); the consolation of His people by the gospel (2 Thess 2:16); the weight of glory to which they are called (2 Cor 4:17), and "unseen things" (v.18); as also salvation (Heb 5:9); redemption (9:12); inheritance (9:15). Surely these occurrences, were they all, would prove that the thought of never-endingness is indissolubly linked with the word in question.

But they are not all. The same word is applied to God's glory (1 Pet 5:10); "honour and power" (1 Tim 6:16); the Spirit (Heb 9:12); and God's very being (Rom 11:26). Can the solemn significance of the fact be denied that this very word is applied to hell-fire (Matt 18:8), future punishment (18:46); destruction (2 Thess 1:9); chains (Jude 7); judgment (Heb 6: 2) and damnation (Mark 3:29)? If *aionios* does not represent 'everlasting' – applying as it does to God and His glory, His covenant and the blessings of the redeemed – then there is no such thought in the Greek language. To go back to Matthew 25: What has settled the destiny of those on trial is, the treatment meted out by them to those whom the Lord calls "these My brethren" (i.e. the faithful ones of Israel, His brethren according to the flesh), whose judgment will then be proceeding before the twelve apostles (compare Matt 19:28 with 25:28). This may seem a small matter on which to hang eternal issues, but it is a small matter which means everything. It shows the true bent of each. Moreover, from Revelation 13:16, we may gather that all on the left hand will have taken the mark of the beast, in spite of God's terrific warnings (compare with this 14:9).

The word used here for "punishment" (*kolasis*) has lost in Hellenistic Greek the remedial sense it once had, for the penal. [See Trench's Synonyms of New Testament, § vii.] If annihilation were meant by the phrase "everlasting punishment" then, as has been well remarked, it would be "ended punishment" not "endless punishment". The future punishment of the wicked will be co-existent with that of the devil and his angels, with the inheritance of the redeemed, with the Being and Glory of God and His Kingdom.

BEYOND THE GRAVE

In Luke 16, in the story of Dives and Lazarus, the Lord lifts the veil of the unseen world as clearly and as simply as language could. Merely to protest that the passage is a parable, which is more than doubtful, proves nothing, for a parable is intended to convey teaching consistent with its terms. Here the Lord affords us a glimpse into Paradise and its conditions, and into Hades and its conditions. Hades though not exactly the same as Hell, is the same in character, and is, if we may so say, its vestibule during the present intermediate state. How then does He describe the two scenes? He shows us Lazarus in Abraham's bosom in conscious comfort, and Dives in Hades in conscious torment, as he himself states twice, and in a state of hopelessness of his own deliverance; for such a thing he does not even suggest. And the Lord excludes it for He speaks of "a great gulf fixed" [*steerizo* - means to fix firmly, to set fast] between the two abodes, which stamps the condition of things with an unquestionable character of finality. Those who tamper with His words here are the wreckers of humanity and will have to answer to the Lord.

One more passage may suffice to complete this brief survey of our Lord's own unequivocal teaching on this solemn subject, the closing passage of Mark 9. The context is well known. The Lord is warning against holding on to sin: "If thy hand, foot, eye cause thee to offend, cut them off (or pluck it out): it is better for thee to enter into life maimed than having two feet, two hands, two eyes, to go into hell, into the fire that never shall be quenched: where their worm dieth not and the fire is not quenched". The antithesis is between "entering into life", and "going or being cast into hell".

The usual way of dealing with this passage by the deniers of eternal punishment is to begin talking about the Valley of Hinnom and the ever-burning fires which they say existed in the place, but this is really so much dust-throwing. It is true there was such a valley to the south-west of Jerusalem, where in ancient times idolatrous rites to Moloch were practised, but this was reclaimed from such uses by King Josiah, and turned into a place where the refuse of the city was disposed of and the dead bodies of criminals cremated. As for the ever-burning fires, authorities like the late Dr. J. B. Lightfoot doubt if they ever existed outside the imagination of these teachers. However, there is no harm in believing that refuse was burnt there, and that the valley had become a symbol of Gehenna. No educated Jew, however, would confound the geographical valley - Gehinnom, with the place of the lost Gehenna. The Talmud makes this plain, "In the valley of Hinnon, - there is a fire issuing from between two palm trees. It is the door of Gehenna". Of course this is a legend, but it is useful as showing the commonly-received distinction between the literal and the invisible. But our opponents deny this and maintain that all that the Lord meant by His words, quoted above, was cremation of dead bodies in the Valley of Hinnom.

But does this explanation adequately represent the Lord's warning words? Not only does it fail to do so, but it actually robs them of all logical weight. For if cremation of the literal body were all that was intended, the conclusion would be the exact opposite of that which the Lord draws. Manifestly it would be preferable for a man that his corpse should be cremated in the Valley of Hinnom with its full complement of limbs, than endure a painful amputation during life. Little it matters what becomes of the body after death. What does eternally and infinitely matter is, what becomes of the man himself. "Fear Him, who after He hath killed, hath power to cast into hell, yea I say unto you, fear Him!"

The doctrine of the apostles

This branch of the subject demands no lengthy treatment, for so complete was the doctrine of Christ concerning it, that little remained for the Spirit to add, and the apostles had only to take it over in its integrity. In their public addresses, as recorded in the Acts, they spoke less of the future state of the wicked, and entered far less into detail than their Lord and Saviour, in whose discourses, as we have seen, most of the awe-inspiring imagery is found, describing the future of the wicked. He took upon Himself to sound forth the warning note, which proves that there was a future danger corresponding to His own descriptions. Nothing short of eternal punishment could justify the Lord's own repeated warnings, not only of unquenchable fire and the undying worm, but, as though to leave no room for doubt, of the solemn fact that the wicked were to suffer the same retribution as the devil and his angels. Not only so, but He, the Saviour of mankind, asserts again and again that He will personally superintend the carrying out of the sentence. Indeed as has been well said, 'Jesus Christ is the person responsible for the doctrine of eternal perdition, and He it is with whom all the opponents of this truth are in conflict.'

The Lord, moreover, clearly teaches that death is the turning point on which all depends, e.g., in the history of Dives, who asks that his brethren may be warned before they die; and this agrees with the plain statement, "After death the judgment." What is known as the Intermediate State, is only intermediate with reference to the absence of the body, not as being a state of further probation of the soul. Death is the boundary line between the two aeons: "the world that now is, and that which is to come". There are really only two, and "If ye believe not that I am He, ye shall die in your sins, and whither I am ye cannot come." The present is always viewed by our Lord as the only time of probation, "He that believeth and is baptized shall be saved; He that believeth not shall be damned."

Before taking up the actual subject of this section, we would deal with one objection to eternal punishment, which is often alleged by the ungodly themselves, and which seems on the surface to have a certain weight. The plea is that eternal punishment is out of all proportion to sin committed in a lifetime. But, the fact cannot be denied that even in this world, a sin which took but a moment to commit, may mar a man's whole life, and entail a perpetual penal sentence, or being for ever cut off by death. As has been said, "Sin persisted unto the end of life, seems to show that, were that life prolonged, the persistence would be prolonged too. Persistence in sin shows an attitude to God; why should this attitude ever change?" Will punishment succeed, where grace failed? Sin persisted in is the rejection of God's only remedy, and the consequences must naturally be for always. If punishment could produce what grace fails to do, then it was unnecessary for the Son of God to become flesh and die. But who can affirm that an impenitent man would ever truly repent? Though actual sin will be impossible in eternity, the will to sin will be present, and would at once be indulged, were the opportunity to recur. The "beast" who will ascend out of the bottomless pit (see Rev 11:7), will be identically the same wicked man that he was before, and even more so! Satan loosed from 1000 years in that same fearful place, will emerge unchanged, the same irreconcilable enemy of God and man, as he had ever been (Rev 20:7, 8.), And so we believe it would be with all the wicked lost, who die in their sins, rejecting the grace of God.

Let us now examine the doctrine of the apostles. In their public preaching the apostles included warnings of judgment (e.g., Acts 3:23; 10:42; 13:41; 17:13), but these did not form the staple of their testimony, but rather forgiveness through Christ. Such warnings are supplemented in the Epistles. Paul for instance warns of coming wrath in Romans 1:18, and speaks of those who treasure up wrath against the day of wrath (2:5), and of indignation and wrath, tribulation and anguish upon every soul that doeth evil (vv. 8-9). Even the blessings of the redeemed have a solemn voice for the wicked, for if there be "no condemnation to them which are in Christ Jesus"; if their sins are forgiven them, for His Name's sake; if they receive "the gift of God which is eternal life", then condemnation awaits the wicked; their sins remain in God's book of remembrance, they will receive "the wages of sin which is death" – the second death. If they are not reconciled to God in this life a fearful moment awaits them when they will be crushed beneath His feet (1 Cor 15:25).

In 2 Thess 1:7-9, the apostle speaks of the days when "the Lord Jesus shall be revealed from heaven…in flaming fire taking vengeance on them that know not God, and that obey not the gospel of our Lord Jesus Christ: who shall be punished with everlasting destruction from the presence of the Lord, and from the glory of His power". In Hebrews 6 eternal judgment is cited among foundation truths, and the question is asked in 10:29, "Of how much sorer punishment, suppose ye, shall he be thought worthy who has trampled under foot the Son of God…?"

With what solemn clearness too do Peter and Jude speak of the coming judgment and the eternal fate of the ungodly: "Against the day of judgment and perdition of ungodly men"; "Suffering the vengeance of eternal fire"; "To whom is reserved the blackness of darkness for ever" (2 Pet 3:9, Jude 7,13).

When we come to the Revelation, the warnings of John, "the apostle of love", as some call him, approach in severity those of our Lord. Thus we read in Rev 14:10,11 of him, who takes the mark of the beast, "He shall be tormented with fire and brimstone in the presence of the holy angels and in the presence of the Lamb. And the smoke of their torment ascendeth up for ever and ever: and they have no rest day nor night." Also (19:3) of Mystery Babylon "and her smoke rose up for ever and ever". Also in v. 20, of the Beast himself and the false prophet, "These both were cast alive into a lake of fire burning with brimstone." Again in 20:10,15 it is written, "And the devil, that deceived them was cast into the lake of fire and brimstone, where the beast and the false prophet are (for these arch-rebels are still surviving), and they shall be tormented day and night for ever and ever," and then of all the wicked dead, "and whosoever was not found written in the book of life was cast into the lake of fire." This is further confirmed in 21:8, "But the fearful, and unbelieving, and the abominable, and murderers, and whoremongers, and sorcerers, and idolaters and all liars, shall have their part in the lake which burneth with fire and brimstone, which is the second death." No doubt it is largely for this that the Book of the Revelation is villified by unbelievers as it is, and yet the closing warnings of 22:19: "If any man shall take away from the words of the book of this prophecy, God shall take away his part out of the tree of life, and out of the holy city, and from the things which are written in this book," might deter any but the most hardened enemies of the truth from tampering with the words of this prophecy. It is not denied that all this is unspeakably awful, but it is more prudent to "flee from the wrath to come", than merely to deny that there is any wrath to come. It is not as though God had provided no way of escape. "He wills all men to be saved and to come to the knowledge of the truth", and has provided redemption for the sinner at infinite cost to Himself, even by the precious blood of Christ – the Son of His love, as "of a Lamb without blemish and without spot", who "died for our sins according to the Scriptures, was buried and rose again the third day according to the Scriptures".

Yes, a Divine Person has fully met all the claims of Divine justice, and provided for those who believe, a way of escape from entering Hell, but no way of escape for those who once enter. It is strange how little one sees of God's way of salvation in the writings of those who oppose the truth we are now considering. They seem to ignore the sufferings of Christ for sinners, and substitute their own sufferings in the flames of "purgatory" or hell. It is as though we read instead of "The blood of Jesus Christ God's Son cleanseth from all sin", it were "the fire of judgment cleanseth from all sin"! It would seem that, much as the natural man hates the doctrine of hell, there is one thing he hates worse – the doctrine of Christ's atonement and the call to repentance and faith in Him as the way of acceptance. But how can men consistently charge God with injustice in consigning them to eternal punishment, when they persist in refusing the only way in which He can justly save them – His unspeakable "gift of eternal life through Jesus Christ our Lord"?

As one has said of the Cross: "It is suffering mysterious, unutterable and inconceivable and in these characteristics, resembling, we doubt not, the eternal penalty reserved for sinners hereafter…But amidst all this intense and perplexing suffering, which utterly confounds the reason, and makes the faculties of man stand aghast, there shine forth love and compassion which stretch into the depths of the infinite, and which ought to make even the hardest heart beat with a responsive echo: 'God gives his all, Sinner! rather than thou shouldest perish'!"

6. UNIVERSALISM – A GROUNDLESS HOPE

"Lord are there few that be saved? And He said unto them, Strive to enter in at the strait gate: for many, I say unto you, will seek to enter in, and shall not be able; when once the Master of the house is risen up and hath shut to the door." (Luke 13:23-25).

Universalism answers, on the contrary, all, including the devil and his angels (though some so-called universalists, I believe, except these), will sooner or later be saved, restored to God's favour and enjoy eternal blessing. This doctrine does not generally deny all future punishment, but only its penal and unending character. It can only, it is argued, be remedial and temporary, otherwise God's love, and His ability to govern the universe would be compromised. But does the fact that there are convicts serving life-sentences prove that the government has failed? No, rather the exact opposite. It only proves that the convicts have failed.

No doubt the universalist conception is very seductive to the natural mind. It paints God as the kind universal Father, only intent on making everybody happy; and relieves the uneasy conscience of the dread spectre of an irrevocable judgment.

But doctrines, however agreeable, if not based on God's Word, are deceptive and dangerous. These not only ignore the claims of God's holiness and fly in the face of our Lord's plain statements, but clash with the facts of life; for the world, in spite of God's love and power, is undeniably full of sorrow and suffering, and it would be hard to prove that this is only remedial. The question is, Did God, when He conferred on angels and men the gift of moral freedom, undertake to make everything come right in the end, whether they used it well or ill? On the contrary, He solemnly warned men (and by inference angels) of the immediate and terrible consequences of disobedience: "In the day that thou eatest thereof thou shalt surely die". He offered no hope whatever in case of disobedience. The angels that sinned did so in full light of heaven and no atonement has been provided for them (Heb 2:16; Matt 25:41). With man the case was different, and God in grace came in with the promise of a Deliverer: otherwise the whole race must have perished, without hope. But what is there to show that for those who refuse to avail themselves of the divine remedy, the effect of sin will ever pass away? God would have made them vessels of mercy to display His grace; they have fitted themselves to be vessels of wrath to display His judgment. An endless hell will not compromise God's love, for He has given full proof of this at infinite cost by the gift of His Son, as a ransom for all: "God so loved the world that He gave His only begotten Son." Must He give a further proof by stultifying His holy claims and saving even those who spurn His gift? Were this possible, the first were needless.

Really 'Restorationism' sets aside the three great factors in the one and only salvation provided for man – Christ's atoning blood, the Father's saving grace, and the Spirit's sanctifying power – and substitutes the flames of a man-invented purgatory, which can never take away sin. How hell is going to produce in the lost, loving submission to God and fitness for heaven when His grace and goodness have failed to do so, is left an unsolved mystery. Sin stereotypes itself: character tends to permanency; the soul in its opposition to God gets fixed even in this life, like clay in the kiln. Habits gather power and volume as they go, and the time comes when "he that is unjust must be unjust still, and he that is filthy is filthy still". Water would sooner run up the Niagara Falls, than evil persevered in rise to good. The Lord's words to certain religious sinners of His day sealed their doom. "Ye shall die in your sins: whither I go, ye cannot come" (John 8:21). To the objection that an endless hell would involve endless sinning, the reply is that though hell will be the abode of impenitent sinners, it will not be a place of sinning. The will to sin will be present, but not the power. It would be a very defective system which allowed convicts to practise the very sins for which they were being punished. But God may cause even the fearful necessity of hell to work to some salutary end. Those who perished in the flood and in the overthrow of the cities of the plain have served ever since as an example to others (2 Pet 2:4,5; Jude 7), so the eternal judgment of the impenitent may serve as a factor in the moral stability of the universe. Could all rebels be restored to blessing apart from atonement and repentance, what would prevent yet another rebellion breaking out at some future epoch of eternity, when the present tragedy had sunk into oblivion? Experience, expedience and revelation cry out against this delusive theory.

Did our Lord teach any future probation ?

Had the vindication of God's love demanded this, would not our Lord have put it beyond question. None spoke so clearly as He of eternal life, through faith in Himself, none so clearly of the perdition of the unbeliever. Where did He give one hint of 'another chance' in a future state? Are His words, taken only from one Gospel, in harmony with such a thought? "Fear Him, which is able to destroy both soul and body in hell" (Matt 10:28). "The Son of Man...shall cast them into a furnace of fire, there shall be weeping and gnashing of teeth" (13:42). "It is better for thee to enter into life, halt or maimed, rather than having two hands or two feet to be cast into everlasting fire" (18:9). "Depart ye cursed, into everlasting fire prepared for the devil and his angels...and these shall go away into everlasting punishment, but the righteous into life everlasting" (25:41,46). Does Christ give any hope in such words of a future probation?

Did our Lord teach universalism ?

What has already been said negatives this, but we may add the following additional proof. When asked by one, "Lord, are there few that be saved?", He might have set the matter for ever at rest by replying, "Certainly not 'few', for all will eventually be saved." Instead, He urged His hearers to 'strive' (lit. agonize) to enter in at the strait gate, for many will seek to enter in and shall not be able, when once the Master of the house has risen up and shut to the door (Luke 13:24,25). The same gate that shuts in some, will shut out others, as in the case of the Ark (Gen 7:16) and the marriage feast (Matt 25:10). The many on the broad way, and the few[5] who find the narrow, are not travelling to the same destination (see Matt 7:13).

We may be sure that wherever God can righteously apply to any soul the infinite value of the blood of Christ, in whatever nation or dispensation, that soul will be brought into eternal blessing, but where the gospel is preached to responsible hearers, the principle holds good, "He that believeth and is baptised, shall be saved; He that believeth not, shall be damned." Is there not a dread finality about such words? Again He speaks of a great gulf fixed between Paradise and perdition; the "comforted" and the "tormented", which none can pass (Luke 16:26). Is it not the merest trifling to hold out the love of God as a possible ground of future hope to men who refuse it as a present refuge? Such words as, "I also will laugh at your calamity, I will mock when your fear cometh" (Prov 1:26), "Vengeance is mine, I will repay, saith the Lord" (Rom 12:19), sound the death-knell of all such vain hopes. The universalist is the murderer of souls; luring on sinners with his false hopes to their eternal doom.

Alleged arguments for Universalism

To meet the clear statements of Scripture, something more is needed than the sentimental reasonings we have listened to. Accordingly, phrases, usually taken out of their setting, are quoted from the New Testament expressing God's willingness to save all, Christ's death

---

[5] Here the Lord is referring to those of responsible state, without prejudice to the multitudes of souls that pass away before they know their right hand from their left, and are therefore not responsible to find the narrow way. All such are lost without knowing it by disobedience of Adam, and are saved without knowing it by the redemptive work of Christ.

for all – e.g., "He gave Himself a ransom for all"; but this is to confuse the potential value of His work, with its actual value. It is sufficient for all, but only efficient for those who believe. The word 'all' is often limited by its context. We must ask, All of whom? All of what? When we read the words, "By Him to reconcile all things unto Himself, whether things in earth or things in heaven" (Col 1:20), we notice a double limitation: it is "things" not "persons". Indeed what persons in heaven could need reconciling. Again, "under the earth", i.e. the nether regions, is excluded here, though, where subjection is referred to as Phil 2:10, they are included. This same limitation applies to Eph 1:16, "that in the dispensation of the fulness of times He might gather together (lit. head up) in one all things in Christ, both which are in heaven, and which are on earth". There is no mention of the nether regions, they will be excluded from the blessing.

Romans 5:19 is another verse quoted as proving the final restoration of all, but it says nothing of the kind: "As by one man's disobedience (Adam's fall) many were made sinners, so by the obedience of one (Christ's death) shall many be made righteous." As one might say of a wreck, "As many were wrecked in the ship, so many were saved in the life-boat" (i.e. all who got in). Repentance and faith have been insisted on all through the Epistle, why divorce them from this verse? Again such phrases as, "All shall know Me from the least to the greatest", and "the restitution of all things", are put forth as teaching Universalism, but reference to Hebrews 8:11 and Acts 3:21 will show that the future blessing of Israel is in view in both passages. What does the phrase, "the restitution of all things" describe, but the antitype of the Day of Jubilee, when every Israelite will return to his home and possessions.

One more verse which is quoted by universalists may be considered, namely 1 Cor 15:24. The words, "when He shall have put down all rule and all authority and power", are interpreted as meaning universal reconciliation to Him, but surely the true meaning is given in v.25: these enemies are "put under His feet" or "destroyed" like death in v.26, for that is the word translated "put down" in v.24. Crushing as a footstool beneath the feet would be a strange way of expressing "reconciliation". It was not thus the father received the prodigal, but with embraces. But when Joshua made his captains put their feet on the necks of the Amorite kings, it meant their total defeat and doom, and they were all hung before nightfall.

The events of 1 Cor 15:24-28 will take place, not at the end of some immense period of time – "the ages of the ages[6]", but at the close of the Millennial reign when Satan and the wicked dead will be dealt with summarily and seriatim. The day of grace will then be passed and nothing but the day of wrath remain for the Christ-rejector.

There are seven Universals in the Scriptures, which universalists ask us to mistake for an eighth, Universal Restoration, which we do not find. We do find the following.

1. The Universal Creatorship of God

"God who created all things" (Eph 3:9). In this sense only is the universal Fatherhood of God true, but it must be distinguished from His Fatherhood of those who believe in His Son (John 1:12; and 1 John 3:1). In this sense His tender mercies are over all His works. He is the Saviour and preserver of all men, specially of them that believe. If 'Saviour', were intended in the Universalist sense why 'specially' of some?

2. Universal Fall of Man

"Through one man sin entered into the world and death through sin and so death passed unto all men, for that all sinned" (Rom 5:12, RV).

3. Universal Propitiation of Christ

Christ is the propitiation – for the whole world (1 John 2:2). The gospel can now be preached to every creature. Salvation is brought within the reach of all.

---

[6] This phrase is the equivalent in the Greek for what we know as 'Eternity' as its usage shows. Thus it occurs in Gal 1:5; 1 Tim 1:17; Rev 1:5 in ascriptions of glory to God, in Rev 4:9,10; 5:14; 10:6, of God's existence, in Rev 1:21 of the existence of Christ. Is it seriously suggested that any distinction is intended between this phrase and eternity? In what other way could the thought of eternity be expressed? Interspersed among these occurrences are solemn phrases descriptive of the fate of the lost, e.g. Rev 14:11; 19:3; 20:10. What can be logically deduced from this, but that as long as God is God, so long will His enemies abide under His righteous Judgment. So with the cognate phrases "to the age of the age", "to the age", which can be no more differentiated, in their ordinary usage than our English phrases, "for ever", "for evermore", "for ever and for ever".

Christ is potentially the light that lighteth every man (John 1:9); the Lamb that taketh away the sin of the world – (1:29); the bread that giveth life unto the world (6:33); but only actually to those who repent and believe the gospel.

4. Universal Goodwill of God to Man

"God so loved the world" (John 3:16); "He will have all men to be saved" (1 Tim 2:4); "He is not willing that any should perish" (2 Pet 3:9). But to some the Lord had to say, "Ye will not come to Me, that ye might have life" (John 5:40).

5. Universal Witness to Man

God has not left Himself without a witness (Acts 14:17). No one is left without sufficient light to repent, whether by creation (Rom 1:20; 10:18), providence (Acts 14:17), conscience (Rom 2:14,15), or the gospel (Mark 16:11).

6. Universal Resurrection of the Dead

There will not be a simultaneous resurrection, for Revelation 20:3 shows that there will be at least a thousand years between the resurrection of the just to Life, and that of the unjust to Judgment.

7. Universal Triumph of Christ

If this triumph is not by grace then it will be by power. The universalists ignore this distinction, but when Christ comes in glory, it will not be to make peace, but war (2 Thess 1:8-9; Rev 19:11).

The present-day apostasy has ruled out the doctrine of Eternal Punishment as 'out of harmony with modern thought', as though human fashions could affect divine truths. The unanimous vote of a committee of convicts that life-sentences were unthinkable would have no weight with those who make or administer our laws, and far less the pronouncements of Modernism with the Great Lawgiver.

The doctrine denied is too terribly in harmony with the aggravated character of sin; with judgments in the past in the case of flagrant and obstinate sinners; with the plain warnings of Scripture; and not least with the remedy provided, the death of the Son of God become flesh. If "God spared not His own Son" to provide an atonement for all, how will He spare the sinner who spurns His proferred mercy? "Now is the accepted time; now is the day of salvation." He who counts on a future chance will find himself one day hopelessly disappointed and for ever lost. To the Annihilationist it is inconceivable that anyone cast into the Lake of Fire should survive; to the Universalist it is inadmissible that anyone cast in there should not be ultimately restored to divine favour. Let these two Satanic systems be consumed one of another! The terrific truth remains, like a clear deep river flowing between muddy and malarious banks - the eternal punishment of the Christ-rejector. If then, my reader, you are a Christ-rejector, cease from this suicidal way. God offers you Christ as your Saviour. Receive Him, and instead of eternal punishment you shall have eternal life.

7. CONDITIONAL IMMORTALITY
– A DELUSIVE ARGUMENT

The many false systems of religious belief, which have sprung up in the last hundred years, have at least one feature in common – they all deny the endless punishment of the wicked, which they affirm to be a mere human tradition, inconsistent with the love of God and foreign to the Scriptures. It is strange, if this be true, that the vast majority of Christians, down the ages, should have read the Scriptures so differently, and believed this solemn doctrine so unhesitatingly.

But while the opponents of this doctrine are agreed as to what the Scriptures do not teach, they cannot agree as to what they do teach. There are many shades of belief ranging from extreme Universalism, which we have just been considering in the light of the Scriptures, and which teaches that all will eventually be saved, to extreme Annihilationism, which teaches that all the wicked will become non-existent. Between them lies the truth of the never-ending conscious banishment from God's presence of all who reject the light, and die in their sins. Nor is this an arbitrary decree, it is inevitable. At infinite cost, God has made a sufficient provision for all sinners, in the gift of His only begotten Son, who died for our sins, was buried and rose again, "that whosoever believeth on Him should not perish, but have everlasting life".

Thus alone can God be justified in saving guilty sinners. Any other ground would nullify the Cross and stultify His own character. Unbelief alone can shut out the blessing: "He that believeth not the Son shall not see life" (which clearly refutes Universalism), "but the wrath of God abideth on him" (which equally disproves Annihilationism, for how can God's wrath abide on some one who no longer exists?). Certainly annihilation would not be an excessive punishment for a life-time of rebellion against God. Here it is often the good who suffer, and the wicked who prosper. What would become of the justice of God, were annihilation all these latter had to fear? Was it to save from nothing worse than this that our Lord endured the pains of Calvary? His own words cannot be made to fit in with any such theory? "Depart, ye cursed, into everlasting fire, prepared for the devil and his angels" (Matt 25:41). Surely such words imply, if language means anything, that those who enter that fire will last as long as it lasts. We are accustomed to the words aeonian and age-lasting on the lips of these teachers, as a translation of the word *aionios* – eternal, but they do not impress us, being meaningless. The usage of a word alone determines its meaning, and the usage of this word in the New Testament certainly stamps it with the sense of 'endlessness', as we shall see later.

In v. 46 of this passage, the Lord uses the same word (*aionios*) to describe the duration both of the life of the saved, and the punishment of the lost. To meet this, some of these agile teachers assert that "eternal life" is not endless, but only lasts the thousand years of the millennial reign; so that to deny the endlessness of punishment they are prepared to sacrifice the endlessness of life. To such extremes are men reduced, who are determined to deny that the Scriptures mean what they say. But as though they knew this would not satisfy, they have another objection, which nullifies the first: the word is not 'punishing' but 'punishment'; it is an endless result, not an endless process. Thus we are treated not only to home-made Greek, but to home-made English. There is no such phrase in English as 'eternal punishing'. It would be a barbarism. Certainly most people connect punishment with something endured. If eternal non-existence could mean 'eternal punishment', then the viper that Paul shook off his hand into the fire at Melita is suffering eternal punishment, for certainly the effect of Paul's action is eternal. The word[7] here translated 'punishment', in the only other place where it occurs in the New Testament means something consciously endured; "fear hath torment" (1 John 4:18).

The expressions "eternal judgment" and "eternal redemption" are quoted by conditionalists to show that "eternal punishment" need not be an eternal process. But though it is true that the sentence of judgment is not always being pronounced, nor the price of redemption always being paid, the wicked will always be consciously enduring the former, and the redeemed consciously enjoying the latter. It is absurd to talk of "eternal punishment" unless someone is enduring it. That convicts should rebel at life-sentences is perfectly natural, but it will not open the prison doors. And He "who is of purer eyes than to behold evil, who cannot look on iniquity", and who "spared not His own Son" to provide an atonement, will certainly not spare those who reject it. This, it is affirmed, would be inconsistent with His love. But if the love of God alone could save, Calvary was superfluous and a cruel mistake. How grave the responsibility of those who tamper with God's truth on the plea of defending His character, and thus claim to be more jealous for God than the Lord Jesus Himself.

To return to the meaning of the word *aionios*, translated eternal or everlasting, expressions philologically identical: deep in it lies *Êi*, meaning 'always', as Aristotle points out. *Aionios* in the LXX Greek version always represents *olam* (from a verb, to conceal) in the Hebrew Old Testament Scriptures, the root idea of which is "mystery connected with unsearchable duration" (the late Dr. Handley Moule). Seventy-six times in the Old Testament is *olam* applied to God – the Everlasting God. In the New Testament, out of about 130 occurrences of *aionios* and its cognates, where the future is obviously in view,

---

[7] *Kolasis* is the word, and some insist on its classical sense here of disciplinary suffering; but Trench remarks that 'it would be a very serious error to transfer this (i.e. the classical) sense to the Greek of the New Testament, where it is the equivalent of *timoria* – "judicial vengeance". (See New Testament Synonyms, vii.). It may be noted that if this sense of chastening or pruning be adopted in Matt 25:46, the argument that punishment implies only an effect, not a process, would have to go, for discipline is a process, but these controversialists do not seem to mind if their alternative arguments are mutually destructive.

fifteen refer to the impenitent, sixty-two to the blessedness of the righteous, and nearly forty to God Himself. Are we then to believe that heaven will last only "for an age"? or that God will exist only "till a new order of things shall come?" This is the sense of the word we are asked by these teachers to adopt for the future of the wicked. One of them lately,[8] with reference to the fullest phrase of all – "to the ages of the ages", which is a perfectly proper Greek equivalent for our "eternity", has written, "This expression in the Bible signifies, ninety times out of an hundred, an indefinite period of time limited by the nature of the object in view." As the expression occurs at most twenty-two times in the New Testament, the above is a misleading way of speaking. Of these occurrences, seventeen are in ascriptions of glory to God, or in descriptions of His being, two of the reign of Christ and His people, and three of the fate of the lost. We must leave the author to reconcile his statement with these facts.

It might help us to form a true judgment of the meaning the Spirit of God would have us attach to this type of word to quote a few more specimens of its use. Thus we have "eternal Spirit" (Heb 9:14); "eternal life" (Rom 6:23); "eternal salvation" (Heb 5:9); "eternal damnation" (Mark 3:29); "eternal glory" (1 Pet 5:10); "eternal God" (Rom 16:26); "eternal fire" (Jude 7); "eternal redemption" (Heb 9:12); "eternal inheritance" (9:15). Surely if ever the meaning of a word could be determined with certainty by its use, it is that of *aionios*. But these teachers sometimes complain that, if endlessness were intended, some word other than the one we are discussing ought to have been used, which would, they say, have avoided all ambiguity. Certainly a very special word would have had to be used to escape the criticisms of conditionalists. Actually the word is the clearest and most definite in meaning that could possibly have been used: its equivalent in Luke 1:33 being "without end" and in Heb 7:17 "endless" (*akalatutos* – indissoluble, perpetual). What stronger word then could be imagined? It is impossible to escape the conclusion that the word by its usage describes that which is endless. I think the inevitable conviction of any unsophisticated mind must be, that as long as God is God, and all glory is His due, so long will

---

[8] Dopo la morte ('After Death') by Dr. A. F. Vaucher of the 'Seventh-Day Adventists'.

His redeemed enjoy their inheritance with their Redeemer, and His enemies abide consciously under His righteous judgment. No doubt the thought of endless punishment makes the mind reel and the heart quake, but it would be foolish for that reason to deny its possibility. We are not the best judges of the nature of sin, or of the holy requirements of God's righteousness. Nor can we know what precautions are necessary to prevent the spread of sin afresh in the universe, as He, the Omniscient and All-wise, must. All must be judged in the light of Calvary. There the love of God toward the sinner and His hatred of sin are fully revealed. Reject the atonement, and God Himself has no other way to save from an endless hell.

In what way did man differ by creation from the beasts? That there is a connection is evident, for one thing the body in either case is built up of the same chemical constituents; also, like the beasts in Gen 1:20, man in Gen 2:7, is called "a living soul", but as "all flesh is not the same flesh" so we may be sure "all souls are not the same souls". Peter recognises this by the Spirit when he records in his first epistle, that at the Flood, "eight souls were saved by water", ignoring the scores of animal souls also saved in the ark, as being of an altogether inferior and, in comparison with human beings, negligible order. Just as a relation exists between God and man as regards moral and spiritual potentialities, the latter being made in His image, though on an infinitely lower level, so between man and the beasts, there exists a relation as living organisms, though here he is far above them. But man was not evolved from the beasts, his creation being definitely separated from theirs. It was a new start. They had appeared in their swarms from sea and land by the fiat of the Creator; for the creation of man the triune God calls upon Himself to operate, "Let us make man in our image, after our likeness". It would be blasphemous to ascribe this moral likeness to a swine or a chimpanzee. Indeed outside controversy, conditionalists would object as much as other men, to be likened to the beasts. "Thou madest him a little lower than the angels" was not said of any member of the brute creation.

Another contrast is that the animals came forth in their completeness; whereas the body of man was first formed, and then something happened which we never read of the lower creation,

"God breathed into his nostrils the breath of life and man became a living soul" (Gen 2:7). The word used here for "breath" is never used of the beasts, but only of God, e.g., "the inspiration of the Almighty", "the breath of the Lord" (Job 32:8; Isa 30:33), and of man, e.g., "the spirit of man", "the souls that I have made", "whose spirit came from Thee?" (Prov 20:27; Isa 57:16; Job 26:4). Indeed there are passages where the possession of *n'shamah* specifically distinguishes man from the beasts. Thus in Joshua 10:31-39: "He smote all the souls that were therein," described in v. 40 as "all that breathed (lit., had *n'shamah*) as the Lord commanded" (see Deut 20:16-17, where the expression refers to the nations of Canaan). But 11:14 shows that this refers exclusively to human beings, for it adds "that they did take for a spoil the cattle", which shows that these have no *n'shamah*, nor count as souls, when men are in question. Moreover, Adam appears as fitted to hold communion with his Maker, and as a morally responsible creature. How could one who "lives and moves and has his being in God" be intended by his constitution for the ephemeral existence of the brutes? Is then endless existence dependent on the possession of immortality? Are they synonymous terms? The conditionalist affirms so, and it is fundamental to his position; but his belief is mistaken, I submit, being based on the meaning which he attaches to "life" and "death", which I shall seek to show later is quite foreign to the Scriptures.

Certainly man, as we have sought to prove, was created for endless existence, and this is described loosely by some as 'the immortality of the soul', but the phrase is never found in the Scriptures, and the fact that man was capable of death shows that immunity from death was not his possession by original constitution. The second death is eternal existence in separation from God.

Had man been immortal by original creation, God's warning, "In the day that thou eatest thereof thou shalt surely die", would have had no meaning. Adam was not subject to death before he fell, but he was capable of death as the event showed. "God only hath immortality" (*athanasia*) by essential constitution of being. This surely is enough to prove, what is sometimes denied, that immortality attaches to the spiritual part of man, as well as to the body, for "God is Spirit". In order to escape from this dilemma an attempt is made to limit the words of 1 Timothy 6:16 to Christ, but it could not be said that "no man hath seen or can see" Him, whom angels and men have seen. It is God as such who is in view.[9] Man died spiritually, that is, became alienated from the life of God, as the direct result of disobedience, physically as the indirect result. "By one man sin entered into the world, and death by sin" (Rom 5:12). To be immune from spiritual death, the gift of eternal life must be received. This happens at conversion: "God, who is rich in mercy... even when we were dead in sins, hath quickened us together, with Christ" (Eph 2:4-5). This same word is used of the quickening of the mortal body (Rom 8:2; see also John 5:24), which again is the equivalent of the putting on of immortality at the coming of Christ (1 Cor 15:53). The immortality in this passage will mark the effect of the Lord's coming on the living saints, the incorruptibility that on the sleeping saints. The result is the same in either case. The latter word is wrongly translated immortality, etc., in 1 Tim 1:17; 2 Tim 1:10; and Rom 2:7. In connection with the body "incorruptible" seems a good enough translation, but when applied to God it must have the wider meaning of not liable to deterioration (see Rom 1:23 and 1 Tim 1:17). Redeemed man, too, possesses the gloriously positive blessing of Eternal Life, to issue in the endless bliss of knowing and enjoying God to the full.

What is death ?

Let us now consider this question in the light of the Scriptures. This is the crux of the whole matter. Wrong here, wrong everywhere, and it is precisely here that Conditionalism is found most conspicuously wanting. It confounds death and non-existence on the one hand, and existence and life on the other.

The late Dr. Bullinger, a well-known advocate of the views combated here, replies, "The dead are the dead; they are those who have ceased to live" ("The Rich Man and Lazarus", p. 5); but as a definition must never contain the word defined, we are not much the wiser. In his Critical Lexicon, however, we read under the word 'live' – (*zao*) to live, not 'to exist', for a thing can exist without living.

---

[9] The passage runs literally: which (not our Lord, but His appearing) in His times (lit., His own times, i. e. which the Father hath put in His own power), He who is the blessed and only Potentate, etc., will show. . .

And so vice versa, by the same showing, a thing can cease to live, and yet continue to exist. When we say that a man is dead, we do not mean that he has ceased to exist, but that he exists under new conditions. Even the body has not necessarily ceased to exist. Lazarus' body still existed in the tomb, but when the Lord called him forth, it was not only the body that obeyed, but the spirit reunited to it, which had not ceased to exist either. There is no such thought in Scripture as the sleep of the soul. It is the body which, in a figurative sense, sleeps. To undertakers, grave-diggers and suchlike the body may be all, but the friends of the departed believer know he is with the Lord, and even the world, for the most part, have the thought of some kind of survival of the departed, which like the belief in the existence of God, seems an innate intuition in the heart of man of every age and race. This agrees exactly with the Bible usage, where death never means cessation of existence, but separation of existence in the case of physical death, between body and spirit, and in the case of "the second death", between the sinner and God. The first occurrence of the word in the Bible is often the key to its subsequent meaning. The word "death" is found first in the Lord's warning already referred to: "In the day that thou eatest thereof thou shalt surely die" (Gen 2:17). [Hebrew, lit., "To die, thou shalt die", the idiom for emphasis, namely the *Kal* infinitive placed before the finite verb. The meaning conveyed by this idiomatic phrase is not at all that they would only begin to die the day they disobeyed, but that they would surely die that very day.]

To this Satan gave the lie direct, "Ye shall not surely die" (Gen 3:4). If Adam did not die that very day in the sense in which God used the words, then the Devil was right. But what happened? They did not lose immortality, for they had never had it; certainly they did not cease to exist, nor even die physically. Indeed no outward change seems to have taken place in them: corporeally they were the same as before, but a marked and mysterious moral change at once took place in them. Their relations with their Maker were profoundly modified. Hitherto they had enjoyed unbroken communion with Him, now when they heard His voice, they were afraid, and hid themselves amongst the trees of the garden (Gen 3:8). A great gulf had yawned between them and their Maker. This is spiritual death.

Physical death, though undoubtedly part of the penalty of their disobedience – "Dust thou art and unto dust shalt thou return" – had to be insured in another way. They were excluded from the tree of life, of which previously they were allowed freely to eat (Gen 2:9-16). "Now lest he put forth his hand and take also the tree of life, and eat, and live for ever" (Gen 3:22), that is, prolong indefinitely his physical existence in a sin-haunted body, "therefore the Lord God sent forth the man from the garden", etc.

The way the 'conditionalist' teachers juggle with this passage is truly mystifying. They do not like to say point blank that eating the tree of life would have atoned for Adam's sin, but they convey an impression that it was partly so. To quote one of them:[9] "This sentence might have been to some extent minimised and mitigated, had the wilful disobedience been followed immediately by partaking of the other tree", and lower down the same writer calls this "the dreadful gaol of an age-lasting life in the state of disobedience to his Creator". How then could it be a 'mitigation'? Certainly there was no virtue in the tree to affect their spiritual condition, but it was apparently just what their bodies needed to counter-balance the natural wear and tear of human existence: it was the true elixir of life, so long sought for since. The fallen ones were henceforth rigidly excluded from this source of bodily renovation, and physical death eventually supervened.

Spiritual death has characterised the whole human race from Adam to our day. To the Ephesian believers the apostle writes, "And you hath He quickened, who were dead in trespasses and sins" (Eph 2:1). This describes their condition before conversion. They were alive man-ward, for "they walked according to the course of this world", but they were spiritually dead to God. And this was their state, when God in mercy quickened them. How clear then that "death" does not stand for non-existence, but for "wrong-existence"! The Lord taught the same truth in John 5:24, the believer "is passed from death into life". Of course he was existing before, but out of harmony with God, it was a state of moral death. One more example may suffice. "She that liveth in pleasure is dead while she liveth" (1

---

[10] 'Truths, Earthly and Heavenly', May, 1930, by A. van Someron

Tim 5:6). She is alive but it is a butterfly existence, not worthy of the name of life. It is what God calls death. How then is it possible to admit, as the conditionalists hold, that death and cessation of existence are synonymous terms?

What is the condition of the dead in the intermediate[11] state?

To learn this we need, not only the testimony of the Old, but of the New Testament. It is true that both are equally inspired, but in the New we have a fuller revelation of life and death from Jesus Christ, "Who hath abolished death and brought life and immortality (Greek 'incorruptibility') to light through the gospel" (2 Tim 1:10). The book of Ecclesiastes is a favourite with the conditionalists, for having been written in the demi-obscurity of a partial revelation, they think they can prove from it their doctrine of soul-sleep or soul-extinction as some prefer. They quote from ch. 9. to show that "the dead know not anything, neither have they any more a portion for ever in anything that is done under the sun" (vv. 5-6). Certainly, as far as the earth goes, that is, "under the sun", the dead know nothing, and have neither further reward nor portion in it, but how does this prove that the dead have no existence? Their bodies sleep in the grave, but their spirits consciously exist in the unseen world – Sheol or Hades (Hades, from two Greek words: *a* - not, *idein* - to see; the Unseen World). The Old Testament distinguishes between these two conditions, "Thou wilt not leave My soul in Hell (Sheol – the place for departed spirits) neither wilt Thou suffer Thy Holy One to see corruption" (i.e. the tomb) (Psa 16:10). Only a few chapters on, we read, "Then shall the dust return to the earth as it was: and the spirit shall return to God who gave it" (Eccles 12:7). In the New Testament the same thing is taught in clearer terms. The body of the penitent thief was buried in the common grave of the executed, but his spirit was in Paradise with Christ, according to the promise. By His death and resurrection, the Lord "hath abolished death" (i.e. for His people) and "brought life and incorruptibility to light through the gospel" (2 Tim 1:10). These are the blessings experienced in the bodies of the living and sleeping saints at Christ's coming. Again, the Apostle Paul speaks of death as of "departing to

---

[11] The period between death and resurrection

be with Christ, which is far better" (Phil 1:23), or of being "absent from the body, and...present with the Lord" (2 Cor 5:8). This can only describe the intermediate or unclothed state, for in resurrection the believer will in no sense be absent from the body, but in a glorified condition. The conditionalists deny the possibility of conscious existence apart from the body, but the Apostle Paul evidently did not share their views. Witness his description in 2 Corinthians 11:2 of his wonderful experience when caught up to Paradise; he was perfectly conscious of where he was, of what was passing around him, of the words he heard, and their sacred character, etc. Evidently, a conditionalist would assert, he must have been in his body, for otherwise, he would have known nothing of what passed. The Apostle on the contrary is at pains to assure us twice that "he could not tell whether he was in the body or out of the body". We prefer to be with Paul in his uncertainties, than with conditionalists in their assertions.

All this is illustrated by our Lord when He lifts the veil of the unseen world in the narrative of the Rich Man and Lazarus (Luke 16). An attempt has been made to discredit this whole passage by saying that the Lord was adopting a tradition of the Pharisee. This is a mere *ex parte* statement, without the slightest proof or probability. Our Lord never adopted what was not true but rebuked it as a lie, and it is an insult to Him to suggest the contrary. To use a tradition which He knew was false, to crush opponents who believed it true, would be an expedient not worthy of any straightforward worldly controversialist, much less of Him who is "the Truth". In it we are shown two souls in the intermediate state, the one lost, the other safe. From this and the other passages quoted, we learn the condition of the dead in the period between death and resurrection.

1. A disembodied state. Lazarus and the "rich man" had died, and had in either case no doubt received some kind of burial, but their spiritual personality survived.

2. A state of conscious existence. These two are no more extinct or unconscious than Abraham, but real and unchanged. One was comforted and the other tormented.

3. A state of active interchange of thought. How, we know not, but evidently distance and being apart from the body, are no impediment to this. Hades is not a place of silence, as Isaiah 14:10 shows, "All they shall speak," etc., and Ezekiel 32:21, "The strong among the mighty shall speak to him out of the midst of Sheol." No one denies that the grave is a place of silence; the body is not conscious, but it is equally evident that this does not prevent certain spiritual activities.

4. *A state of recognition and remembrance.* "Father Abraham, send Lazarus." "I have five brethren." "Son, remember!"

5. *An immediate state.* That is, it ensues at once on death. "The rich man died, and was buried, and being in hell, he lifted up his eyes, being in torment." "Today shalt thou be with Me in Paradise."

6. *A state of blessing for the believer; of torment for the impenitent.*

7. *An irrevocable state.* "Between us and you there is a great gulf fixed."

What will be the eternal state of the impenitent?

These teachers insist on resurrection, but what they call resurrection is really, as they deny the survival of the soul after death, the re-creation of an extinct being, with no guarantee of continuity of personality or responsibility. The Lord met the Sadducees in their denial of resurrection by showing that Jehovah's words, "I am the God of Abraham, of Isaac and of Jacob", implied the survival of these patriarchs, for "God is not the God of the dead, but of the living"; and to prevent all misunderstanding the Lord adds, "for all live unto Him" (Luke 20:37-38). The conditionalists change this to "will live" in order to make the words refer to resurrection, but the tense is present, and the argument depends on the patriarchs existing somewhere, when Jehovah spoke to Moses.

Again in Revelation 19:20 we learn that "the beast and the false prophet", the two human leaders of the rebel hosts in the great closing scene, will be cast alive into a lake burning with fire and brimstone. According to the older annihilationists they must at once be consumed, as any material object would, if cast into a furnace; but I believe their latest theory says something else: it will take time; every one will suffer a certain amount and endure proportionately. It is really a go-as-you-please system of doctrine, to which any teacher may add to or subtract from as may seem convenient. But could not the God who preserved Shadrach and his friends in the furnace at

Babylon intervene and prevent these two wicked men from being consumed? The words "Every one shall be salted with fire," seem to contain an ominous intimation of this. That this will be the case is proved in the next chapter (20:10) when the devil will be cast into the same place as the two lost men[12] who will be found still existing there, and as we read of the three, "they shall be tormented day and night for ever and ever" – a conscious, endless state, where their worm dieth not and the fire is not quenched, and I think it is only too clear that these awful personages are representative of those who have followed them, and who will share their fate. In Rev 20:15 it is written, "Whosoever was not found in the book of life was cast into the lake of fire," not to be annihilated, but to "have their part" there (21:8), and that according to their character and works, whether "fearful or unbelieving, or abominable or murderers or whoremongers or sorcerers, or idolaters or liars". This fearful condition is described as "the second death", – eternal separation from God, the source of all life and good.

When we turn to the Gospels and Epistles the above testimony is borne out in many solemn passages. What is called, in order to discredit it, the 'figurative', 'hyperbolical', language of the Apocalyptic visions, finds its exact counterpart in the language of our Lord and His most prominent servants. Listen to John the Baptist: "He will gather His wheat into the garner, but He will burn up the chaff with fire unquenchable" (Matt 3:12), clearly figures in both cases; but why "unquenchable fire", if the wicked are to be consumed like literal chaff? Paul speaks of those who shall be "punished with everlasting destruction from the presence of the Lord". "Destruction" is from a root (*ollumi*) signifying utter ruin, but never annihilation. The same root is used of "the marred bottles" of Mark 2:22. Not annihilated, but spoilt for their original purpose, "the lost sheep of the house of Israel" (Matt 10:6), the lost money of Luke 15, the lost men whom the Son of Man came to save (19:10). They are not "annihilated", but if they refuse the seeking Saviour, their destroyed, ruined

---

[12] Some Conditionalists assert that the beast and the false prophet are not men but systems. It would be strange that two systems should be cast alive into fire and be tormented there. The idea of the Devil, a real personality, being tormented with two systems is quite incongruous.

condition can only be perpetuated in the future state. Those who refused His "Come!" will hear His "Depart!" and be banished for ever from His presence. Now 'banishment' conveys the thought of exclusion from blessing, rather than of extinction of being. Peter and Jude both write of certain ones "to whom is reserved the blackness of darkness for ever". Such words imply a conscious experience to eyes that fain would see the light. To quote once more from John, he affirms of the one who takes the mark of the beast that he will be "tormented for ever and ever" (Rev 14:11). Does our Lord's teaching, then harmonise or clash with such words?

Surely the conditionalists must at any rate find support for their views in His words! Nothing can be further from the truth. "Fear Him, which is able to destroy both soul and body in hell" (Matt 10:28), the same word as above. The lost might have become in the hand of a "God who is rich in mercy", "vessels of mercy". Alas! they have fitted themselves to be "vessels of wrath". Later, the Lord, the embodiment of love to those who repent, says He will carry out the dread sentence in person. "The Son of man shall cast them into a furnace of fire, there shall be (not extinction of being, but) weeping and gnashing of teeth" (Matt 13:42). In another place He warns men that it is better to enter life, having one eye, hand or foot, than, having a full complement of members, be cast "where their worm dieth not and the fire is not quenched" into Hell (Gehenna) (Mark 9:43-49). A persistent attempt is made to confuse this with Ge-Hinnom, the literal valley on the outskirts of Jerusalem, into which the 'bins' of the city were emptied. If our Lord were in fact referring to a literal burning in the valley of Hinnom, His argument, as we have already seen, would lose all force or indeed be reversed.

But if our Lord was speaking of Gehenna, 'the lake of fire', His argument was most convincing. It would certainly be better for a man to suffer any loss now, than keep his sin and be damned for ever in hell. The symbols are terrible, the reality infinitely more so, for it will be for always. Such are but samples of our Lord's most terrible warnings. Those who, under one plausible pretext or another, seek to evade these plain teachings of Scriptures, seem to claim a monopoly of love, and charge their opponents with scaring sinners away from God by setting up a fearful caricature. They claim in fact to be more jealous for God than our Lord Jesus Christ, for He was at no pains to avoid language which lends itself to what has always seemed to Christians and others to be the inevitable meaning of Scripture. But surely there is more true love shown in warning sinners, who refuse to repent, of the terrible alternative of an endless hell than in assuring them that they have nothing particular to fear beyond suffering extinction of being.

Such teachers are truly like their friends, the universalists, murderers of men's souls, and, like them, are running the terrible risk of bringing on themselves the divine judgments pronounced on those who take away from the Scriptures. "God shall take away his part out of the tree of life, and out of the holy city, and from the things which are written in this book" (Rev 22:19).

We may leave this solemn subject with the enunciation of four principles:

first, "Let God be true, but every man a liar" (Rom 3:4);

second, "God is love" and "wills that all men shall be saved", so that wherever He can righteously apply to a soul the atoning blood of Christ, which cleanseth from all sin, He will (1 John 4:8; 1 Tim 2:4);

third, "Shall not the Judge of all the earth do right?" (Gen 18:25);

fourth, "Flee from the wrath to come!" (Matt 2:7).